ADAM BY ADAM

ADAM BY ADAM

The Autobiography of Adam Clayton Powell Jr.

FOREWORD BY

ADAM CLAYTON POWELL III

KENSINGTON PUBLISHING CORP.
http://www.kensingtonbooks.com

DAFINA BOOKS are published by

Kensington Publishing Corp.
850 Third Avenue
New York, NY 10022

ISBN: 0-7582-0195-8

First Kensington Trade Paperback Printing: January, 2002
10 9 8 7 6 5 4 3 2 1

Printed in the United States of America

Foreword

Adam Clayton Powell III

We are one generation removed from Adam Clayton Powell, Jr.

I do not write this as his son, obviously one generation removed, but as an inhabitant of late twentieth-century America, less than a quarter century after my father's death.

All around us are echoes and legacies of him and of his era: Laws now of long standing that were the products of protracted struggle, in the streets and in Congress, in the 1950s and 1960s, are now part of everyday life, almost taken for granted: Wages and working conditions that have improved for all Americans, not just blacks, are the result of pioneering labor laws he introduced in Congress. Also with us are increased funding of public education for American children, black and white, that may serve some poorly but serve most well. And most important, while many remain powerfully isolated in the backwaters of inner city ghettoes and rural poverty, our shifting social and cultural assumptions have swept most African-Americans, as well as Latinos, Asian Americans—and poor whites—into the economic mainstream of the country.

These are among the legacies of postwar America, and they are specific legacies of the work, in Congress and in the streets, of Adam Clayton Powell, Jr.

Yet we are also just one generation removed from a darker time for America, for this was also a time when a member of the U.S. House of

Representatives was refused service in a restaurant in the nation's capital because he was black. This was a time when residents of Harlem, however well educated, were excluded from jobs in stores along the community's main thoroughfare, 125th Street, and from jobs on the buses that carried black passengers up and down Harlem's boulevards. And this was a time when the white political leadership excluded African-Americans from participating in the central democratic experience of the country, in the North just as in the South, to prevent black citizens from voting and to prevent black voters from selecting black candidates.

This is all very recent history. In the pages that follow, we can trace the history of twentieth-century America, of how far we have come and of how far we have yet to go, all refracted through the history of a man who considered himself a quintessential citizen of America, fighting for the betterment of his people and of his country.

For that is the theme that will run through these pages, though rarely stated: If we look beyond the tactics, the strategies, the struggles, the accomplishments, and the disappointments, we can see the classic American story. It is a story of democracy, of mass movements, of protest and power.

The story of Adam Clayton Powell, Jr., is unique to America. And far from ending at his death, its epilogue surrounds us and suffuses the American culture and fabric.

Contents

Prologue

All truths proclaimed by man are relative. My search has been for the absolute truth that comes only from what Einstein called "the inspired leap."

As the media of public opinion have become the great streetwalkers of their owners, I have turned more and more to the absolute. In my preaching the shafts are ever aimed at the brainwashed horde. I never wholeheartedly accept anything that man writes or proclaims unless I feel that that man has taken the "inspired leap" that can come only when the Absolute beckons with the uncommon word.

There is something within me that I cannot explain—all that I know is there is something within. This benign growth of the spirit has given me the power to speak what I have been told to say, regardless of whom it offends. It has given me a tremendous stability and security that make it totally impossible for any power or combination of powers of man to disturb. It has come to me oftimes in life with increasing frequency, with a touch of prophecy. And as I journey with this awesome, and yet gladsome, inner power, more and more I feel the faint brush of mysticism across my thinking and feeling. I am a mystic. I am a mystic because I have touched the intangible . . . heard the inaudible . . . and seen the invisible.

Mysticism is not something to be feared. It is not another-worldliness, nor fantasy, nor an apparition, nor an illusion. It is like putting out your hand and seeing and feeling the sun warm it and not having to look into

the heavens to find out whether the sun is shining. It is a breath that is
wafted across one's thinking and purposes, a breath as real as the unseen
wind that hits one's face with sharpness and turns one's cheeks pink.

This warmth, this breath, this innerness is growing steadily as I practice
the presence of God with my fellow men and with myself. I know I shall
never comprehend it in all its fullness . . . this frame could not stand it.
The very thought is beyond comprehension. But it will grow, and with it
I will grow. All I hope for is a contagiousness that will infect others
. . . for this is our judgment.

I believe in judgment. Not a Last Judgment . . . but a continuing
judgment. I am not the slightest bit concerned with the judgment of man.
It means nothing. But there is a responsiveness within me that vibrates with
the judgment of the One. That One sits in continuing and eternal judgment of us all . . . and we know it. The façade of skin may not indicate
it, but the horrors or the blessings are what we really live with.

Whether there shall come a Last Judgment or an Armageddon I do not
know. But one thing I do know, and all the drift of history supports me:
that both man and men are under judgment, and with them all society—
whether in the form of an era, a civilization, a culture, or a nation—is
judged. And because of this I tremble for my country.

I tremble for it right now. It is not that the perfidies of other countries
are any worse than ours, for no man is judged on the basis of comparison
with his fellow man. The eternal One sits in judgment on each one. And
he evaluates us on the basis of our opportunities, where we came from, and
our privileges. The only relativity within the economy of the Absolute is
the relativity of judgment. This is why I tremble for my land. For no land
has had such privileges and opportunities. We have squandered them on
nothingness, and still, small voices come closer.

ADAM BY ADAM

1

Adam Clayton Powell, Sr.

In the 1860s a terrible war was waged in the United States. More Americans died in that war than in all our other wars put together. Those Americans died trying to determine the future of blacks in America—whether they were to be slaves or free.

The great, bloody Battles of the Wilderness had taken place in Virginia from May 5 to 7, 1864. More than thirty thousand men were killed, wounded, and missing.

Jeb Stuart had fought gallantly at Yellow Tavern, and had been defeated and killed in that battle. Grant had crossed the James Ridge River and marched on Petersburg. The weary Robert E. Lee had sent Jubal Early to hold the Shenandoah Valley, and there in the bright late days of September, with the red apples hanging on the trees in Winchester, at Fischer's Hill, and at Cedar Creek, Sheridan thrust his way to fame as he brought the Union victory closer.

Once again Jubal Early was pushed back as Custer captured Waynesboro. The Confederates evacuated Petersburg and Richmond, and on April 3 Jeff Davis retired to Danville. And it was near there, scarcely a fortnight later, that my father, Adam Clayton Powell, Sr., was born in the year 1865.

Somewhere on those battlefields in Virginia were the mortal remains of a slaveowner named Powell, from whose loins had sprung the seed, the seed we know not how received, whether in joy or in abject submission, by a Cherokee Indian squaw. She was my grandmother. I never saw her. I never knew her last name. As she wandered through the countryside during those awful nine months, eating anything she could find for survival and to support her growing pregnancy, there came in April the insistent knocking. A former slave, named Dunn, took her and her unborn child in.

And so, through the kindness of a branded ex-slave, my father was born at the junction of two creeks, Maggotty and Soak, in Franklin County, Virginia, at Martin's Mill, of a German father, whom he never knew, and a tall, rather fierce Negro-Indian woman named Sally. He was born in a day when a whole region had been so destroyed that both poor white and poor colored suffered together. No one for a score of miles around could pay even fifty cents a day to a man or twenty-five cents a day to a woman for work. There in the South anarchy had come to pass. Nothing stood between black and white men except hunger. On one hand were those with the land and no money; on the other were those without land or money, but they knew how to farm. And so sharecropping was born.

One Albert Martin rented to my father's family a one-room log cabin for a dollar a month and all the land they could till, on condition that one-third of their produce went to the owner. Yet they were scarcely able to meet the rent and pay for the oxen that pulled the plows. It took my father's family six years to pay for these oxen. By the time the animals were paid for, they were worn out. Then, as a last tribute of respect, the oxen died, leaving as their testament their hides from which all in the family were able to have shoes for the first time.

The entire family lived in this one-room log cabin with a mud floor; there were seventeen of them, two or three of whom I saw in my early life. From their looks and my memory it seemed that Dunn took in all those who came knocking at his door when "there was no room for them at the inn."

I saw Dunn only once, when my father had brought him North. He was very shy, illiterate, a small dark-brown man. I was ten then and had already gone to bed, for it was late at night when he arrived. My father awakened me and brought me in to meet him. I can remember tracing down his brown back the scar left by the branding of the letter "P." Powell, the man who sired my father, had been Dunn's master and had branded him with the letter "P" as a penalty for running away.

Dunn was a deacon at the local church—local meaning five miles away. Every Sunday morning the whole family would go walking with their shoes in their hands, Deacon Dunn leading the way with his jug of corn liquor. Just as they got within sight of the whitewashed log church, they would rinse their feet in the brook and put on their shoes, which would be taken off at the same spot when they started the walk back home.

My father, up to the time he started school at the age of seven, had only one piece of clothing—a shirt made of a bleached flour sack. In that he worked, played, ate, and slept every day and every night. When he went to sleep, his bed was a bag filled with cornhusks. In the morning he always rose at five o'clock and ate a breakfast of fried fatback, cornpone cooked in the ashes of the fireplace, and coffee made of rye grains. Once the crop had been so poor the preceding year that all the usual foods of corn and wheat were gone. That year, for about two months, he lived off nothing but dried apples and blackeyed peas.

In October of 1871 my father went to school for the first time. He wore his same greasy shirt as well as a pair of pants woven by his mother. The school was five miles from the cabin and was taught by a Jake Bowles. On the way to school the young Adam Powell would stop where cows were lying on the ground and thrust his feet under them for warmth. He learned his alphabet on the first day and could say it backward on the second day. On the third day young Adam was promoted to the spelling class and, as a reward, received a paperback of the Gospel According to St. John from his stepfather, Dunn. He told my father that if he could read the Gospel According to St. John by the time school closed on March 30, 1872, he would somehow scrape together money, get him a scholarship, and send him away to school when he became twelve years old.

Although he was only seven, my father memorized that book. He also memorized Webster's blue-back spelling book, the first reader, and the second reader. And on that last Sunday in March, 1872, he sat under the walnut tree in front of the family cabin and read the entire Gospel According to St. John to his mother and stepfather and the astonished men and women who had been invited from all around to hear the seven-year-old illegitimate son of a former slave read.

My father never saw a clock or train until he was ten years old. In 1875 Dunn sold all the mules, cows, hogs, and chickens he had accumulated during the last three years of a rising tobacco market, and pushed on with the entire family to West Virginia. There men were reputedly being offered the fantastic pay of $1 a day, and women $12 a month. For two days and nights Dunn and his family traveled by train, landing on the banks of the Knawha River, at Coldsburg, West Virginia, where they found jobs at the Tompkins Farm.

For working the farm, my father was paid $50 a year. His mother received $12 a month, and his stepfather $30 a month.

Going to school one morning when he was thirteen years old, my father encountered a little girl of six who was just starting school and was having trouble crossing an open bridge covered with ice. From that time on he would pick her up and carry her over every morning. Many years later, when she was eighteen and he twenty-five, the girl, whose name was Mattie, became Mrs. Powell.

I know more about the lives, the histories, the births and the parentages of the Presidents of the United States than I do about my own grandmother's background. I was never told where she was born or the names of her mother and father, and for some reason I never really inquired until later in life.

When my mother was born in 1872, Ulysses S. Grant, the West Pointer who had entered the Civil War as a colonel and emerged five years later as General of the Army, was in his second term of office. The only bipartisan national ticket in the history of the United States had ended its great and tragic period in office. One fanatic's bullet had done more than a whole army and an entire region in rebellion. Lincoln was dead, and Andrew Johnson, a Democrat nominated by the Republicans, became President. Grant succeeded him as the youngest President to be elected up to that time.

My maternal grandfather was Col. Jacob Schaefer, of the brewing family, founder at the end of the war of the Christiansburgh Academy for the education of Negroes. My maternal grandmother, whose name I do not know, was his mistress during all of their adult lives. I have seen pictures of my grandmother which reveal that she and my mother were identical in appearance, only I do think my grandmother was more beautiful. In one picture they wore their hair in the same style, piled in great rolls on top; and both were dressed in leg-of-mutton sleeves, the nipped-in waist, the high close-fitting lace collar held up with stays, the rich, heavy fabric.

When a legal battle was raging some years ago over the fortunes of the

Schaefer brewing family, I repeatedly urged my mother to participate in it as one of the direct heirs. She refused because, she said, a considerable sum had been settled upon her many years before.

I never saw any of my grandparents. My paternal grandmother died when my father was very young. And I saw Dunn, the very gentle soul who raised my father, only the one time.

During the eight years my father spent in West Virginia he was, according to his own account, a bum, a drunkard, a gambler, a juvenile delinquent, and possibly more. He always carried with him a pistol and a pair of brass knuckles, and had a jug of hard liquor on hand at all times. I don't think he ever told me half of what he really did. In August, 1884, he had to leave West Virginia during the night to keep from being murdered. From there he went to Ohio.

Rendville, Ohio, was a company town run by W. P. Rends, a coal mine owner. The town was a cesspool. Despite the fact that my father was making a $100 a month as a miner, he never had a penny because he lost everything, including his clothes, gambling. Then, during the first week in March, 1885, something happened to him.

He went to bed drunk, forgetting to open the window. Waking from his stupor, he took his shoe and threw it at the window, heard the glass break, felt the cool air surge into the room, and then slept the sleep that comes to the just or to those who are drunk. In the morning when he reawakened, he found that it was not the window he had broken but the mirror in his room. As he sat there, staring at the broken mirror, he began to think about the power of suggestion.

Walking down the street that same Sunday morning, something reached out and stopped him as he passed the Baptist church, where a revival was in progress. He hadn't been to church since he was a child. He tried to go on past the church but could not. He went back up the road again, crossed over and again started down the street, but once more as he reached the church something stopped him. He fought against it, but was pulled into the church as the Reverend D. B. Houston rose to preach the sermon. My father walked down the aisle, joined the church, and was baptized. Out of that revival came such power that saloonkeepers rolled their barrels into Main Street and emptied them into the gutter, and gamblers made bonfires of their gambling apparatus. In one week every place of ill-repute had disappeared, and out of that one-week revival not only was a new town born, but there came five preachers and one of them was my father.

In two months my father had paid back all the money he borrowed, had purchased new clothes, had become secretary of the Sunday School, and was reading the Bible. He began attending the Rendville Academy, working for his tuition by serving as janitor. Later he was appointed Deputy Marshal of the town by Mayor Tuppins. And in his own words, "was on my way" even though he had been "against the tide."

He became determined, at the age of twenty, to be a member of Congress, and even went so far as to apply for admission to the law school of Howard University in Washington, D.C. Fortunately, he was turned down. Fortunately, because if he had gone into law, America would have lost one of its greatest preachers and prophets. In 1888, when he was twenty-three, his mind shifted from the law to the gospel and he found his way to Wayland Seminary and College situated on Meridian Hill in Washington; the school is now known as Virginia Union University and is located in Richmond, Virginia. He was accepted at Wayland and given a full scholarship. In the postbellum days whites broke their backs educating Negroes and my father took advantage of this. He decided to enter all departments of the Seminary: normal, academic, and theological. He finished all three departments in four years by studying nine subjects two days a week, and seven subjects three days. His marks were so high that he was offered a $1500 scholarship. The scholarship would have paid his entire way through college, had he been willing to teach and preach only in the South and only in those places to which the donor would send him. He refused, and accepted a job cleaning the school toilets instead.

He moved to the great Immanuel Baptist Church in New Haven, Connecticut, in September, 1893, after a bitter summer pastoring the Ebenezer Church of Philadelphia at a salary of $8 a week. Of this $8, $4 went to rent a room with kitchen privileges; $2.50 went to my mother, Mattie, for food; and $1.50 was allotted for clothing, carfare, and miscellaneous expenses.

After that summer in Philadelphia he took his vacation in Atlantic City, where he worked as a waiter while my mother worked as a seamstress. Of the money they made there $150 was for books purchased on time from Funk & Wagnalls. They also got enough to eat to rebuild their rundown bodies.

In New Haven the tide began to change for my father. His preaching at Immanuel Baptist drew the largest crowds of worshipers in the city. He began studying at Yale University. He also served as secretary of the Baptist Ministers Conference with George Barton Cutten as chairman. Cutten was not to be seen by him again until many years later, when my father took me to Colgate University on my freshman day and discovered that Cutten was the college president.

My father was one of the most gifted preachers of his day and he was a manuscript preacher. He prepared his sermons in advance, carefully working them over; then finally, on Friday, he dictated them. He worked on the last draft on Saturday and sometimes even Sunday morning. His carefully prepared sermons are still as fresh as tomorrow. And he was a commanding figure: the same height as I—six foot three; and the same weight—a hundred and ninety pounds. He remained the same size to the end of his life. In fact, all his proportions and measurements were the exact same ones I have today. I am not a chip off the old block, I am "the block itself," living again, a reincarnation!

Pictures of my father in those early days show him wearing clothing very similar to that worn today: the pencil-lined slim pants with no cuffs, and the three-button, narrow-lapel Brooks Brothers jacket with the cuffs of the sleeves turned back. He was a man of great vanity, and he had something to be vain about. He was a handsome figure.

Despite the tremendous number of hours he spent studying, he never let his shoulders droop. He taught me a trick as we went for long walks together: "Turn your palms outward, let your arms swing, and your shoulders will have to be erect."

My father loved the good things in life—food, home, clothes, books, friends, and travel. In 1900, two years after the birth of my sister, Blanche, he was elected a delegate to the World's Christian Endeavor Convention held in June of that year in London. I remember his describing Queen Victoria to me a number of years later: "She was so tiny, so old, so tired, so prim."

His wanderlust grew like a virus and it has infected me too. New Haven became too small for him; even the inexhaustible riches of Yale were not enough. The big city beckoned. In the very month I was born, November, 1908, the Abyssinian Baptist Church in New York, mother church of the Baptists of the North—then celebrating its centennial—called the tall prophet to be its seventeenth minister.

But some did not like my father's preaching. He was a man who did not hold his tongue. The gospel was not a sugar-coated panacea, an opiate of the people. To him it was "sharper than a two-edged sword." He cut men! He plunged the probing, incisive finger into his own conscience and so disturbed himself that he would give no one rest until he found a relief for his own sins.

He constantly criticized Negro people. But they were the criticisms of a man who loved them, and the criticisms that would build them into a stronger group.

He knocked at every closed door, and when the knocking was not answered, he refused to go through the back but instead thrust his shoulder against the door until it gave. If doors were cracked, he would put his foot in the crack, refusing to move until the portals were wide. His voice from the pulpit was one of thunder—not the thunder that rolls and disappears into the void, but the thunder that marches until the walls of Jericho fall.

His every word was so sought after that he published as many sermons and lectures as possible; all the proceeds were used to send Negro youths to college. He never could remember exactly how many he put through school but estimated it at more than twenty. As these graduates have come to me through the years the number seems closer to fifty.

In 1908 there was no Harlem for Negroes. Negroes were concentrated in the roaring Forties of midtown New York City. The Abyssinian Baptist Church was located just down the street from the famous gambling house of Arnold Rothstein and across the street from some of the city's worst brothels. Gambling took place on the steps of the church on Sunday evenings, and whores stood across the street from it, seminude, soliciting men as they left the church.

The Mayor of New York was William J. Gaynor, and the corruption during his term of office made Jimmy Walker's administration look like the Second Coming. Mayor Gaynor told my father, in front of the Police Commissioner and other clergymen, "I will not close down a brothel until one of your men pays a woman for the privilege of having a relationship with her, and then you must bring a witness that she accepted the money and that the relationship was consummated."

Conditions improved when John Purroy Mitchell was elected Mayor. He sent for my father and at City Hall said to him, "Doctor, the Police Force and the detectives of the Vice Squad are at your disposal. What do you want us to do?"

My father replied, "Give the gamblers and the whores thirty days to clear out!" And this they did.

On the last of the thirty days, as I was walking down the street with my father as a little tot, one of the last prostitutes on 40th Street, standing on a rooftop, threw down a paper bag filled with human waste. Aimed at our heads, it missed my father and struck me on my white Little Lord Fauntleroy suit. As my father later said, it was a parody of Christianity that the last woman carried out of the block by the Police Department to serve four months in prison for prostitution was not only a member of the Abyssinian Baptist Church but one of the loudest "Ameners" in the Sunday morning praying band. Her twelve-year-old daughter was taken to prison with her because she had taught the child prostitution; this poor girl died two years later of syphilis.

Some idea of my father's masterful preaching and its effectiveness can be gained from an account of his success in Indiana. In October, 1909, he accepted an invitation to conduct a citywide campaign in Indianapolis. For two weeks the battered old church there was packed every night with fifteen hundred people seated and many others standing. Close to six hundred people were converted during the two weeks my father preached there. According to the Indianapolis *News*, "The Reverend Mr. Powell has proved an unusually strong speaker, and appeals to people of all classes. He is not a sensational preacher, but appeals directly to the thought and conscience of the individual."

My father's great love was the church; and the church was the Abyssinian Baptist Church, which grew tremendously under his guidance. During his early ministry at the Abyssinian Church, my father received invitations and calls to many other churches. Although they were then of greater size and with larger financial inducements, he never gave up his first love.

The world-famous play *Green Pastures*, by Marc Connelly, was packing them in on Broadway from 1930 to 1932. The man who played the part of De Lawd, the gifted actor Richard B. Harrison, was from the Abyssinian Baptist Church. He was also head of our School of Drama and the Creative Arts. *Green Pastures*, after winning every award for its playwright and its star, and after breaking many records, finally closed. A fabulous sum was offered and accepted for it to be filmed in Hollywood but, alas, Richard B. Harrison died. It was agreed by all concerned that the play could not be successfully transformed into a motion picture without Richard B. Harrison, that something would be lost.

Finally, the inspiration came to Marc Connelly that my father would be perfect for the lead. I remember sitting with my father and Marc Connelly in the penthouse above the community center of the church and listening

to the offer. To me, as a young man, it seemed like a tremendous opportunity. Marc Connelly went over the play carefully with him, even though
my father had seen it. He said my father would be in absolute charge of
rejecting or accepting all lines, situations, and so on. The price Connelly
offered was considerable, later to be increased several times until even by
present standards it was a fabulous offer.

Marc Connelly entreated my father from the spiritual standpoint, saying,
and I remember his words distinctly, "Doctor, there is no man who can
play the part of De Lawd except you. If you don't play this part, it will lose
the spiritual impact that Richard B. Harrison brought to it."

Daddy answered, "Let me pray it over—not think it over." Mother
begged him. I entreated him. Marc Connelly kept pressing his point. At
times it seemed as though my father was bending to the pressure.

One morning, with a haggard look on his face, indicating that he had
not slept that night, he called Mr. Connelly and asked him to come once
again to our apartment. I sat in on the conference. Daddy said, "Mr.
Connelly, I have talked with God and He does not want me to take this
part. Not because it is not valuable, not because it will not do some good,
but because I married the Abyssinian Baptist Church, for better or for
worse, and I will not leave this church because of any financial offer,
however valuable the new position may be. I will leave this church only
when I feel that the time has come for me to retire from public life."

The months rolled by into years. Finally, the motion picture was completed and the world première was held in New York City. My father and
I were guests at the opening. As the clouds rolled back the voice cried,
"Make way for the Lord God, Jehovah!" Rex Ingram came walking in as
De Lawd. Rex Ingram was magnificent. *Green Pastures* was great entertainment. But as Marc Connelly had prophesied, the spiritual touch was
missing. It was just a rollicking good movie with God handing out ten-cent
cigars and smacking his gums at an eternal fish fry.

At last the day came in 1937 when, after twenty-nine years, my father,
at the age of seventy-two, literally forced the church to accept his resignation. After having worked by his side for seven years, I became the eighteenth minister of the historic Abyssinian Baptist Church.

For a man who had retired, my father was busier than ever before.
Lectures, sermons, books, pamphlets, and above all a new relaxed way of
life under the guiding hand of Inez, whom my father had married after my
mother died in 1945. Forty years younger than my father, Inez was a skilled

nurse, and I always felt that the combination of her personality and her skill kept him alive during his last years. A blue-eyed blonde who looked white, Inez used to buy Bull Durham tobacco and roll us cigarettes on her own cigarette-rolling machine, and she loved her Scotch and water.

Sunday was always the gathering day at home after my father's retirement. People dropped in, young and old, for he was ageless. The jokes were never repeated; the stories were always fresh. He held the center of attention. Drinks were served, food was always there in abundance, and wonderful times were spent. No one ever had the feeling he came to cheer up a man in the extended twilight of life. Rather we all came to share the sheer joy of living that he possessed, the secret of which we were struggling to find.

What a spectrum the life of my father encompassed: from the surrender of Robert E. Lee to almost the centennial of the Emancipation Proclamation; from illegitimacy to acclaim as one of the outstanding preachers of the day; from squalor to all the creature comforts one could ask for and life could afford. He had come from illiteracy to many degrees; from the inability to read or write to the authorship of five books and innumerable pamphlets; from a one-room log cabin to fine brownstone houses in New York City; from a stepfather who was a slave branded with his master's initial to a son who became a senior member of the United States Congress.

He had experienced the love, adoration, devotion, and dedication of two women—the love expected in his youth and the love unexpected, but fortunate to have, in his old age. Life had been good. But more than that, God had been good.

My father was a kingdom-seeker. He believed that the mere act of seeking the kingdom brought all things you needed unto you. His life proved it. I am another witness that when a man seeks a kingdom on earth and puts that trust into his life, loves the people of the earth, friend and foe, black and white, the beautiful and the ugly, even if in that loving he sometimes is unable to have the time to love an individual, then "All things will be added unto him."

The memory of my father, the hatred suffered by my people at the hands of the South, and the memory of a branded slave named Dunn all combine to deepen for me the plot of life's never-ending drama of love and hate.

When educated and wealthy Southerners tell me today of the bleeding wound left by the War Between the States, a wound that knows no healing and one they will never forget, I think of the slave named Dunn who took in my father's pregnant mother, even as love hemorrhaged and hate filled the very veins of the South.

I think of Dunn's branding. A branding worse than that of cattle because in the branding of a man there is not only a memory that man shares with beasts, there are teachings of the Man of God that disturb a memory that the beast does not have. How can God make a man black and bid him to sing the Lord's songs in a strange land? For here was Dunn, not a "little lower than the angel," but a little above the "beasts of the field." Yet when Sally came to him, bearing the knocking embryo of the very man who pressed an iron so hot that it had turned from red to gray against his back, he, like that Man of the twice-smitten cheek, took them in. My father loved him so for this that it was not until Dunn's death that he told me that Dunn was not my grandfather. Speak to me no more, my Southern friends, with your minds made keen on our Northern campuses, from the summit of your positions of affluence and influence, saying that you cannot forget the bleeding wound nor staunch its flow. Over a century has passed and here once stood a black man, twenty-five days removed from Lee's surrender and a few score miles from Appomattox Court House, who forgave while the wound of the flesh and the wound of memory were yet warm.

2

Adam Clayton Powell, Jr.

"**A**dam, where art thou?" With this cry as ancient as man himself, which God used in the Garden of Eden to call for His erring man, would my father humorously call me all through the earliest years of my life.

"Adam, where art thou?" Nearer and nearer the voice came. All I could manage was an incomprehensible grunt. The door opened and into the room he came. Tall, six foot three, black hair and moustache, looking, as I was to learn later, like Mark Twain. Gray-blue eyes looked at me and then a deep laugh came from his groin. He reached down, pried the bars apart, picked me up and said, "Never let anyone keep you contained and never let anyone keep your voice silent." This is my earliest recollection in life. I was three, and my head had been caught in the iron crib as I pushed it through the bars trying to find out what was on the other side of the world.

No child knows anything about race, whether he is as black as sable breast of darkness or as bright as the noonday sun. Homer Price Rainey, chancellor of the University of Texas, once said to me at his home in Austin, in the presence of a then relatively unknown and skinny colleague of mine in the House of Representatives named Lyndon Johnson, "If we would just leave these young people alone for one generation, they would solve all the race problems." If I had been able to think about race, I would have looked around and thought I was in a white world.

I was born Thanksgiving Day, 1908, in New Haven, and every birthday has been Thanksgiving ever since. The calendar says only once every several years, but for me every November 29 was my Thanksgiving Day. I could always have what I wanted and clearly remember demanding and getting knockwurst for one Thanksgiving Dinner, maybe because my mother was of German descent. Mattie Fletcher Schaefer was a beautiful woman in anybody's *"Seelenbild"*—exquisite features, chestnut-brown hair cascading down well below her knees, possessing all the *"Hochmut"* that Germans have. And I recall my "Princess" with blue eyes and blond hair, my sister, Blanche, ten years my senior. Between the two of them I was spoiled, utterly and completely. There was also a third woman, Josephine. Josephine was a self-indentured servant who started working for my family when she was in her early years and knew no other employers. Even when she reached the age of eighty she was still fighting to keep from being retired. Josephine was the only one who obstinately, and without reason, continually contradicted my father, claiming complete equality with him on the grounds that she was born the same day as he—namely, twenty-five days after Robert E. Lee surrendered at Appomattox Court House. My father, of course, did not spoil me, as he loudly proclaimed and consistently contradicted. But let me blame it on the women, if you will, because women have always spoiled me. And I have done everything within my power to assist them.

When I was six months old we came to New York to live, living always in private houses uptown except for two years in a slum apartment adjacent to the church on 40th Street and a few years in a ten-room penthouse on top of the new church buildings uptown. There was always a backyard for me to play in and a room of my own. There was never any consciousness of race and there still isn't; for race today in my mature years is no longer a question of pigmentation but a philosophy of life, a modus vivendi. How wonderful to have been raised in such an atmosphere, filled not with luxury but with all the creature comforts of living, and not to have the stigma of wealth nor the problems of the poor. Or should I say, the problems of the wealthy and the stigma of the poor?

West 134th Street between Seventh and Eighth Avenues back in 1909 was a place of importance. Harlem then was almost totally white. The Jews were concentrated around the 120s and Lenox Avenue. The Irish ran Eighth Avenue as their private domain; Scandinavians were centered about 125th Street and Fifth Avenue. And all the brownstone houses, designed for the most part by Stanford White, were for the upper class or middle class. I went to school just across the street from our home. Harlem was such a wonderful place then that I don't remember a thing about it, because I think children in their fourth and fifth years remember with sharpness only the bad things. How some parts of the world have spun backward! Today I consciously and subconsciously try never to drive through 134th Street. It has become a place of squalor. I have even erased from my mind the address of the house I lived in—but the home I cannot forget.

I was born more than half a century ago, when it was a disgrace to bring in bread from a store and, for that matter, anything that was already baked. A big black stove was a place of magic where the coal fire always glowed and from which good things came. Cooking was my mother's private bailiwick, totally inaccessible to anyone else, including Josephine, who therefore always remained a terrible cook. Father was allowed into the kitchen only early in the morning at about six or seven, when strong black coffee was served. A hand-cranked coffee grinder hung on the wall. I would sit with them as they drank their coffee. Nowadays when I am with my Puerto Rican friends drinking their *café con leche*, it reminds me of my infancy because what they drink now is what I drank then—a cup of hot milk with a drop of coffee.

The bathroom was mammoth. The tub was wonderful—a big long iron thing sitting on four legs; no fancy modern sunken tub that you can't get into without bumping your chin against your knees when you sit down. I could swim in this tub and I had sailboats, motorboats, and all sorts of celluloid animals, and here I had a glorious time every night before going to bed. The toilet in the bathroom was too high for me. In fact, toilets in those days were built like thrones; they were something you squatted on with a sense of security, with a chain that led to the big wooden box over your head, and when you pulled the chain the rushing of waters was such that you had no doubt that this machine spoke with authority. The seats were not plastic but good solid oak properly varnished, and one had to be careful not to sit on them when they had just been varnished, for toilet seats had to be varnished every three or four months. The chain was brass and had to be polished every week along with the doorbell, the faucets, the nameplate, and the mailbox outside.

I lived in a room next to my mother and father on the main bedroom floor until I graduated from the crib stage; then how wonderful it was to live on the top floor next to Josephine, in a room all my own.

Many rooms in the house were not used. The parlor, which sat so stiff and dustless, with all the pictures covered up in the summer and the horrible horsehair furniture covered with summer slipcovers was one of these. Why it was not used I do not know, except that it was very fashionable to keep one's parlor shut up like this. Then there was the study, where no one went but my father; and the sitting room, where no one went but my mother; and the dining room, where everyone went because that was the forum, the life, the living, the everything of our home.

After breakfast I would sit in my father's lap while he read the Bible to me, reciting strange long names. There was much I did not understand, such as Methuselah. Why should a man be so important because he lived almost a thousand years? What complete boredom! Every now and then my father would look at his magic gold chronometer given him by his former church in New Haven. Then, at one minute after ten, he would rise gruffly, carrying me in his arms, and call down the dumbwaiter shaft, "Mattie, you are late." And this would be the real beginning of the day.

Our lives centered on the two main meals—breakfast and dinner. Prayers, in which all freely joined, preceded both meals, of course. Mine, unfortunately, grew longer as I grew older because my appetite wasn't as keen. But in the earlier days I regretted the presence of visitors because that meant a longer wait before I could get to the food. I don't know how we modern men live on such paltry offerings—food then was food. For breakfast we had a different hot bread every morning—muffins, biscuits, corn bread, loaves of hot oatmeal bread with handfuls of raisins and blueberries sprinkled through them; pancakes so big that they seemed to be a yard wide but, in fact, were only the size of a big frying pan because pancake griddles had not yet been invented; and popovers so big you could put your hand inside, which meant there was room for plenty of butter. Butter was butter. Not crushed into a machine and cut according to the metric system, but carved out of a barrel or sometimes even churned by Mother from cream that she bought by the dipperful from the local grocer.

My father always ate salt mackerel for breakfast. How he could stand it

I do not know. Eggs I never liked and do not like now. For about thirty years I wouldn't touch one because my father one day had forced me to eat some against my mother's wishes. That was the end of my eating eggs and the end of his talking about it. Mattie's Teutonic wrath took care of his soft Virginia gentleness. And, of course, Josephine and Blanche supported her.

But back to breakfast: codfish cakes made the preceding night and tossed up in the outside air to make them "light"; baked beans cooked all night long on the back of the stove with plenty of black molasses on top and huge hunks of salt pork inside. But with all of those goodies, the main goody was a "discussion" preceding, during, and following breakfast each morning. This revolved around the morning paper, and all could take part in it, with respect shown for everyone's point of view. I would guess that breakfast always took about an hour and was usually concluded by my taking the oatmeal bowl and turning it upside down on my head—and I still don't like oatmeal.

Then I was taken for a walk. Oh, how I hated that. Josephine always fixed my pale-yellow hair in curls. Yes, curls! I wore Little Lord Fauntleroy suits, Buster Brown collars, and flowing black ties. I was shocked the first time I saw Senator Tom Connally of Texas, because he was wearing the same sort of tie I wore when I was three. I even had a gray Persian lamb coat for the winter. And my hat! The first time I went to Venice and saw the gondoliers, I said, "They have on my childhood hat." Yes, they were exactly alike—broad-brimmed with streamers. And I wore patent leather shoes. No wonder when Roi Ottley saw me for the first time, being led by Josephine, very much the governess in her correct uniform, he turned to W. C. Handy, Jr., and said, "My God, is that a boy or a girl?" I was apparently the only one in the family who knew what I was with unmistakable conviction.

Dinner, which was always even more wonderful than breakfast, was nevertheless founded upon the principle of the law of diminishing returns. That is, whatever was bought for Sunday was always bought with the objective that it should last in some form until Friday or Saturday, and it did. A fifteen-pound leg of mutton on a Sunday ended up on Friday or Saturday as lamb croquettes; during the intervening days it appeared as a ragout, stew, hash, and various and sundry other inventions that only the combination of a thrifty German and a pennypinching Yankee could produce. Fresh bread on Saturday and Sunday ended up as bread pudding around Thursday. A whole boiled cod, which I loathed, with its head and eye balefully looking at me, always offered its bones, tail, fins, and again that head as the basis of a New England fish chowder. And when things were "in season," they were really in season. When Daddy started fishing in the spring, we had fish four or five times a week until the cold weather rolled in. When the hucksters drove through the blocks with barrels of rabbits, we had *Hassenpfeffer* every day. Quarts of Lynnhaven oysters were sent us from Virginia. Huge smoked country hams came from West Virginia, sometimes with little white worms crawling around in them, and then my father would say, "It's in good shape." Fresh greens were always cooked with this ham, from wild watercress in the spring to winter kale. But too much of a good thing can be too much, and I think that's why I called for knockwurst one Thanksgiving Day.

But, alas, we just don't eat today the way we did then. When we had corn on the cob, there was a pot filled with it, two and three ears for each person. Watermelons were never sliced but were always quartered, and I would eat mine flat out on the kitchen floor with newspapers spread out underneath me so I could spit the seeds wherever I wanted to.

Dinner was served at four o'clock. The peculiar hours of eating in our house were arranged according to my father's convenience because everything revolved around him, but not with any subservience on my mother's part nor servility on Josephine's. It was just that he was an important man undertaking an important task and needed the full marshaling of all the resources of the Powell menage, and so we ate dinner at four o'clock.

Whereas breakfast was always a minute or so late, dinner was always at least five minutes late. Every day, without fail, my father remarked, "Dr. Lowell of Harvard says that any man can read the Harvard Classics if he just takes the period between the time dinner is supposed to be ready and the time he actually sits down to eat." And he was right, because he read the Harvard Classics every day during that period. He never sat down to eat at any time until every single person was in his or her seat, napkins taken out of their silver rings upon which each one's initials were engraved and tucked into the collar of one's shirt or the neck of one's dress—who would dare to spread them across the lap? Then father would arrive, fully dressed in his black suit, white starched collar, stiff-bosomed shirt with detachable cuffs, stonily starched, hooked on with clasps. He always removed his cuffs so that he could carve the meat with aplomb and convenience.

I will never forget the first time I was conscious of the fact that my father was going away to speak or to fish, I can't remember which. I broke out in tears. After I was quieted, I asked, "Now who is going to carve the meat?" It was a wonderful question because my father was the only human being in the world, I am sure, who could take an ordinary duck, usually served in quarters, and carve it so that eight people would have more than enough to eat. I never doubted for once the miracle of Jesus feeding the five thousand when I saw the way my father could carve and feed our family and the unexpected guests who always dropped in. These guests always came on Sunday, in droves; they were fed first before any of the family, and so it was not until much later in life that I learned that a chicken, which was very often Sunday fare, had anything more than a neck or giblets— for I naturally was served last.

Next to the Bible, the most important book in our household of prolific readers was a huge dictionary that stood on a revolving stand. At dinner the Bible was placed on the dining-room table and the dictionary on a small table next to my father. He read to us from the Bible before eating and from the same good book after dinner. He would correct our pronunciation. Sometimes there was a dispute over pronunciation between him and my sister, who was then in high school. He would write to the *Literary Digest,* which ran a column called "The Lexicographer's Easy Chair." They would hand down, from their self-appointed place on Mount Thesaurus, the correct pronunciation.

Snow was snow and heat was heat in those days in New York. Although school was just across the street at the time of which I'm thinking, I can remember my father shoveling a path across the sidewalks and through the street in order for me to get to school. He made huge snow piles which we tunneled out and used as caves. Matt Henson, who had been at the North Pole with Perry and had planted the Stars and Stripes there because Perry was too ill to get up off the sled, used to tell me strange and wonderful stories about that land. And, of course, when I built my snow house I always knew I was at the North Pole and expected to dig up a frozen Eskimo at any moment.

When summer came, it came to stay. It stayed summer all day and all night. As soon as the sun set we would go out and sit on the stoop. Backyards were for daytime, and the front steps—or stoop, as it was called then—was for nighttime. There was always the comforting lap or bosom of my mother or Josephine to fall asleep on. The two lullabies I liked best were:

Little fishes in the brook,
Daddy caught them with a crook,
Mama put them in a pan,
Adam ate them like a man.

The other, of course:

Rock-a-bye baby, in the treetop. . . .

There I would sleep in those citadels of security until the first breeze of night came. I can remember waking up just a little sometimes, to learn with a shock that I had stayed up as late as ten o'clock before being put to bed.

In September of 1914, when I was two months shy of six years old, I became sickly, and my parents spent the next six years and all the money they could get together to keep me alive. The illness was a tremendous shock to me. Until that time I had been a strong, husky youngster, growing rapidly—a lusty little animal. Now I was prohibited from paying games with the other children, and was always being virtually carried about by mother or my sister or Josephine, and was kept in the open air most of the time. When I was going to school on 40th Street, my mother and I would meet daily to walk across to Bryant Park behind the Public Library even in the coolest weather and sit there in the sun during lunch hour. When I went to school uptown, I was taken daily to St. Nicholas Park.

As Inez was to extend my father's life, so my mother, devoting herself almost exclusively to me, kept me alive. Each day at school she brought me a tall bottle filled with cream, raw eggs, sugar, and sherry, and four times a day I drank nothing but that rich mixture. Later in life X-rays revealed that I had scar tissue on my lungs, and to this day my respiratory system is blotting paper for any passing virus.

And so because of my illness I was enfolded in the attentions of the three women who figured so importantly in my childhood. What a wonderful womb to live in. It made the cutting of the umbilical cord later in life so difficult. But I have not a single criticism. What a home should be was all there. I got spanked and had my mouth washed with soap several times for telling lies. A cat-o'-nine-tails always hung threatingly in the kitchen but was never used—it consisted of a wooden handle from which nine long leather strips were suspended. This was a medieval instrument designed to scare children, and it was actually used in some families. But when I was spanked it was usually with a firm hand and sometimes, for some unknown reason, a small hand towel. I was never shut in closets but often hid in them with my sister, who was afraid of thunder and lightning.

I almost always had a live pet. There was a wonderful friend of my mother's from Willimantic, Connecticut, whom I knew as Aunt Effie, who was always giving me something—fantail pigeons, white rabbits, kittens, canaries, goldfish, and these I loved with a consuming passion. One morning, believing my kittens were cold, I put them into the oven to be rescued just in time by my mother. Another time one of my white bunny rabbits had such big cute ears and a pink nose that I literally loved it to death, and I was forever dipping into the goldfish bowl to catch the goldfish to bring them out to get some air!

My first revolt in life began when I was put into my crib for my afternoon nap. I knew that I was being put in that crib of iron bars to prevent me from hearing or seeing something wonderful that was happening in the world just outside that stockade. In the next room I could hear mother and father laughing and murmuring in low voices and, of course, I was insanely jealous of him. I could hear the footsteps of Blanche, my Princess, upstairs in the room above me and wondered why she would leave me alone when I loved her so much, and downstairs was Josephine, scrubbing the floors on her hands and knees with a brush and croaking in her crone's voice some awesome church hymn such as "Let Your Lower Lights Be Burning." What a horrible thought! But I won that fight against the iron crib and no one has been able since then to shut me in or to still my voice.

3

My Education

The first influence on my education was Josephine, who, though only semiliterate, agonizingly taught me, when I was between three and four, the alphabet and how to read from the newspapers. On the long trolley-car or elevated trips between our home on 134th Street and the church on 40th Street, Josephine taught me not only to read my ABCs but to print them.

Of course it was not true, but it seemed that in the nursery, kindergarten, first years of school, all the teachers were beautiful angels. And there was one I definitely knew to be an angel. I fell in love with her instantly. I hadn't been in her class long before I was skipped to the next class, 1-B. Thereafter, I skipped term after term, entering college when I was sixteen.

In those days the old brick school on 134th Street seemed to have such huge rooms and oversized windows—windows with sunlight pouring in over potted plants into the room that had all sorts of pretty cutouts pasted on the walls. And I loved school . . . I always have. I've always worshiped at the shrine of knowledge, knowing that regardless of how much I study, read, travel, expose myself to enriching experiences, I still remain an intellectual pauper. In Socrates' last words, "I know nothing."

When we moved from our home on 134th Street to the apartment next to the church on 40th, I didn't like the year or two I had to spend in a school downtown, and was glad to get back to Harlem, to our new home on 136th Street—number 227. I was either nine or ten then, I don't remember which. But I do remember that it was shortly after moving into the new house that Roi Ottley, the gifted author of *New World A-Coming* and *Black Odyssey*, saw me for the first time and was confused about my gender because of the way my mother dressed me, the big straw hat with streamers, the way they carried me around by the hand, my blond hair that hadn't yet darkened much. Roi never could get this first picture of me out of his mind. Although he remained one of my closest friends for over a quarter of a century, when he wrote a chapter about me in *New World A-Coming*, he described me as blond-haired and blue-eyed. My hair had long since turned brown, and my eyes were never blue—they are hazel.

I was younger than any of the fellows in my neighborhood, but the terms I had skipped in school put me in the same class with them or only half a year behind. In order to get to school we had to cross Eighth Avenue, where the Irish were always waiting for an old-fashioned gang fight. No zip guns and switchblades, just good iron fists and now and then maybe a bottle. We later refined this technique by filling the bottles with sand, which caused a lot more damage.

Mother made me wear short pants until I looked like a German child in *Lederhosen*. Finally, when short pants could no longer be found that would cover me with any semblance of decency, I was graduated into knickers and long black stockings. There were two schools of thought concerning knickers—the above-the-knee. school and the below-the-knee school. If you wore them above the knee, you were still a sissy and not entitled to the company of grown boys who smoked cigarettes made out of cornsilk. Of course, my mother made me wear mine above the knee, but as soon as I turned the corner, down they would go as low as I could drip them, and then I could smoke my cornsilk cigarettes and steal potatoes from the vegetable market on the corner.

There were no such things as Idaho potatoes or any other kind in those days; all potatoes were Irish potatoes. And because the Irish on Eighth Avenue were called Micks, we called the potatoes "mickies." It didn't matter how stuffed we were from the best dinner we ever had at home; we always stole a couple of "mickies," lit a fire in the gutter, and roasted the "mickies." And with great delight, without salt, pepper, or butter, we ate the half-raw things. One day I was told that if I continued to do this, I would get colic and die, and that's the only thing that helped me kick the habit.

The first night that my father sent me out to buy the evening paper in our new neighborhood, on 136th Street, a gang of Negro boys grabbed me and asked, "What are you, white or colored?" I had never thought of color. I looked at my skin and said, "White!" Whereupon I was promptly and thoroughly beaten. The very next night I had to go to Eighth Avenue to get something from the store for Mother, and a gang of white boys grabbed me and demanded, "What are you?" Remembering my answer, and my beating, of the preceding night, I answered, "Colored!" Whereupon I again was bloodied. On the third night, another group of colored boys grabbed me on Seventh Avenue and asked the same question, "What are you?" Remembering once more my previous experiences, I said, "Mixed!" One of the boys yelled out, "Oh, he's a Mick!" And I was sent home crying for a third time.

That was my first real brush with racism. It sowed the seeds of my belief that it's not the color of your skin but the way you think that makes you what you are.

Since I had to cross Eighth Avenue to get to school, and since I was still a skinny, puny fellow, I made a practice of meeting on the corner of 140th Street and Seventh Avenue with the other boys from that area, and then, as a group numbering sometimes ten or fifteen, we would go to P.S. 5 together. But if we missed that group meeting, if we were late, or if we forgot and went directly up 140th Street to Eighth Avenue, the Irish were always there, ready to beat up anyone who was alone.

On top of the hill, near City College, was the Hebrew Orphan Asylum. Kids from that institution also went to P.S. 5, and as they came down the hill on 141st Street, the Irish would meet them there and beat them up. And at school itself there was a hulk of a man named Paddy Walsh who taught arithmetic; he was a real anti-Semite. It was easy to distinguish the Hebrew Orphan Asylum boys, for they were always dressed in their uniforms—dark knickers, white shirts, and black socks. Morning after morning Paddy Walsh would take a ruler and deliberately go around the room and crack the knuckles of these boys whenever they failed to do an equation correctly. On the other hand, if anyone else in the class was wrong, he merely received a severe admonition and was then given assistance so that he could do better. I personally had no problem with Paddy because I was always good in arithmetic and later majored in mathematics at college.

One of those great teachers who formed the straight line in my education, from Josephine on through to John Dewey, and who influenced me by their personalities and their philosophies more than by what they taught, was Mrs. Winterble. She taught eighth-grade English with her voice, with her dress, with her manners, with a grand aura. Day after day I was thrilled to sit in her class.

A struggle was going on at that time between a fellow student, Frank Battaglia, and myself to see who would graduate at the top of the class. Frank beat me by one point on his average. But in our graduation play I got even with him. The play depicted the victories of the allies in World War One. I was chosen to play Uncle Sam and Frank Battaglia was chosen to play Italy. At the graduation performance Uncle Sam marched in and threw Germany down—then Italy. I remember pushing Frank just a little too hard, and when I put my foot on his chest, which was part of the act, I pressed that just a little too hard, too, until he cried "Ouch!"

Just as my father had a voracious intellectual appetite that was never satiated, so had I. I read the newspapers every day. My favorite was the old New York *World*. And from cover to cover, as soon as Daddy finished it, I read the *Literary Digest*. I also read all of the Rover Boys and Horatio Alger series. Then I came across *The Nigger of the Narcissus* by Joseph Conrad. When I finished it, I laid it down with a thrill. Here was something I wanted to go into further. This was Life!

That very week in the *Literary Digest* there was an advertisement: "All Joseph Conrad's works, twenty-eight volumes, sent free to your home. If after ten days you are not satisfied, return at our expense, or otherwise pay a dollar a week." I immediately mailed in the coupon without consulting my mother and father, and the books arrived one day while I was at school. When I came home my father said, "You should have discussed this with me. If you really want the books, clean all the bathrooms in the house [there were three] and I'll pay for them." I did, and by the age of twelve I had read all of Joseph Conrad's works. These volumes still occupy a prominent place in my library.

Of course, the great standard literary works were part of the very fabric of my thinking. I read all of Mark Twain's books because everyone said my dad looked like Mark Twain . . . and because I liked him. O. Henry was absorbing. But my favorite was *Ivanhoe*. I was always the knight on the charger, of course.

The older boys, Roi Ottley, Frankie Steel, and Bill Handy (son of W. C. Handy, the "Father of the Blues"), would steal books from the older people in their families and we would sit and read in a den we had set up underneath the steps of Roi's house on 136th Street. There we also read all the pornographic literature we could beg, borrow, or trade. This was our club.

After graduation from P.S. 5, I was accepted at Townsend Harris preparatory school for the College of the City of New York, which accepted only students with an elementary-school average of A. Senior high school extended over four years, but anyone who could get through Townsend Harris in three years was automatically accepted at CCNY.

I didn't do too well at Townsend Harris—I was beginning to change physically and the pendulum had swung back to good health . . . the age of puberty had arrived . . . I had been introduced to sex . . . I was deeply in love with a girl . . . and all this at the age of thirteen. But I did well enough at school to get by. And Townsend Harris needed me; since it was a place where only the brilliant went, there were very few athletes and I was developing into a fairly good basketball player. There I earned my first letter, jumping center as a member of the varsity basketball team.

By this time, 1923, the gymnasium of the Abyssinian Baptist Church had been built and there we assembled the best basketball team in town. Year after year we won all the championships of The Inter-Church Athletic League. Finally, since there was no competition because of our repeated victories, the Inter-Church Athletic League was dissolved.

While I was playing basketball at Townsend Harris, the director of physical education at City College and greatest basketball coach of all time, Nat Holman, used to drop in to watch me. At that time I still didn't know which college I was going to attend. I knew my folks had had a rough time of it during my illness and didn't think they had the money to send me away. Nat Holman begged me to come to City College because "I have no tall men and we need a tall man on the squad next year to jump center." Basketball in those days was very different from basketball today. It was not a competition for giants, with an adding machine needed to keep score. There was one tall man to jump center, two short fast people we called ponies to play forwards, and two heavier men to play guards. Games rarely went over thirty-five or forty points. We wore long stockings and big leather kneepads.

So, at Holman's urging, when I finished Townsend Harris, barely squeezing through, I went to CCNY, a good, tough school, which was free to residents of New York. I promptly tried out for the freshman basketball team and made it. I received my freshman numerals that year.

When I entered City College, I was sixteen years old, turning seventeen that November. It was 1925. I began using the time that should have been devoted to my college work for the extracurricular—having a good time, going to parties, drinking, smoking, being spoiled by women in new ways —so that at the end of the first semester I failed three subjects. This automatically excluded me from the college. But the president of the college, Sidney Edward Mezes, was a good friend of my father's, and my dad went to see him and begged him to give me another chance. Mr. Mezes did the unheard-of, breaking the rules, and I was allowed to return to City College for the second semester, in 1926.

My father, who worshiped scholarship and who had always idolized me because of my brilliant marks in elementary school, could not understand the transition I was going through. He did not remember his teen-age experiences as a bum, a gambler, and a drunkard back in Rendville, Ohio. And I, not knowing at that time he had gone through a similar period in his own life, rebelled against his "holier-than-thou" attitude and his "Calvinism."

During that second semester at City College my sister, Blanche, died. That was the end . . . of college, of church, and of faith! Whereas I had gotten three Fs in the first semester at CCNY, I got five Fs in the second. I was kicked out. My father washed his hands of me. My sister was dead. And I just didn't give a damn!

My real love, my passionate love, had always been my sister . . . my Princess. When I was still very small, I loved her so much that, of course, I used to beat her. Since she was much taller than I, the best I could do was to kick her as she held me off, my kick usually landing on her shins. Nothing my mother and father could do would break me of this, until one day my father said that wherever I kicked her I would have to kiss her.

And I said, "I might get germans"—meaning, of course, germs.

He said, "It does not matter. You will kiss her wherever you touch her."

This stopped me for a long time, but after a while I forgot. One day I kicked her, and promptly had to kiss her on the leg. I will never forget that terrifying scene. It was wintertime and her flesh was so cold that I remembered it many years later when I kissed her on her lips just before they closed her casket. Her lips were cold, too. But, at any rate, that kiss on the leg broke me of fighting with my sister.

I loved her so, I told everyone I was going to marry her when I grew up, and I meant it. At the ages of six and seven I thoroughly believed this, convinced that one day I would marry this graceful, elegantly beautiful girl and we would live happily together forever. She was about five foot ten and her blond hair never changed in color as mine did. She looked totally white, with blue eyes like Daddy's, my mother's skin, my father's mouth, and my nose. She always smelled so good. I don't know what fragance she used but it was always the same one. Sometimes at night, if I had gone to bed when she wasn't at home, she would come into my room while I was asleep and kiss me good night; and I would know that she had been there because when I awakened, there was a lingering perfume.

Now and then through the years I have smelled this in odd places, and there would come tiptoeing into my mind the tall, beautiful, long-legged girl that I never got to marry.

Blanche was well educated and worked for a member of the Stock Exchange downtown, where she passed for white. She married very young and had a baby. The marriage meant nothing to me because I knew it couldn't last. Sure enough, the divorce was granted in a very short time.

Everything new in the world of fashion was introduced to me by Blanche. She was the first woman I knew who shifted from cotton to lisle stockings, and then from lisle to that wondrously sheer, beautiful stocking called silk. In the flapper age she cut her extremely long hair, much to the sorrow and even tears of my mother, my father, and myself. She was the first to step out of the heavy-handed world of brocades, velvets, and broadcloth to shimmery chiffons, georgettes, and crêpes de chines. And away with high collars—wonder of all wonders, a dress cut so low you could actually see her throat and a little bit of her shoulder! No more long white kid gloves, but instead short little white lacy things or plain cottons; a tiny parasol over her head; ribbons in her hair instead of hats. Sometimes as she came walking toward me down the street as I sat on the stoop, my heart would jump right into my mouth and hang there and wouldn't beat and I couldn't breathe. I would be scared to death that I would get dizzy and fall down right there in the street, but by then she would be close enough to kiss me. Not a little peck on the forehead but a real good buss right on the cheek, and I didn't care whether the guys on the block saw it or not because she was my girl, the personification of sweetness.

When Daddy took me away on a facts-of-life trip to Maine, that was really the first time I knew absolutely for certain, deep down in my heart, that we could never get married. I was sorry to learn there was such a thing as sex and that, therefore, my sister and I could never be married.

When Blanche married the second time and moved away to her own home, her home became the place where she taught me that which I had been denied in my parents' home. We went to the movies together, to Coney Island, and the Palisades. She and her husband taught me how to play cards and, wonder of wonders, they had a gramophone! A real Victrola with the trademark of the little dog sitting with his head cocked to the side and underneath the words "His Master's Voice." And they had all the latest records. Blanche taught me to dance. By the time I went to college at sixteen, I was ready for the social world. I knew poker from one end to the other and liked nothing better than straight five-card stud. As far as I can remember, I was the only member of the graduating class of Townsend Harris High School who could do the Shimmy, the Black Bottom, the Charleston, and, under pressure, a slightly personalized version of the tango. I used to bring my girls up to my sister and brother-in-law's apartment.

At home my parents had brought me as far as they could; they were not able to take me any farther. The puritanical Calvinism of my father, sharpened by his gentleness, and the Teutonic starkness and rigidity of my mother, softened by her love, still were not enough for a boy in rebellion against his day and about to enter college. Dad could no longer help now. He had neither a philosophy of life nor a religion at that time that could meet the acids of the post-World War One world. My mother saw the age of puberty emancipate me from my world of sickness so that within one year I grew heavy and tall and her ministrations, much to her sorrow, were no longer necessary. Josephine had led me by the hand for the last time and the story of "The Three Bears" was no longer of interest in a world of dirty jokes and four-letter words on the walls of the school toilets.

This was a strange year in which my dependence upon my sister became almost absolute. It was a year of great shock, when just as I was managing to struggle to the crest of this new hill, desperately anxious to look beyond and see the new horizon, Blanche died. She died of a ruptured appendix while stupid doctors diagnosed her as suffering from "female trouble." This particular death, this shock, this particular moment in my life turned me against everything and everyone without reason or logic. I began to hate, mistrust. God was a myth, the Bible a jungle of lies. The church was a fraud, my father the leading perpetrator, my mother a stupid rubber stamp. The smiling good people of the church were grinning fools.

All the girls I knew, as many and as fast as possible, were only something to be used as a hopeless catharsis to rid me of Blanche's death, and I found myself about to be kicked out of college almost as soon as I had entered.

In this tremendous vacuum and this aching void, my mother came back into my life for the second time. Through my early years she had kept me alive physically. Now she moved in again, not as well lettered as my father, but with a compassion and love and understanding based on her knowledge of my father's behavior during a similar period in his life. She began to pray with me. This bored me, but because I had nowhere to go any more— Blanche was dead—I had to come back to Mother.

I got a job that summer, working as an errand boy for "Wolf, the Clothier" on 125th Street and Madison Avenue. I was hired for forty hours and worked seventy hours the first week, so I quit . . . receiving $12. Then a member of the church got me a job as a busboy at the Savarin Restaurant in Penn Station. After I had been there for a couple of weeks Roi Ottley came to me and said, "We've got jobs as bellboys at the San Remo Hotel on Central Park West!" There, as bellboys, we made around $60 to $75 a week—in those days, tremendous money for seventeen-year-olds.

Two stars of the Ziegfeld Follies lived at the San Remo: Frank Finney and a girl named Imogene, who was later to change her name and start a new life in Hollywood. About once or twice a week Frank and Imogene staged orgies. They would bring home chorus girls from the Ziegfeld Follies, hide five- and ten-dollar bills around their apartment; after the girls became drunk they would all take off their clothes. Then Frank would beat them with a switch, and the closer they came to the money, the more he would beat them—the old game of hot and cold. I tended bar and always received a $25 tip.

Living in one of the towers of the San Remo was the family of a Latin American diplomat. During that summer we went through the wife, the daughters, and the two maids. Whenever the husband left town, the word was flashed downstairs. Nearly every bellboy in the hotel was intimate with someone in that family. The set tip to us was $10 a man.

I played the numbers that summer for the first time, and I played them only once. I hit for ten cents and the banker wouldn't pay off.

While I was drifting, making money, spending it, broke all the time, Mother was praying and planning. When I came home one evening, there waiting to see me was a mountain of a man I vaguely remembered from my childhood. A lifelong friend of Mother and Dad, Charlie Porter was the biggest mass of muscles and bones I have ever seen in my life—about six foot six, two hundred and sixty pounds. He had been one of the head trainers of the American Olympic Team and was the right-hand man of Chick Meehan, then football coach at Syracuse University.

Mother said to me, "Come here, Adam. Charlie and I want to talk with you." We sat around the dining-room table.

After we talked a while, Charlie said, "I've been handling men all my life, Mattie. Nothing's wrong with this boy—he's just grown up overnight. His sister's death shocked him. What he needs is to get away from this family. I love you all, but I can't stand you myself sometimes . . . with your holiness attitudes."

"What do you suggest?" Mother queried.

"Send him away to an all-male school. Far away from here where he can really be forced to live on his own and live with men. And I've got the school for you; it's Colgate University."

He was right. Nine hundred men; thirty-five miles from the nearest town in the Cherry Valley in upstate New York. But where would the money come from? I never knew all of the truth. All I do know is that my mother always had money . . . she had it then . . . she had it every year while I was at Colgate. I never received a scholarship. I never had to work my way through college. I worked in the summers only because my father forced me to.

My father personally drove me to Colgate that fall. As we walked in to meet the president, the latter said, "Hello, Adam!"

I thought he was talking to me, but then noticed it was my father he was looking at. My father, astonished, said, "Why, it's George!" And it was, the same Dr. George Barton Cutten, who seventeen years earlier in New Haven had presided over the Minister's Conference of which my father was the secretary.

The Dean of Personnel placed me in the freshman hall with a roommate named Patterson. We got along wonderfully. We would go down the valley about five miles to Randaville, where we would drink needled beer with the football greats like Eddie Tryon, Duke Shaughnessy, and a Negro named Ray Vaughn. Sometimes we would climb into the old Model-T Ford that we bought for $25 (and sold two years later to an unsuspecting freshman for $50) and go up the hill behind Colgate where a farmer made the best applejack I have ever had. Sliced potatoes fermented under our bed and we drank that. We mixed pure alcohol, stolen from the chem lab, with ginger ale. We bought jugs of hard cider from the local farmers and hung them out the window to get even harder. Poker games, crap games, floated all over the dormitory on weekends. There was only one rule at Colgate: "Don't get caught drunk." When a man was caught drunk, he was promptly expelled.

Chapel was compulsory. In the early spring my father was invited to be one of the chapel speakers. He came and talked from a prepared manuscript. The boys loved him from the start. When he turned the first page, page two was not there. He fumbled through his manuscript looking for it. Finally, totally deadpan, he took off his glasses, looked at the boys and said, "Gentlemen, you must excuse me. I must have gotten in between the wrong sheets." From then on, for many, many years, even after I was graduated, he was one of the most popular chapel speakers at Colgate.

He talked that first time about race relations. He presented the cause of the Negro. He said things that at that time no one but he would dare say. When chapel was over and my father and I had finished lunch, I went back to my dormitory suite. There was a note from my roommate, Patterson, saying, "I can't live with you any more because of the way your father defended Negroes today—you must be a Negro!" Colgate University agreed with Patterson and moved me out of the room. This was the first time in my life that deep discrimination had touched me directly. It came as a tremendous shock to me. Patterson and I had been such good friends . . . buddies. And just because my father, logically and factually, presented the cause of the Negro people, he refused to have me stay in our room any longer . . . and the University Dean had agreed to put me out.

At Colgate there was a saint of saints—Doc Alton. He was next in the line of Josephine, my nurse, Elizabeth Jackson, my Sunday School teacher, and Mrs. Winterble in elementary school to make a profound impression upon me. He counseled me during those bitter days. He was head of the Philosophy Department, and he lived what he believed.

Gene Bewkes, now President of St. Lawrence University, was another professor who registered an impact on my life.

I can remember one day when Bewkes asked me to prepare a term paper on sociology, and after I had presented it he said to the class, "I prophesy that this man, Adam Clayton Powell, Jr., will one day be one of the greatest men in the United States."

The first summer after I entered Colgate, in 1926, the man who had been bell captain at the San Remo Hotel when I worked there became bell captain at one of the most elegant summer resort spots, the Equinox House in Manchester, Vermont. I went to work there, making even more money than during the preceding summer.

The son of Abraham Lincoln, Robert Todd Lincoln, drove up to the Equinox House nightly for dinner. He hated Negroes and whenever a Negro put his hand on the car door to open it, Mr. Lincoln took his cane and cracked him across the knuckles. The manager asked me if, at a special increase in salary, I would take care of Mr. Lincoln's car each night when it arrived. So promptly every day, when Robert Todd Lincoln's chauffeured car rolled up with the son of the former President of the United States, I, whose father had been raised by a branded slave, would open his door. And Mr. Lincoln, looking at my white hand, was satisfied. For this service I received $1 a day from him and $10 a week from the inn's management.

During the previous spring the Daddy Browning and Peaches scandal had erupted. Edward W. Browning, one of the wealthiest real-estate holders in New York City, in April of that year had married a fifteen-year-old girl, Frances Heenan, known as Peaches. They came to the Equinox House for the summer. Another bellhop and I were assigned to take care of them. They arrived with four trunks and twenty-six pieces of luggage. It took all day to get the bags and trunks up to their suite, unpack, press and hang clothes, and get the champagne iced. Daddy Browning gave Peaches a hundred-dollar bill to give us as a tip and he went to take a nap. When we were finished, Peaches, dressed only in her wrapper, walked to the door with us. She gave us a ten-dollar bill, casually letting her wrapper fall open, and smiled. But we were too tough for her; we had been around this business too long. I reached out and grabbed her other hand, pried it open, and took the hundred-dollar bill.

Daddy Browning liked me and I worked for him all that summer. Sometimes he would give me $20 to get him cigarettes and sometimes $1 for working all night, serving at a party. But I never minded his capriciousness because at the end of the week he was always good for about $100.

When I wasn't chasing the Vermont girls, I was at the employees' bunkhouse shooting crap with tremendous success. When I came home that fall I had more than $1000 in big bills, and I set up my own savings account.

My marks began to pick up in my second year at Colgate. I made the honors list, and remained on it for the rest of my time at the university. If it had not been for some low marks in my freshman year, I would have made Phi Beta Kappa.

There were no summer vacations because my father insisted that I work every summer, and he was right. And I gave up athletics while I was at Colgate, trying to vindicate my mother's faith in me and because my father's faith in me had returned.

I was on my way to Harvard Medical School. In the last half of my senior year Colgate began to install the Humanities system. I worked as an assistant to Doc Alton, who continued to influence me. I had studied even more than necessary and my marks jumped to As and Bs. I moved to Andrews Hall, a new dormitory near the golf course, and my friends on campus began to make my place their headquarters. At that time I was going with the outstanding star of Broadway, Isabel Washington, who had come out of the Cotton Club to make a drama called *Harlem* a big hit on Broadway. Bunking with me in my room at Colgate, although not a student, was Al Campbell, who was hiding from something in New York. He had a Pierce Arrow, and each weekend we would drive it to New York City. Isabel arranged for Connie Immerman, fabulous night club impresario, to fill my empty suitcase with all kinds of whiskies and gins, which I then brought back to Colgate to sell at fantastic prices to unsuspecting freshmen, and for the usual bootleg prices to my friends.

One particular night in February of 1930 I'd worked late at my desk in my room in Andrews Hall on some papers for Doc Alton. It was two in the morning. I turned out the light, looked out over the snow-clad golf course through the leaded-glass English casement window, with the moon shining in my face. Suddenly there came a voice. Something like my father's, but softer, and yet more insistent. A still, small voice: "Whom shall I send? Who will go for me?" And there in that room in that quiet, for the first time in my life God talked to me. That day I began my first steps into areas of mysticism. And ever since, in every way, I've tried to maintain a sensitivity and an awareness so that this voice would always be heard.

Early the next morning I telephoned my parents, who had never advised me or encouraged me in the slightest to go into the ministry and had no idea I was even thinking about it—because up to that time I hadn't been —and I told them I had decided to change my life's program and intended to enter the ministry. The tears of happiness flowed over the phone. My father was so incoherent that I don't even remember what he said. My mother just kept repeating, "God bless you, sonny boy. God bless you, sonny boy."

On Good Friday night, 1930, I preached my trial sermon. It was a strange crowd that listened—all the girls from the Cotton Club, others from the downtown night clubs, girls of every color, bootleggers, gamblers, all the fantastic array of acquaintances I had accumulated through the years. I can still remember the sight. They all came to laugh. "Adam's going to preach!" Adam, who played one of the best games of stud poker, who had bet every cent he had in his pocket on one roll of dice, who had slept with more women then anyone could count, and who could hold more liquor than anybody in his circle, was going to be a preacher!

My text was "I am the vine, ye are the branches, and my father is the husbandman." The final appeal of the sermon was shaped around billboards I had seen coming down from Colgate. The then-popular ad was "I'd walk a mile for a Camel." I traced this slogan as I saw it from city to city, on down to New York, and concluded by saying, "How many will walk just a few feet tonight for Jesus?" Thirty-seven people joined the church that night.

The following week the Board of Deacons and my sainted father granted me a license to preach. After Easter I went back to Colgate, was graduated, and left immediately for my first trip to Europe on the maiden voyage of the Hamburg-American liner *Bremen.* I had $2500 in my pocket and a round-trip ticket. I also had a job as business manager and assistant to my father on my return in October, and had been accepted at Union Theological Seminary.

4

My Religion

On my return from Europe I took up my work as assistant minister of the Abyssinian Baptist Church. I had not been on the church staff more than four or five weeks when my father suffered a nervous breakdown. When the doctors had finished examining him, they told me that he must go on a regime of total rest. As one doctor put it, "Don't let anyone speak to him about anything connected with work. No news, no advice, no opinions—nothing."

My father's illness could not have come at a more difficult time. There was the great Abyssinian Baptist Church with its huge flock, needing its pastor more than ever now that the Depression was beginning to make itself felt. And there I was, an untried twenty-one-year-old who had preached only a few sermons. Nevertheless, the deacons met and appointed me acting minister. With no experience, I had to step in and take my father's place all through that winter. I knew that my preaching was far below what our church was accustomed to, but I was pleased when the crowds did not fall off and offerings maintained their usual level.

At the same time as my father's illness forced me to shoulder the burdens of his ministry, I was attending Union Theological Seminary. Union is one of the fine liberal institutions among those preparing individuals for the ministry, but I found its then president, the eloquent Dr. Henry Sloane Coffin, to be not only conservative but reactionary. He invited me to lunch one day, after I had been a student for some weeks, in order to dissuade me from going with and becoming serious about Isabel Washington.

"Of course," Dr. Coffin told me, "no minister could marry anyone who is on the stage, much less a divorcee."

"Henry, that's none of your business," Mrs. Coffin told him—and of course, she was right.

My real break with Union came as the result of Dr. Coffin's reaction to a prayer I had written for his class in Prayer. As each member of the class was required to do, I had written a prayer and submitted it to him. He sent it back with the comment "Of no value." I asked myself then how any man could decide on what was or was not of value concerning another man's conversation with his God, and it was this incident plus the Isabel Washington matter that decided me on leaving Union. I felt that my studies there were not equipping me for the job the church required of me.

When my father recovered, I decided that what I really needed was training in religious education so that I could operate our community center, a four-story building next to the church, with a full-time, morning-to-night program, seven days a week, as it should be operated. I enrolled at Columbia's Teachers College, where I got my Master's degree in religious education. My studies included all religions, not just my own, and I felt that this enriched my understanding greatly.

At the time I was going through Teachers College the climate there was one of great ferment; George Counts was there, Margaret Mead, John Dewey, William Kilpatrick, and I studied under all that host of brilliant teachers who made Teachers College in the 1930s the most significant graduate school in the United States. Today I know that most of my thinking has been influenced by these prophets of Columbia University.

When I look back now upon my ministry, I take particular pride in the fact that to the best of my ability I have carried out my father's hope for his church. As he wrote in one of his books: "I built this church, but my son will interpret it"—and this I have done, am doing, and will do. I call my brand of ministering the outreach of the church, which means to me not just a Sunday-go-to-meeting church but a seven-day, twenty-four-hour-a-day church, and I am critical of those who claim to be Christian but do not carry out in their daily life this kind of religion.

Next to our foreign policy no institution in our American life is more hypocritical and therefore does more to hurt the cause of God and the cause of democracy than our so-called Christian church. Next to our lack of an adequate foreign policy stands our lack of Christianity, twins of hypocrisy walking hand in hand.

Dr. Gaganvihari Mehta, the brilliant Ambassador from India and one of the apostles of Gandhi's passive love, was refused lunch at the Houston, Texas, airport because of his dark skin. The whole future of our foreign policy in Southeast Asia depended upon his religious reactions to that un-Christian hatred. Fortunately, his religion was superior to that of the Bible Belt and its refusal to practice the principles of Christianity.

The Finance Minister of Ghana, Komla Agbeli Gbedemah, was refused a glass of orange juice at a Howard Johnson's restaurant in Delaware. We could have been in serious trouble with the entire west coast of Africa and the newly emerging nations as a result, but *his* sense of religious values prevailed over our twisted and perverted form of Christianity.

When the seven houses of God were bombed in Montgomery, Alabama, and none of the perpetrators of this outrage was ever arrested, it was the Negro Christian who, without rancor or bitterness, cried out through prayer for help. When Emmett Till, a young boy, was killed in Mississippi and his murderers sold their confessions to *Look* magazine, nothing was done. The Department of Justice did not even appear before a Congressional committee to ask for a Federal anti-lynching law. While the country was wringing its hands in hypocritical horror, Jesus was hung on the cross again.

Little Rock! Out of all this hatred and hypocrisy, bitterness and blood, in a land where legalized persecution had reached heights exceeded only by its pretensions of Bible-pounding, only one man stood in the street one day with his arm around a little child and walked that child down the streets of Little Rock . . . he was white and he was a preacher! Yet all the while not a voice cried out in continuing and sustained indignation from the white pulpits of the South.

Then why do all these things happen? When I was hungry You fed me, and Dr. Mehta is not allowed to eat; when I was thirsty You gave me drink, and Howard Johnson's would not serve a glass of orange juice; when I was in prison You came and visited me, and Emmett Till was beaten to death; upon this rock I built my church, and it was bombed. Inasmuch as you have done it unto one of these, the least of my brethren—little boys and girls were kept from going to school. Why?

These acts were performed by those who belong to churches. These were the deacons, the Sunday School teachers, the good white Christians who went to their good white churches and worshiped their good white God, and yet would not allow the man from India and the man from Africa and the little boys and girls to come inside. These people who practiced prejudice during the week were the same people who occupied the pews on Sunday. Congressman Graham Barden of North Carolina once told me, "We have two Christmases in my county."

Naïvely, I asked, "Why?"

"On December 23 for colored people, and on December 25 for whites." I again showed my naïveté. "Why?"

"So they can work for us on Christmas Day," he replied.

This is anthropomorphism. There is never any religion in which man makes God in his own image. Where there is anthropomorphism there is no God. Therefore the voice of God is silent in that area of our land that needs it most, because God has no other voice than our voice. There are no shepherds to hear the voice from a burning bush any more.

We even have degrees of prejudice. When the seven churches were bombed in Montgomery, I sent a letter to the five hundred members of Congress asking them to make a contribution toward the rebuilding of those churches. The letter told my colleagues the story and gave the name of the building fund's treasurer in Montgomery. Only two members sent money to Martin Luther King, Jr., to help rebuild these houses of God. Yet when the synagogue was bombed in Atlanta, President Eisenhower personally ordered the FBI to move into the situation immediately. We Christians deplore the bombing of all houses of worship, but at least we want the equality of prejudice if we cannot have the equality of love.

After thirty years of ministry, preaching to four and five thousand on Sunday mornings, serving communion to 2,500, adding hundreds to the church membership every year—what is my interpretation of religion?

This is my personal credo: There is no heaven or hell in the sense that they are places to which one goes after death. The heaven or hell to which one goes is right here in the span of years that we spend in this body on this earth. That is the life I believe in.

I preach a strong personal gospel, which begins by trying to get man to have a sense of sin. Each of us knows when he is doing wrong or right. There is an Inner Voice that speaks through conscience and gives us all the correct evaluations of our thinking, of our thoughts, and of our sins. But we try to suppress this Inner Voice, to rationalize our wrongdoings, so the first thrust of my preaching is to give man a sense of sin—to preach that no man is better than any other man, that every human being is a sinner, that we are constantly in the process of sinning, that we sin by omission, we sin by commission, and we sin by permission.

Once man comes into the knowledge of his humanness, admitting his inherent weaknesses and frailties, expressing to himself his predilection to sin, then the process of salvation can begin. But it is very important to be careful that in giving man a sense of sin, one does not in turn give him a guilt complex. At the same time, if one meets a man who already has a guilt complex, the preaching thrust must constantly be shaped to meet this. While I recognize the validity of psychiatry and appreciate its contributions, nevertheless I believe that no man can be permanently cured of his guilt complex without the power of God in his life. All that the psychiatrist can do is reveal the guilt complex and its causes, but the salvation from the guilt itself can come only from the power of God.

When one has received the sense of sin, it is necessary to have a sense of conviction. Not just to accept that one is a sinner and that all people sin and are likely to continue, but to have a conviction that sin is wrong, that there is no such thing as partial sin; that sin is sin, and that there is no such thing as one sin's being greater than another. With this sense of conviction concerning sin there will come the ancient cry: "What must I do to be saved?"

There is only one answer: one must attain an awareness of God.

The awareness of God—nearer than one's hands and feet, closer than one's breathing, the eternal Hound of Heaven. What is God? All the beauty and truth and goodness in the world! No one has ever been able to improve my religious thinking on this simple definition of my mother's. So what we preach is an awareness of these things: beauty, truth, and goodness —then we are opening up the way to the awareness of God.

The way to the awareness of God is not the monopoly of the church nor is His inspiring spirit its captive. The church is of no value except to serve as an avenue or a way to this awareness. One can preach about this God only when he knows Him. Not when he knows *about* Him from what he can be taught from books and men in the theological seminaries. When one knows Him in His fullest sense, not only from reading and teaching but also from agonized searching, then one can walk through the world looking for beauty in all things. For all things have within them some element of beauty. One can also look and listen for truths, not the truths that the world proclaims as truths, for these truths are relative, but the truths that are absolute, the truths that one must find because only through finding the absolute can one be free. These absolute truths lead one into the ways of goodness.

So with this awareness of God one looks beyond the beauty of the superficial and the truths of the relative. One looks for beauty in all things because all things come from the Creator of beauty. A chain reaction is set up, not the chain reaction that comes from the beauty of the superficial nor the truth of the popular word, but a chain reaction that leads to goodness from the beauty that is within and the truth that makes one free, rather than the truths that make one captive. This is the eternal struggle of man against the unliberating truths that are self-evident, and toward the freedom-giving truths that must be agonizingly sought after. (Nor does this goodness consist of something that someone else purchased through a cross two thousand years ago.) This is the kind of preaching that came to my father in a vision in his later years. It came after many years of preaching about the outer man, so popular in my father's early days and about whom he preached with such power.

How can one increase the awareness of God? I cannot depend upon anything because God is not a thing. We are not, therefore, to be judged by the position that we hold in the church, nor by our years of membership, nor by our race or class, and not ever by the contributions that we make to our church life. For if God looks not on the outer man, how can we?

This is one of my great struggles in preaching: to try to convince people that they cannot be better Christians than Jesus. All too many of them think that they are. Religion, therefore, does not depend upon the visible. For this reason I have encouraged people through the years to come to church in any attire they desire, as long as that attire is decent. Why should religion depend upon whether one wears a hat or stockings, a necktie or a jacket? How can we set up rules for meeting in God's house when God has no rules for man to meet him except the hunger and the thirst?

This drawing near to God, this increasing awareness, cannot be accomplished, nor even the initial steps be taken, until one has purged himself of all hatred toward all fellow men. This is why I view askance the average white man's religion; and in this religion of his I include not just his church but the whole priesthood of believers and of preachers, his institutions of theological learning and his outer projection of his religion into community and world life. There is absolutely no Christianity of any type in any church where there is not active and equal participation at every level of church life and every level of religious institutions by all the sons of God. When for any reason whatsoever any participation of any member of the family of God is prohibited at any level, then there is no Christianity present, regardless of the pretensions.

Therefore, America is not a Christian country. It is a country of pretensions, of "churchianity," where the institution of Christianity has been perverted into an instrument to perpetuate if not to propagate, directly and indirectly, anti-Christian doctrines of segregation and discrimination. The only Christian churches in the United States are those churches that, at all levels, welcome and encourage the participation of all the sons of man.

The Negro is no better than the white man, but his awareness of God, his techniques to approach His nearness, and his unsegregated church undeniably indicate that his religion is more mature. His religion is obscured by his emotionalism, judged by the cults and their leaders, however, and most objective thinkers in the field of religion look down on the Negroes' church.

Emotionalism has its place in religion, for it is a part of the drive, the dynamism. Religion is a joyful thing. If one can scream because a man runs ten yards through the mud with a piece of pigskin in his hand, then there is no reason why a sincere "Amen" cannot be uttered when the breath of God is felt. The white man's Christianity has become ritualized; ferment of the religion of the Pilgrim Fathers has been aborted. Where once men practiced the continuing presence and sought an ever approaching nearness to God, they now reduce it to one Sunday morning service where the ears may be fastened on the preacher, but the eyes are on the clock.

Even going to church has become a fad. We proudly, as Americans, point to the statistics of growth in our various churches, fully aware that there has been a shrinking in the depths of our hearts and an increasing parsimony of the soul. God has always been sought most avidly during crises. When there is not a crisis, we merely "belong." But the reason the Negro is more mature in his religion than the white man is that because of the white man's oppression of him, the Negro has been forced to make the search for God an everyday, twenty-four-hour job.

To indicate that one cultivates the presence of God does not necessitate the outer symbols of the pious look, the somber clothes, the ostentatiously carried Bible, the dangling cross; but it does necessitate the bringing of more beauty, truth, and goodness into the world and into the lives of others—of all peoples in all places, wherever one can find them or their need.

It is at this point that the members of the Abyssinian Baptist Church register their fullest impact. For them, to practice the presence of God demands a continual witnessing in all areas of life at all levels with all peoples in all places. Vast as is this church, ancient as is its history, built in the heart of an unfriendly ghetto, it is a place of warmth and love—it is a friendly place. The outreach of its members, therefore, is a friendly outreach. From its portals stream thousands who go into every area of the life of our town carrying the Abyssinian spirit of friendliness. The outreach of our church is the outreach of a heart, as we move into the areas of our secular life—the mill, the factory, the office, the school, the bar, the club, the dance, politics; it does not matter where, we take this spirit with us.

We move with the calm inner assurance that we possess something so good that nothing outside can disturb it; so rare and wonderful that we want everyone to share it. The witness that we give, as we move through our town, is as meaningful to the semiliterate who walks by our sides as it is to the skilled surgeon or the captain of industry who works with us. We do not walk with the proclamation "I am a church member! I am a Christian!" We walk knowing that this sensitivity within His exuding awareness is speaking, and that when He speaks, it is with a thunderous incisiveness far beyond our stumbling proclamations.

We do not believe in the Bible as the word of God. It is too filled with contradictions. We believe in the Thomas Jefferson Bible. Carefully, that brilliant Founding Father cut from the New Testament only those words that Jesus spoke. Then in logical and chronological order, he put them together until he had created a new Bible, a new Bible of old words, only the words of Jesus himself. This is the Bible from which I preach.

I love the prophetic atmosphere of the Old Testament, I love the lyrical witness of Paul, but there is only one word that I feel is of God; and that is the word of the Son of God as it was recorded in Matthew, Mark, Luke, and John: "This is my Bible!" I reject all else, even the other words of Matthew, Mark, Luke, and John; and all of the Bible from Genesis to Revelations must be measured in terms of the words of Jesus Christ alone.

For us God is a God of truth and that truth is absolute. Yet how can He contradict Himself? And the Bible is filled with contradictions. I believe that the men who penned the words of the Bible were inspired, but all inspiration varies. Some inspiration does not reveal the final truth; some inspiration is so wrongfully received that no truth is revealed at all. Here and there as God speaks to man, as man becomes increasingly sensitive and aware of Him, man is privileged to be the recipient of the immortal flashes of the Absolute. Therefore, I believe that the Bible is still being written. I believe that whenever any soul at any time in any place comes close enough to God to hear the still, small voice—that is the moment when God speaks and a truth is told, or a beauty revealed, or a way to goodness is shown. Then that is written.

This, then, is the Bible; a continuing book of the inspiration of God to man. This is the continuing Bible as it was continued in some of Paul's letters. It was the continuing Bible that spoke to the first-century Christians in the Book of Acts and in the Apostles; it was the continuing Bible that came to John in the twilight of his life, on the isle of Patmas, and it was the voice of Logos itself.

I am not concerned with the theological disputes over the events preceding, during, and following the life of Jesus. All that I am gloriously certain of is that once a man walked this earth and spoke with such uncommon power that He separated history into B.C. and A.D.; that the teachings He proclaimed become newer and more challenging as the centuries roll. Any man who will actively preach, practice, and pursue those teachings and continuingly practice the presence of God will be making an active contribution to the world as he passes through, and that man is a Christian.

I do not preach a belief in the Virgin Birth nor do I preach against it. If an individual wants to believe in it, and if by that he does not tend to separate himself from his fellow men, then I say believe in it; but under no conditions must one base his religious faith upon whether or not he can believe in such incidentals as the Virgin Birth.

I am against all theological incidentals that through the years have not strengthened and united the family of God but rather torn it asunder. I am against infant baptism because my religious faith and my modern mind rebel against the concept that an infant must be baptized in order to be saved. I am against all doctrines that emphasize outer symbols. If we preach symbols, we are in danger of obscuring the all-important inwardness. Outwardness and symbols have been used to exclude, not include. As soon as one raises a symbol, a doctrine, a creed, then immediately there fall away, however few, those who do not agree. Therefore, I say that any church that in any way preaches or practices anything that will exclude anyone from membership is negating the power of Christ.

For twenty years I have refused to baptize. This act is performed by my assistants. Not that I disbelieve in baptism, but I disbelieve in any church that says its form of baptism is the only form. I hope that the day will come, before I retire from the Abyssinian Baptist Church, when I will see in front of the marble baptism pool of the Abyssinian Baptist Church a marble font, so that when individuals join the church, they can elect whether they should be baptized by immersion or by sprinkling.

5

The Abyssinian Baptist Church

During Thomas Jefferson's last term a group of traders who were in New York City from the country of Abyssinia, now called Ethiopia, wished to go to church on a Sunday morning. They went to the nearest one, which was on Gold Street and was the only Baptist church in the city. Abyssinia, incidentally, is the oldest Christian country in the world. Long before the first Anglo-Saxon had passed a comb through his matted hair, long before the first Anglo-Saxon could read or write, the people of Abyssinia had accepted the institution of Christianity and had developed a culture.

When these men came to the Baptist church to worship on that Sunday morning, they were promptly ushered into the slave loft. Wealthy, educated, world travelers, proud human beings, with a well-defined philosophy of religion that matched that of anyone in that auditorium, they resented this and walked out in protest. The Reverend Thomas Paul, a liberal white preacher educated at Harvard, left with them.

They then pooled their resources and in June, 1808, bought property on Worth Street on which they established the Abyssinian Baptist Church—the second oldest Baptist church in New York and the first Baptist church in the entire North to establish a nonsegregated membership.

The Abyssinian Church's history parallels the history of the development of New York City, which from a population of only a few thousand in 1808 has expanded to a population of some 8 million today. Scarcely four institutions still survive in New York City which antedate the Abyssinian Baptist Church: the oldest drug firm in America, Schiefflin & Company, the Bank of New York, the *New York Post,* and Tammany Hall.

From the beginning this church attracted people from all over New York. Some would come by boat from New Jersey and others by boat from Brooklyn, because there were no bridges then. So many members were coming from Brooklyn that on May 18, 1847, the Abyssinian Church sent the Reverend Mr. Samson White to organize the Concord Baptist Church there. The Concord Church has grown today to the point where its membership, attendance, budget, and wealth are almost identical with those of the Abyssinian Church.

In the early part of the nineteenth century the Abyssinians did not have a permanent church home, having sold the Worth Street property several years after they purchased it. For a time they met in various halls. But in 1856 Father William Spellman purchased a permanent church at Waverly Place in Greenwich Village. Its membership rose to sixteen hundred. Father Spellman was an aristocrat and an autocrat who introduced the system of rented pews. No one but the wealthy and the aristocratic attended.

In 1885 the Reverend Dr. Robert D. Wynn was called to the ministry. He dreamed that one day the Abyssinian Church would be built in Harlem. When he told the church members of this dream of moving to Harlem, they pronounced it a nightmare. He was so sure that he was right that when he resigned his ministry, he left behind $16,000 toward the building of this new church in Harlem.

Charles Satchell Morris, eloquent and brilliant, came as the sixteenth minister. He added $9000 more to that $16,000 and with this the Abyssinian Baptist Church bought the Dutch church on 40th Street and two adjacent apartment houses, selling the Waverly Place property. On the occasion of the centennial of the Abyssinian Church my father was called to the pastorate.

Mr. P., as my mother called my father, came to the Abyssinian Baptist Church on December 31, 1908, a month and two days after I was born. He found that the church was hopelessly bankrupt, owing $146,354, and that its bank account had been overdrawn by more than $300. My father instituted a foolproof bookkeeping system; preached to the members that they should give 10 percent of their income to the church. He found that they had become accustomed to starting church services anywhere from fifteen to twenty minutes late. He began services on time, and in twenty-nine years was "late at church" only once, having been delayed by a blizzard. Mr. P. was quite a man.

During my childhood the old red-brick church on West 40th Street was a playground for me, and despite all the good food at home, for a long time I thought the church was a place where people came primarily to eat. In those days everyone ate in the church after services. The Sunday dinners were one of the most lucrative forms of income for the church's treasury. All during Sunday School, which was conducted in the basement, you could smell, at the back of the room near the furnace, the tantalizing odors of delectable food. The fragrance arising from great mountains of fried chicken, hills of potato salad, and vats of greens cooked with ham hocks was integrated very nicely with that of baking hot bread.

For most people Sunday was a great day of rest, but for me it was merely the end of the week. We started out early in the morning, went through Sunday School, church service, Sunday dinner, Women's Christian Temperance Union, Baptist Young Peoples Union, and evening service. Occasionally attendance at the church itself was interrupted with a visit to a private home, where we prayed and sang hymns. In addition, all of Saturday and sometimes even Friday were spent preparing for Sunday.

Each Sunday my father left our home on 134th Street around five o'clock in the morning to attend the Sunday Morning Praying Band, which met at the ghastly hour of six o'clock. The Band, it seemed, predicated its meetings on the theory that God was more available at that early hour and man was in better condition to talk to him.

My mother usually went with my father, taking my sister, Blanche, with her. Josephine would bring me along later, leaving home about nine-thirty, and then we would all walk into church together. When my mother swept down the red-carpeted aisle of the church, trailed by her teen-aged daughter, with golden curls and starched dress, and me dutifully bringing up the rear, dressed in white in the summer, blue serge in winter, she was a sight to behold. I can still see her in a wide-brimmed Dolly Varden hat, with maybe an ostrich feather, a voluminous dress of that period, with cloth-topped high-buttoned shoes, and always her impeccable white kid gloves.

It took Josephine and me one hour to get from 134th Street to 40th Street if we went by trolley. That, of course, was the only way to go in the summertime. Trolleys were thrilling vehicles—especially if you could ride on the front seat with the motorman. All the seats on the summer trolleys were wooden benches with wide-open sides; when it rained, cloth curtains were pulled down.

As the weather grew colder and the winter trolleys were placed on the tracks, the only comfortable way to travel was by elevated. But the El was much too fast for me; we got downtown in almost forty minutes. What's more, Josephine always had to pay more for me on the elevated because at the age of five I was as tall as a nine-year-old, and by the time I was eleven I was as big as a fifteen-year-old. On the summer trolley the conductor collected the fares after we had taken our seats, so I would slouch down next to Josephine as small as I could. But we always got caught on the elevated because we had to walk past a man in the booth, and regardless of how low I crouched, Josephine had to pay the full children's fare when I was still under six and the full adult fare when I was still under twelve. This double taxation without representation always irked me.

When my father stood in the pulpit, he was awesome in his Prince Albert coat as he thundered his holy invectives against the sins of that day. He preached so hard that his starched collar and cuffs always wilted. Finally, my practical mother bought him celluloid ones.

Everything my father preached about I believed word for word. As I played or walked the streets with Josephine, I was always turning from side to side to see where this Jesus was who "walked with me" all the time. But church was so long—innumerable announcements, offerings, hymns—that by the time my father rose to preach I was either asleep or ready to compete with him. I felt I had a right to compete with him by talking out at any time I wanted, since all over the church others were continually doing so. "Amen!" "Hallelujah!" "Praise the Lord!" continually punctuated the service with stiletto sharpness. One old lady said "Hallelujah!" so often that we called her Sister Hallelujah. She even said "Hallelujah" when the announcements were made concerning the offerings of the previous Sunday.

Then there were the shouting sisters. How I used to love to watch them work out. Some would run up and down the aisles. Others would begin to jump with such strength that even three or four men from the ushers' board couldn't hold them down. But the one I liked best of all was the one who would suddenly jump up at just about the climax of my father's sermon, lean over backward, and slide slowly over the pew into the lap of whoever was unfortunate enough to be seated behind her. Every Sunday as she did so she revealed a set of lovely lacy underwear. Naturally she was a subject for constant discussion, but no one knew how to cope with the problem. One Sunday, however, as she slid over backward, staging her customary act, the bench broke. The church's Board of Trustees promptly sent her a bill for the repair of the bench and she never came to church again.

My mother and my sister, of course, never shouted or said "Amen" or "Hallelujah." This was part of my mother's way of demonstrating that we were slightly above those who gave way to such emotionalism. But I knew she wanted to. Many times when my father was thundering, his long, curly, black hair falling across his brow, his arms wide-stretched in appeal, she would start to cry. Then her left leg would begin to jump a little. That was my signal to put my hand on her leg and an arm around her and say, "Now don't cry any more, Mother." This always helped her to regain control.

As I grew older, I was a hell-raiser in church. Once I was so bad in church that my father stopped in the middle of his sermon to a packed auditorium and made me go up and stand in the pulpit with him for the rest of the service. And I'll never forget another day when I was in a particularly hell-raising mood, and no one could quiet me as my father was preaching. I was obviously distracting him. Mother very quietly and leisurely took off one of her spotlessly white kid gloves and holding it by the lining only, so that the outer part would not get soiled, she took her free hand and slapped me right across the face. Then just as calmly and coolly, she replaced the glove, button for button, and sat there impeccable again in her unsoiled white kidskin gloves.

As early as 1911 my father caught the Harlem vision. Few Negroes then lived in Harlem; most were still concentrated in the Forties downtown. My father recognized that the restless push of business along Broadway, and Seventh and Eighth Avenues in the Forties would eventually squeeze the Negro people out, and they would have to move uptown because there was no place betwen 40th Street and 135th Street where they were wanted or would be allowed to live.

A black leader had caught this same dream before my father. He was Marcus Garvey, the semiliterate, short, squat, heavy-set Jamaican, who, on his arrival in Harlem in 1914, said, "Where are your black lawyers? Where are your black judges? Where are your black mayors? Let us proceed now to set up a black empire in the United States." He immediately set up a Black United States within the United States of America. He was the Black President and he had a Black Vice President, Black Cabinet, Black Congress, Black Army with Black Generals, Black Cross Nurses, a Black newspaper called *The Negro World*, a steamship line called the Black Star Line, and a Black religion with a Black God. Negroes all over the South and in the West Indies began to say, "Let's go to Harlem to see this Black Moses." Marcus Garvey was the first man to ever make "black" Negroes proud of their color.

One of the greatest thrills of my life when I was about ten or twelve years old was to sit at Garvey's feet, or roll down Seventh Avenue with him as he paraded in his white-plumed hat. But he was railroaded to prison in the United States, railroaded to prison in London via an agreement with the British government after his term was finished in the United States, and he died of a broken heart in London. But today if you go to Jamaica you will see in Queen Victoria Park a statue of Queen Victoria—and staring her straight in the face is a statue of the first hero of Jamaican Republic, Marcus Garvey.

Father kept pushing to make the Abyssinian Church Harlem-minded. At last, when I was scarcely twelve years old, the church purchased land on 138th Street between Seventh and Lenox Avenues, and there, next door to Marcus Garvey's Black Freedom Hall, Daddy pitched his tent. For two summers, under that canvas, thousands were packed in every night as he preached. The membership of the church jumped to four thousand; tithing money increased to $35,000 a year; the regular offerings doubled. The Harlem push had picked up momentum.

In those days, from 137th to 138th Streets, and from Seventh to Lenox Avenues, there was a farm where I played as a ten- and eleven-year-old. An Italian squatter lived on the hill on Seventh Avenue, and from the hill to Lenox Avenue he farmed, producing fresh vegetables that he sold in the neighboring community. He also kept a herd of goats. On the land the church later bought he allowed us to play baseball. One day when my father came to watch us play ball, he said, "This is the spot upon which I want to build our church!" And upon that rock he did build the church. Up to this time no Negro church in the United States had cost $100,000 except the Union Baptist Church of Philadelphia. Yet, on that rock my father built a church that cost almost $340,000. It was built of rock, steel, brass, and marble. Mr. P. was indeed quite a man!

On the first Monday in July, 1922, the editor of the religious department of the New York *Journal-American,* Mr. Joseph Gilbert, wrote: "Work on what will be the largest Baptist Church in the country is now under way on 138th Street between Seventh and Lenox Avenues."

I helped to clear the land upon which the first tent was pitched. The land was cleared by volunteers from the church, and while they worked the ladies served them food. I ran back and forth with a pail of lemonade to refresh them as they toiled under the hot sun. Though still a boy, I helped to drive the first peg that put the guys of the tent in place. I stood by my father as the masons laid the cornerstone. I helped plan the gymnasium of the community center. Every step of the way I was part of the building of that Tudor-Gothic structure, even to running downstairs sometimes, late at night, to throw the switches that turned off lights the sexton had left burning. This was my church. It was my eternal mother.

On June 17, 1923, the new buildings on 138th Street near Seventh Avenue were completed at a cost of $334,881.86. The insurance today on these buildings is more than $1 million.

At one time $60,000 was needed to pay off the balance of the indebtedness. John D. Rockefeller, Jr., a staunch Baptist and the major contributor to the Riverside Baptist Church, agreed to give the entire amount, but on condition that one member of the Board of Trustees be appointed by him. My father brought this news back to the United Boards of the church, which turned it down unanimously. Within four and a half years the church was free and clear of any mortgage and also from any outside control.

The church and the community center were too small from the first day they opened. The church was built of solid rock, Italian marble, windows imported from Germany and England. The community center, built as part of the main building, was packed from basement gymnasium to rooftop, morning and night, throughout the week.

Long before the concept of Social Security had been introduced by Franklin D. Roosevelt's New Deal, the Abyssinian Church bought and furnished a white limestone townhouse at a cost of $40,000. It was dedicated on July 4, 1926. Here all members of the church, when they were no longer able to work or support themselves could live out their old age free of charge.

The church became so affluent that it was able to give $1000 a year to the National Baptist Foreign Missions Board; $1000 to the building of the Medical Center in New York City; $2000 to Virginia Union University; $4000 to Fisk University; $1000 to Tuskegee and Hampton. Nor did any new church ever come to Harlem to buy or to build without receiving a large financial gift from our church.

A school of religious education, set up under the supervision of Columbia University, included teacher-training as well as weekday and Sunday religious education classes. Adult education provided elementary English, citizenship, designing, dressmaking, home nursing, and business courses, and the famous school of dramatic arts directed by Richard B. Harrison, "De Lawd" of *Green Pastures.*

When my father received the Harmon Award in January, 1928, for notable achievement in religious service, Herbert Hoover, then President of the United States, sent him a personal letter of congratulation.

In September, 1937, my father resigned and was named pastor emeritus with a pension for life. Under the ministry of my father, during his twenty-nine years, the church budget, originally $6000, was increased to $55,000; under my father's ministry and mine the original indebtedness of $146,000 was converted to the present assets of $400,000; the original membership was seven hundred, the present membership twelve thousand.

Because of the inauguration of two Sunday morning services early in my ministry, I was preaching to twice the number of people my father had reached. So many people passed through the community center, now named after my father, that a dean of theology from a West Coast University said, "You don't have to tell me that you work here. I can look at your floor, your walls, and your furniture and see that it is used."

We have never had enough room. Soon after I became pastor I closed down the ten-room penthouse apartment on the top floor of the church, turning it over to community activities. Within one week that too was overcrowded. Social Security had by now been born and I asked the church to place our home for the aged, the white limestone townhouse, on the market because there were no more applicants. Rather than encumber the church with purchasing a house for the minister to live in, I asked the accountants to figure out the average yearly expense for maintaining a parsonage over the previous ten years and accepted that in lieu of a parsonage.

The Abyssinian Baptist Church reached another milestone early in 1961 when we finalized plans for the purchase of three YMCA buildings adjacent to the church, at a cost of approximately half a million dollars.

No important Negro has come to Harlem from any of the far corners of the earth without being honored at the Abyssinian Baptist Church. When Haile Selassie, Emperor of Ethiopia, came to the United States for the first time and decorated President Eisenhower, I also was decorated. The Emperor gave the Abyssinian Church, through me, a solid-gold seven-foot Coptic cross; the gold alone is worth $20,000. The President of Liberia, the President of Haiti, the Acting President of Indonesia have worshiped in our auditorium. Before Ghana was known to the world, a young black seaman sailing in the Merchant Marine and shipping out of New York visited the church. His name was Kwame Nkrumah, and he later became Prime Minister of that young country. Dr. Agokiane, who became a leading political figure in Nigeria, ofttimes worked with me back in the 1930s, worshiping in church and helping to picket stores that were not practicing democracy.

In November, 1983, the Abyssinian Baptist Church will celebrate a hundred and seventy-five years of service to its people. I will be marking my seventy-fifth birthday. And as long as He is willing, we'll celebrate together as we have most Sundays since 1937.

6

A Pioneer
Marching Black

In 1930 the national debt of the United States was $15 billion. The entire cost of our participation in World War One was slightly more than $30 billion. Yet in a very few brief weeks, the stock market had blown $30 billion into the air. The Great Depression had arrived.

This state of economic affairs meant nothing more to me than a few cold words of print. It all had happened while I was safe in the security of my senior year at Colgate University, with all bills paid and a doting mother waiting on graduation day with a ticket to Europe in her hand and a command to "go see the world and don't come back until your money is gone." There was no opportunity even to taste some of the salt of the bitter tears of the unemployed.

I was graduated on the morning of June 7, 1930, and left at midnight that night. In the four months I was away everything tumbled in the United States. When I returned on October 1, one-fifth of Harlem was unemployed. But as I stepped off the boat I had my job waiting for me: business manager of the church and my father's assistant minister. For this reason I had no feeling or sensitivity for the suffering around me. I had spent four years in a small, select, and expensive college, had had months of good times in Europe, and had a job prepared for me—a job I could have the rest of my life. What, then, did it matter to me that in Atlanta 65 percent of the Negro people were on relief; in Birmingham 63 percent; in Charlotte, North Carolina, 75 percent; in Norfolk, Virginia, 81 percent?

One day I stopped my father's Pierce Arrow limousine at a red light on Prospect Avenue in the Bronx and saw hundreds of women huddled against the wall in the rain. I turned to my companion in complete amazement and asked, "What are they doing?"

She answered, "Those people are unemployed domestic workers who stand there from six o'clock in the morning till late at night, selling themselves to whoever comes by for ten cents an hour for a day's work."

I began to find out more of what was going on about me. I learned that as the result of the Depression, 63 percent of the schoolchildren in the Abyssinian Church neighborhood were suffering from malnutrition, while I lived—and lived well—in our ten-room penthouse. Slavery had returned to the United States. In Jonesboro, Arkansas, actual slaves were living on one of the plantations there; and in McClelland, Florida, a whole community of Negro workers had been found under guard at the turpentine camp. Poor whites were beginning to suffer as much as the Negro. Deep in the heart of Florida and Alabama the legs of thousands of little white kids began to shrink and their bellies became distended. Mothers and fathers of the poor South knew nothing but a hopeless rage.

When men are driven by frustration and wrath, when hope dies completely, when there is nothing to do, not even to dream about, scapegoats are eagerly sought after—just someone, anyone, who can be beaten lower than the level to which he has already been pushed.

Twenty-three-year-old Claude Neal of Florida was arrested for alleged murder, and America was invited to attend his lynching. Headlines screamed the invitation from the *Miami Herald*, the *Peoria Journal*, the *Kansas City Star*, the *Shreveport Times*, the *Tampa Tribune*, the Louisville *Courier-Journal*, the Bismarck, North Dakota, *Tribune*, and the *Raleigh News and Observer*. The radio station of Dothan, Alabama, broadcast an invitation around the clock and, as a result, seven thousand white people came from eleven states to witness a man, made in the image of God, having his genitals cut off and being forced to eat them. This was the kind of world I started to work in, completely insulated from it, knowing about it only what I read in the newspapers.

One night early in 1930 there came a knock at the door of our apartment. When I opened it, there stood five of the outstanding doctors of the Harlem community: U. Conrad Vincent, Marshall Ross, Sidat Singh, now dead, Peter Marshall Murray, later to become the president of the New York County Medical Society, and Ira McCown, later to become the physician of the New York State Boxing Commission. Dr. Vincent got right to the point and said, "We need you, a flaming tongue, to fight our battle."

They had just been banned from Harlem Hospital because they were Negroes, despite the fact that it was the only public hospital in Harlem, but it served a totally Negro community with an all-white staff. These eminent practitioners had been kicked out only because they were Negroes.

"What can I do?" I asked.

They said they wanted me to organize the masses to help them fight their battle. Dr. Vincent urged, "You have got to be what Clarence Darrow said Mayor John P. Altgeld of Chicago was to the maimed and beaten, the sightless and voiceless! The eyes and ears, and a flaming tongue crying in the wilderness for kindness and humanity and understanding."

And so for the first time I heeded the call of the masses and became part of the struggles of the people of Harlem—not through any wish of my own, not through any divine call, but simply because I had been born to begin my work in the Great Depression.

I immediately rallied to the task set before me by the doctors' committee and called together as many people as I could, representing a cross-section of Harlem life. We organized the Committee on Harlem Hospital and I staged my first mass meeting. After that I marched in my first picket line in front of Harlem Hospital. I headed delegations that went to the office of the medical director, Dr. John Connor, who was bitterly anti-Negro. I went to the superintendent of the hospital, who refused to see me; and to the Commissioner of Hospitals of the City of New York, who ridiculed our efforts. No one took our drive seriously because Negro people had always gotten excited through the years about a cause, but they had never learned the lesson of sustained indignation. Even the national Negro organizations, with their headquarters in New York, refused to cooperate.

But something had happened to me. The people of the streets, the failures, the misfits, the despised, the maimed, the beaten, the sightless, and the voiceless had made a captive of me . . . and I was to know no other love but these people. Whenever they commanded, I followed, but fol-

lowed only to lead. It was a mutual contagion, a mass empathy on their part
and an undeviating allegiance on my part.

In that spring of 1930 I led a mass delegation of six thousand people to
City Hall demanding reforms at Harlem Hospital. Six hundred policemen
had been called out by the city fathers to handle the crowds. It was a
dramatic sight—all over City Hall Park hundreds of mounted police and
plainclothesmen mixed with our masses; patrolmen in uniform were drawn
up, shoulder to shoulder. Riot squads were hidden in various buildings and
riot equipment had been issued. But the six thousand moved as one with
me, for in the few short months that we had lived together I had taught
them the power of non-violence. On that day at City Hall no words were
spoken, no curses hurled, no sticks or stones or weapons were used. We
carried nothing except the massive strength of our unity.

I was the first to arrive at City Hall, with just the two or three others
who rode down in the car with me. We stood on the sidewalk and waited.
Suddenly—up from the subways . . . down from the elevated lines . . . and
out of the buses . . . our people streamed We had expected a few hundred,
but after the first thousand arrived, we had to move from the sidewalks into
City Hall Park. Then two or three thousand more came. I had to stand on
a bench and, finally on top of a car in order to talk to them. These were
six thousand people marching together; they were my people, and I belonged to them. On this day we stepped up the tempo of democracy in
action in New York City.

The Board of Estimate of the City of New York was in session when we
arrived at City Hall. Seated in the main chair was Acting Mayor O'Brien.
He was a fat, big-headed, and bald-headed man who would not heed our
demands to see him. The policeman wouldn't let me in, but the president
of the Board of Aldermen, a member of the Board of Estimate, Joseph V.
McKee, demanded that I be heard.

Joseph V. McKee was one of the pillars of the Roman Catholic Church
and Cardinal Spellman's personal lawyer. He was later to be Franklin D.
Roosevelt's choice to run for Mayor of the City of New York and I was
to be the chairman of his uptown campaign. A friendship was forged
between us that day at the Board of Estimate meeting that was never to
be broken except by death, and only a short time before he died we traveled
together to Panama on the Panama Line. He lost in the mayoralty race to
Fiorello H. LaGuardia, but he went on to great fame and fortune.

When I stood before the Board of Estimate and stated our demands, I knew at last the power of the masses—as long as I could keep the thousands on my side united, it mattered not who opposed us because we would win. The Board of Estimate launched an investigation and finally all five doctors were reinstated, and Harlem Hospital was given an interracial staff, with a Negro as the Medical Director. The surgical and medical facilities, which had been so filthy that the hospital for years had been referred to as "The Butcher Shop," were cleaned up. The Nurses' Training School at the hospital was investigated and overhauled. And later I had the privilege of standing by Mayor LaGuardia and helping him lay the cornerstone of the hospital's new women's pavilion.

This victory was very heady wine for a youngster of twenty-two. All my life I had been preparing for this moment and yet had never been conscious of it.

During the early 1930s there was no Department of Public Welfare in the City of New York. Not a single agency of any type—city or state—even indirectly, much less directly, existed or had been set up to cope with the problem of the Depression. Then financiers Seward Prosser and Harvey Gibson organized a citizens' committee. These deans of industry and finance had been impressed by my control of the masses in the Harlem Hospital fight, and in the spring of 1932 they called me to meet with them in the board room of one of the important banking houses of Wall Street. I was not yet twenty-four.

The room where we met breathed opulence and understated elegance. The portraits of men who had made America and who had in turn become legends looked down upon us. After we had been seated, Prosser and Gibson asked me what I thought they should do to relieve the suffering in Harlem. "Get together all the available money you can for Harlem," I told them. "We will not give one penny of it away but will make people work for the money. Even if I have to put them in one spot and have them scrub that same spot all day long, they will work for the money."

They believed in my proposal and we set up the committee headquarters in the Abyssinian Baptist Church. It was the first relief program, private or otherwise, in New York City. Every Saturday an armored truck would arrive and give me $2000, sometimes $3000, in cash. I had from one hundred and fifty to two hundred men and women working. They were scrubbing, painting, and conducting adult education classes. No one loafed. But it was not enough to meet the need. Even though men who had gone to college jumped in and gave their time and formed the first staff, it was still not enough. Thousands would line up every day, asking for just "something" to do for a few dollars.

My father gave me a $1000 gift and we set up a free food kitchen in the gymnasium of the church. It was staffed by volunteer workers, led by Albert Jordan who years before had been the maintenance superintendent of the Knickerbocker Theatre. With contributions from meat markets and grocery stores, we were able to feed a thousand people a day. I was reminded of an incident during my childhood, when one daÿ a panhandler came by to ask for a handout. Mother had no money but gave him a hot loaf of freshly baked bread she made every Saturday morning. He threw it into our trash can as he walked away cursing us. But in 1932 men and women, black and white, a thousand a day, stood in line for a slice of bread and a bowl of soup.

I learned something in those days that I will never forget: there is such a thing as gratitude. People have often said to me through the years, "Why do you work so hard for the masses? The masses are never grateful for what you do. When you need them, they will forget what you have done."

This is totally untrue. The bread that we literally cast upon the waters in 1932 returned, and every man and woman to whom I was able to give even a small sum on Saturdays, and every man and woman who was able to get a little something to eat each day, has remembered—to this day.

For every one person I helped over the years, a score rose up to stand by me. The sons and daughters of the parents we helped in the 1930s have gone on to high places, but they have been taught the story of what happened back in those days, when all their parents wanted was someone who cared . . . and I did care. And there is a reward when one gives of oneself wholeheartedly and without stint. Deep within there comes an inner glow that nothing can purchase and no one can steal.

The Great Depression continued to increase in intensity. People were being evicted by the thousands in the dead of winter with snow on the ground. Morning after morning the curbstones of Harlem were lined with the miserable, battered, broken remnants of what was called furniture. What could I do? What should I do? An average of a hundred and fifty people a day would stand in line in my office with eviction notices. My heart was sick from the suffering of these people.

By this time the city had set up its first Department of Public Welfare, but it was ill equipped and poorly staffed. Public relief was a new thing, and even though we sent delegations to the relief bureau to demand money to cover rents for those in need, it was unobtainable. Dr. W. Adrian Freeman, brilliant Western Reserve University traumatic surgeon and member of the Abyssinian Baptist Church, who maintained his offices adjacent to the community center, suggested a new idea to me: "Why not organize a rent strike?"

I then developed the following technique. I would walk the streets looking for an evicted family, and when I found one, I immediately sent a protest committee to the owner of the building, saying "Put that family back in their home or we will have every family in the building refuse to pay their rent."

No one paid any attention to our threats, so we carefully organized our first house. When we had finished organizing the building, all the tenants in the house went on a rent strike. A treasury was set up into which they paid their rent as it became due. The landlord dared not evict the entire house because the expenses to the City Marshal, the loss of rent, and the cost of painting and fixing required for new tenants would have been prohibitive. Before long the landlord gave in. So we moved our first family back into the very apartment from which it had been evicted. The rent strike idea spread and Donnellan Phillips, one of my co-workers, organized the Consolidated Tenants League. The day of the avaricious landlord had started to come to a close.

On March 19, 1937, Harlem burst into flames of riot. The winds of the ghetto had fanned resentment and an igniting spark was all that was needed. On that afternoon the rumor spread that a Puerto Rican boy, allegedly caught stealing in Kress's five-and-ten-cent store located on Harlem's major thoroughfare, West 125th Street, had been beaten by the store manager. Mobs poured into the streets. Groups collected that ranged from three to ten thousand persons each. The first race riot started by Negroes in the history of America was under way. It lasted for only one night, but when it was over there were dead and wounded and property losses worth millions of dollars. The damage to plate glass alone amounted to $200,000.

Why? Harlem was a community that had been built to house about eighty thousand whites, mostly German and Irish. Within one decade it became the world's largest racial ghetto because three hundred thousand Negro people from the South and the Caribbean had poured into it. Despite the fact that Harlem had quadrupled its population, not a single new school or hospital had been built in the district; and to aggravate matters, the private hospitals in the Harlem area refused to accept Negro patients. At the same time, not more than twenty new apartment houses had been built. And so, in this compact area, three hundred thousand Negro people were forced to live, serviced by institutions created for only eighty thousand.

Naturally, with the ancient law of supply and demand working, Harlem-ites had to pay a tax on being black. Rents were 20 percent higher than for similar accommodations elsewhere in New York City. Foodstuffs were 17 percent above the general level. Life insurance rates were doubled. Credit clothing stores thrived on usury rates of 100 percent.

Resentment in Harlem was also fanned by the fact that into the community each morning came shopkeepers whose coffers flowed with the black man's money, and who left in the evening taking all that money with them, because not a single store in Harlem owned by a white would employ a Negro except as a porter or maid. I made a survey in 1936 and found that out of five thousand people who worked on 125th Street, from river to river, only ninety-three were Negroes, and they were all menials.

This, then, was Harlem in the Great Depression. It had no real leader-ship and no mass organization. It was exploited by politicans, victimized by merchants, and hampered by woefully inadequate educational and health facilities. The important Negro mass organizations—the National Urban League and the National Association for the Advancement of Col-ored People—were living in their downtown ivory towers, totally insulated from the sufferings of their people.

On March 20, 1937, the morning following the riot, a group came to me and asked, "Why should we allow these 125th Street merchants to take our money and not give us employment? Look at what the Negro people have done in the Negro section of Chicago."

As a result of this meeting I organized the Coordinating Committee for Employment. This was the first time a mass organization had been created on the basis of group rather than individual memberships. By this time masses of people had already been organized by me and had been marching with me for seven years. Now, I felt, the time had come to stretch out and bring in other organizations. They came: the Garvey Black Nationalists joined us because I had always preached that Negroes must have self-respect before they can demand respect from others; the West Indians came because I had worked hard to abolish the artificial barrier between them and the native-born Negro people; the left-wing organizations stepped into line because I had cooperated with them in the fight for the freedom of the Scottsboro Boys. And, naturally, our first meeting was held in the Abyssinian Baptist Church, the great foundation upon which so many people's movements have been built.

The Abyssinian Baptist Church, then as now, gave us office space free, and therefore no money was necessary to underwrite the expenses of our mass movements. The vast membership of the church, over ten thousand, always stood as the united primary task force to give the initial backing to my mass meetings and to spearhead the initiation of any worthwhile cause.

The Coordinating Committee for Employment was shunned by the national Negro leaders—leaders who wouldn't be recognized by five people if they walked down Lenox Avenue on a crowded August night.

The co-chairman of our committee was the brilliant Reverend Dr. William Lloyd Imes, minister of St. James Presbyterian Church and president of the Alumni Association of Union Theological Seminary, later to be president of Knoxville College in Tennessee. I was young and Dr. Imes was mature. I acted before I thought and he thought before he moved. I was impetuous and impatient, but Dr. Imes always paused to reason. He was a great man, with the mind of a scholar, the soul of a saint, the heart of a brother, the tongue of a prophet, and the hand of a militant.

Then there was Arnold Johnson, executive secretary of the committee, a black Cuban, suave, handsome, young, radical, and always dressed impeccably. Arnold at heart was a revolutionary, against everything and everyone he felt was wrong.

The treasurer of the committee was Mrs. Genevieve Chinn, a West Virginia socialite, wife of Harlem's leading eye, ear, nose, and throat specialist—a handsome young woman who presided over her luxurious Whitestone Landing mansion with all the dignity of a person to the manner born. Yet in her heart Mrs. Chinn was a passionate fighter, side by side with us, for the uplifting of the masses.

It was a strange group. James W. Ford, the perennial Vice Presidential candidate of the Communist Party, was working side by side with Capt. A. L. King, head of the remnants of the nationalist Garvey movement. And because the police were watching our every move and rumors had come to us that the Department of Justice had assigned agents to infiltrate, we never again met in Harlem. Instead we gathered in the Greenwich Village apartment of a Wall Street broker, Sascha Iskander Hourwich. Though we dreamed different dreams, we all had but one objective: the full emancipation and equality of all peoples. Because we were operating in the period of the Great Depression, we took as our first goal economic equality.

We began to picket 125th Street stores from river to river. We made it a disgrace for anyone in Harlem to cross a picket line. One Saturday we closed down Chock Full O'Nuts, a New York restaurant chain, thus forcing them to employ their first Negro salesgirl. Today the vast majority of their employees are Negroes and Jackie Robinson, a Negro, served for sometime as a vice-president of the company.

I developed a technique for hitting similar types of stores that were in competition with each other. We would pick off only one, leaving the other free to do business, even though its policy was just as bad. For example, we picketed Grant's and let Woolworth's go unpicketed; in two weeks Grant's capitulated. Then we hit Woolworth's . . . and it was all over in one weekend.

Our slogan, as proclaimed from picket signs, sound trucks, and picketers, was "Don't Buy Where You Can't Work!" Our campaign increased in power. One Saturday alone we closed ten stores that later signed contracts with us overnight. The Coordinating Committee became so powerful that the president of the Uptown Chamber of Commerce, Col. Leopold Philip, for the first time in United States history signed a contract with the consumer guaranteeing employment of the consumer. Two hundred and seven organizations were represented in the committee for a total membership of 170,000 people.

The Coordinating Committee accomplished all this, yet never had more than $300 in its treasury. We never bothered to conduct a real membership campaign, because we acted on the assumption that all Harlem belonged. As the victories came to us, the bandwagon crowd began to jump on. In Harlem, at the height of our campaign, merchants were appealing for so many Negro Workers that the Harlem YMCA, the Urban League, and the African Patriotic League set up classes to train Negroes as salesclerks.

Herbert Lehman was then the Governor of New York State. This liberal decided that action concerning the problems of the urban colored population should be taken by the State of New York. He therefore appointed a committee which held hearings all over the state. I can remember one that was held in New York City, in the local courtroom on 150th Street between Convent and Amsterdam Avenues. Governor Lehman was present that day. Members of the commission and experts in their fields sat on the judge's rostrum. The witnesses were the executives of the utility companies.

The vice-president in charge of personnel of the telephone company stated that he would never employ Negroes because Negroes and whites could not get along together. Privately, he had told us that he didn't favor the employment of Jews or Catholics either. The executive vice-president of the Consolidated Edison Company, Colonel Stilwell, similarly testified, and the Governor of New York could not force them to change their hiring policies.

The idea of a Fair Employment Practices Commission had not yet been born, but we had the power to make these giant utilities do what was right. We began to picket the offices of Consolidated Edison. We gave Con Ed an ultimatum: either start hiring Negroes or we will declare Tuesday of every week as lightless night. Though we did not advocate violence, we made it clear that there might be some in the community who would resent seeing lights buring in any window. The merchants in the Harlem community, including the operators of the big chain stores, demanded that Con Ed change its hiring policy because they could not afford to turn out the lights in the windows of their stores, yet could not risk having those windows broken. And so Consolidated Edison succumbed.

At about this time the telephone company was installing the dial system. One of its principal offices, located in Harlem at the corner of 146th Street and Convent Avenue, had been remodeled into a dial system office. The operators who had previously worked there had been moved to other areas during the remodeling. We told the telephone company that unless they hired Negroes for this branch we would start dialing "Operator" on the machines. This, they knew, would throw their dial system out of order. They did not believe we would do it . . . but we did. In three weeks the telephone company changed its hiring policy. Today over seven thousand Negro women work for that company as operators.

Our next problem was the Negro pharmacist. Scores of Negro pharmacists in New York were unemployed or working at other operations. To help them get work in their own field, we began a picketing campaign against the drug stores. We succeeded in getting the Liggetts chain to sign up first, and by the time we finished our campaign—within four months—there was not a single unemployed pharmacist in Harlem.

In the late 1930s none of the companies of the beverage industry hired Negro salesmen in Harlem—not only Hoffman's and Canada Dry, but the liquor stores as well. In 1938 I helped organized the "Cork and Bottle Club," composed of the Negro representatives of companies doing business in Harlem. This group has grown to be one of the most important groups of salesmen in the New York area.

On and on we moved, and in 1939, when Grover Whalen was named chairman of the New York World's Fair Corporation, we went to ask him for employment at the Fair for qualified Negro people. He offered us a few token jobs. We refused them. The slogan of the Greater New York World's Fair was "Building the World of Tomorrow," and I can remember telling Grover Whalen, "You cannot have a World of Tomorrow from which you have excluded colored people."

Mr. Whalen, suave and urbane, smiled beneath his carefully trimmed moustache and said, "I do not see why the world of today or tomorrow of necessity has to have colored people playing an important role."

For the first time we moved our picket line downtown, picketing the Empire State Building, where the New York World's Fair Corporation had its headquarters. Every Thursday night we held a death watch. It was there, on those all-night death watches, that unity reached out and brought into the ranks more "makers of the dream." Chorus girls from Ethel Waters' Broadway hit would come to walk the picket line at midnight; the Cotton Club girls would come over between shows; the first Negro General Sessions Judge of the City of New York, Miles Paige, picketed every Thursday night. As a result of this picketing we received close to six hundred jobs at the World's Fair.

It was in 1941 that our committee gained its greatest victory. The Omnibus Corporation, which operated the buses in the streets of New York, had refused to employ any Negroes except as cleaners in the garage. On February 26 the Transport Workers Union, under the fiery Mike Quill, who was carrying his shillelagh, began their picket campaign to unionize the company. Mike Quill and I had a meeting in a downtown restaurant. "If you will support me after you have won your organization drive, then I will support you now," I said to Mike. We agreed and shook hands on it. As we were leaving, I added, "Mike there is only one thing I want you to do. When you see that victory is coming your way, call me just a few hours before so I'll be ready to roll with my program."

On March 10 I received a phone call from Quill saying that the twelve-day-old strike was finished and that the settlement announcement would be made in a few hours. Five hours after the Transport Workers Union's victory had been announced, we struck. Our signs had been prepared while we were waiting for the word from Quill, and we now began to March back and forth with them at the crossroads of Harlem—125th Street. Our signs read: "We stayed off these buses for twelve days that white men might have a decent standard of living. Keep on staying off them now for the rights of black men." We had seventy pickets the first night, nine hundred one week later, two thousand the third week. In the fourth week, when we began to send thousands of pickets downtown, the company began to weaken. The white bus drivers refused to drive through Harlem—not out of fear, but because we had helped them in their own days of campaigning. From 110th Street south along Fifth Avenue, Eighth Avenue, every avenue, hundreds of buses were left vacant, night after night.

One night at the Golden Gate Ballroom ten thousand people showed up to volunteer to picket. The next morning John D. Ritchie, an official of the bus company, sent for me. I went to his office in the Omnibus Corporation Building at 138th Street just off the Hudson River. He was visibly shaken. "Reverend Powell," he said, "I have not slept all night. Your people are ruining my business. If those thousands of pickets you gathered together last night go downtown and start picketing the downtown areas, we will probably go bankrupt. What do you want?"

I told him, "I want integration of people on the basis of ability,' not on the basis of color." So lawyers were appointed—one from the company, one from the Transport Workers Union, and Harrison Jackson representing the consumers of Harlem. An agreement was drawn up listing every phase of employment in the company and laying down my formula that "for every white man employed, two Negroes should be employed," until a decent and democratic number had been hired. Since that day we have had absolutely no trouble or complaint. Today more than ten thousand Negro people are working in the New York City transit system in every capacity.

During this entire period of conflict I used everyone I thought might aid us, everyone I could enlist to help in this mass struggle. My critics have often cited the names of many Communist-front organizations with which my name was associated. Let it be a matter of record that no man ever used me, but in order to help my people I used everyone that had any strength whatsoever, including the Communists. The proof of this is that the membership of the Communist Party in Harlem never exceeded five hundred out of the section's three hundred thousand Negroes. Yet there were times when I could get a thousand or two thousand Communists to picket for our cause.

In 1941 the war was almost upon us, bringing with it artificial prosperity.

We had broken down the economic walls of Jericho, but I began like Alexander of old to feel a strange emptiness—"No more worlds to conquer." But then in the early part of 1940 Wendell Willkie, who was to be the Republican Presidential candidate that year, sent for me. I went to his office in New York City. We were closeted alone. He pointed out his dreams and his hopes and he almost won me to his cause. These are the Willkie words that seared me: "Powell, I would like you to be a part of my team. I would like you to play a major role. I like independents. But whether you join my team or not, Powell, remember this—always keep yourself independent. Don't let any of these political parties control you."

As I rode back uptown, I began to think about Willkie's words. The population of New York City now included close to half a million Negro people. Not a single Negro-elected official really represented the people. Harlem itself was so gerrymandered that it was impossible to elect a Congressman or a State Senator. A piece of Harlem was held by Representative Sol Bloom; another by Representative Vito Marcantonio; still another by Joseph A. Gavagan; and even a small corner was allotted to the Bronx. Negroes in Harlem were blindly Republican or Democrat—there was absolutely no independent, liberal thinking. What Wendell Willkie told me that afternoon convinced me of the new possibilities and objectives which changed my course of direction.

At my urging the Coordinating Committee for Employment organized now into a new group aimed at political equality. We called ourselves the Peoples' Committee and its slogan was "One People, One Fight, One Victory." The Reverend Dr. Imes had left New York to become president of Knoxville College. Dr. Channing Tobias, the senior secretary of the National YMCA (later to be chairman of the board of the NAACP), was elected to fill the vacancy left by Dr. Imes.

Under the proportional representation system by which the City Council of New York was elected, no Negro had ever been seriously considered as a Councilman. It was virtually impossible even to think that a Negro could be elected. Under the city's electoral system, by which an individual must run citywide, no Negro could be elected without the complete unity of all of Harlem, plus considerable support of whites in other areas.

On September 25, 1941, I announced my candidacy for the City Council. I refused to accept the support of either party. Although a registered Democrat, I ran as an Independent. Other candidates were being set up to run against me. Dr. Tobias had been selected by the Republicans as their candidate; Dr. Max Yergan had been picked by the American Labor Party; and Tammany Hall had selected one of its faithful, Herman Stoute, who was nothing but a Negro district captain being used by Tammany to divide the Negro vote. I went to Dr. Tobias and to Dr. Yergan and pointed out that if we rallied around one candidate, we would have a chance. They withdrew.

I had no money, just workers. A few days before Election Day the County Chairman of the Republican Party sent scores of thousands of pieces of literature to the Republican leaders in Harlem for distribution. Harold Burton, dean of the Republican leaders there, refused to accept them. Burton went to Thomas J. Curran and said, "I would be run out of Harlem if I asked my people to go out and distribute literature for Stanley Isaacs for City Councilman with Adam Powell's name being in the same leaflet." All the other Republican leaders—William Cornelius, Charles Hill, and Carey Blue—supported him. Curran tried to use his power to persuade them otherwise, but they refused. Finally in exasperation, he said, "Well, if you want to put Powell's name on the literature, then he will have to print it himself."

I had no money, but I had a friend named Maurice Rosenblatt, now the chairman of the executive board of the National Committee for an Effective Congress, with whom I had been working to raise funds for an underground terrorist organization in Palestine. At this time David Ben-Gurion was trying to work out a compromise with the British government. There were two groups in what was then Palestine, now Israel, who refused to go along with Ben-Gurion. One was the Stern Group, the other was Irgun. I worked with Irgun, for which I raised close to $150,000 at a rally at Madison Square Garden. At the rally I raised a hundred-dollar bill in my hand and said, "If a black man will give a hundred dollars for the freedom of Israel, what will you Jews do?"

Maurice and I got into a taxicab and he took me to see four of his friends. The next morning I had $1200 to pay for campaign literature and to get some sandwiches and coffee for my workers. This was all the money that I raised and all that I spent.

When the returns of the election came in on the first day, the *New York World-Telegram* ran a front-page headline that said: "POWELL LEADS CITY." When the final ballot was counted, I had come in third out of ninety-nine candidates and had the right to sit on the council of the largest city in the world as an Independent.

7

First Bad Nigger in Congress

I stood on the Floor of the House of Representatives at the opening of the 79th Congress, on January 3, 1945, and lifted my hand along with my four hundred and thirty-four colleagues, swearing to uphold the Constitution of the United States. In that Constitution there are certain guarantees based upon the Bill of Rights and the Declaration of Independence: "We hold these Truths to be self-evident. . . ."

Far off in strange lands men were fighting to make this world safe for democracy, yet they fought with complete and rigid segregation in the armed forces, sustained by the Supreme Commander of Allied Forces in Europe, Dwight David Eisenhower: "Negro and white soldiers could not fight together." But in the Battle of the Bulge, Hitler's Panzer divisions, striking with power, began to penetrate and decimate the white fighting man. In desperation, all thought of segregation was lost. Black men, who had hitherto been confined to waging this war in the 310th Quartermaster Corps, the 238th Salvage Collection Company, and the 303rd Rail Head Company, men who had been denied the opportunity to learn the intricacies of modern arms, suddenly had guns thrust into their hands. With the courage that all men are heir to, regardless of color, they fought and they bled and they died, side by side, with whites and the bulge was turned back and victory came closer.

This, then, was our country fighting a war to preserve democracy, but with an undemocratically segregated Navy, Army, and Air Force. Abroad the United States was preaching "the century of the common man" and the "Four Freedoms," yet it was denying any of these freedoms at home, even in the nation's capital. America was talking about the creation of a new world while its conscience was filled with guilt.

In that capital, along the banks of the quiet and muddy Potomac, witness and testimony were given by night and by day to the emasculation of the Bill of Rights and the Constitution that I had sworn to uphold, even when there was no upholding being done by those in high places. The dream of the Founding Fathers was becoming a faint mirage and "these truths" were no longer self-evident because truth had been banished from the land. There was evil there in Washington on January 3, 1945—the evil that comes when one preaches and fails to practice, when one proclaims and does not act, when the outside is clean and the inside is filled with filth. This was Washington, D.C., capital of the "sweet land of liberty."

And in all the "sweet land" there was but one Negro Congressman, William L. Dawson. Arriving from Chicago in 1943, he found not a single hotel that would give him a room. Nor was there a restaurant where he could eat or a lunch counter where he could buy a cup of coffee. Black men were dying for good far afield, for a good they themselves didn't know and that some would never know. High above Washington on the great dome of the Capitol, was the statue of Freedom, and yet below that statue there was no true freedom for people with the "wrong" skin color. For this man who had come from Chicago, a member of the United States Congress, was even discouraged from eating in his own dining room, although the sign read "Reserved for Members of Congress Only." Even the black men and women who toiled for the government could not eat in the government employees' dining room, but stood abjectly in the corridor, waiting for their handouts from a window—even while some received the fateful wire, "We regret to inform you that your son. . . ."

Under the massive, glittering chandelier, reflecting its myriad prismatic lights, with his own polished dome, sat "Mr. Sam." The room was not too large. It had only one large desk and two chairs, but there was a smell of

greatness in the air. Through the doorway had come all the men of the
centuries whose names little boys sitting in stiff chairs behind plain wooden
desks were taught never to forget. I sat there one early January day, thrilled
but not awed, nervous but not afraid, excited yet inwardly calm, and the
Speaker of the House of Representatives, the Honorable Sam Rayburn of
Texas, said, "Adam, everybody down here expects you to come with a bomb
in both hands. Now don't do that, Adam. Oh, I know all about you and
I know that you can't be quiet very long, but don't throw those bombs. Just
see how things operate here. Take your time. Freshmen members of Congress are supposed not to be heard and not even to be seen too much. There
are a lot of good men around here. Listen to what they have to say, drink
it all in, get reelected a few more times, and then start moving. But for
God's sake, Adam, don't throw those bombs."

I said, "Mr. Speaker, I've got a bomb in each hand, and I'm going to
throw them right away." He almost died laughing. Meanwhile he was
chewing tobacco—and how he could spit: it was said that he could hit a
spittoon six to eight feet away without missing.

After that first exchange Mr. Sam and I became close friends. Over the
years we had many chats about religion and finally I talked him into joining
the church. He was baptized about a year or two before he died.

The New York *Herald Tribune* reported that on December 17,1944,
over four thousand people packed the Golden Gate Auditorium in New
York City to send me off to Congress. In my platform I outlined that I
would push for fair racial practices, fight to do away with restrictive cove-
nants and discrimination in housing, fight for the passage of a national Fair
Employment Practices Commission and for the abolition of the poll tax,
fight to make lynching a Federal crime, do away with segregated transportation, undergird the Thirteenth, Fourteenth, and Fifteenth Amendments
to the Constitution, protest the defamation of any group—Protestant,
Catholic, Jew, or Negro, fight every form of imperialism and colonialism,
and support "all legislation, one hundred percent, to win the war, to win
the peace, pro-labor and pro-minority."

The two symbols of the fight against this program were both from
Mississippi: Bilbo in the Senate and Rankin in the House. I said, finally,
that I was going to Washington to "baptize Rankin or drown him." John
E. Rankin was the smartest parliamentarian in the House of Representatives, except for Vito Marcantonio. Just a little taller than Marcantonio,

he had a shock of very curly gray hair and a swarthy complexion. Because of the texture of his hair and his color, I always felt he fought Negroes so much because he might have had Negro blood in his veins. Many a time when Rankin was waving his arms and giving vent to one of his tirades against "nigras," Marcantonio would walk down the middle aisle, pass in front of the well in which Rankin was speaking and whisper out of the corner of his mouth, "You look more like a Negro than Powell." Invariably this caused the old man to turn even darker with rage.

Rankin was against everything progressive. Moreover, he had missed killing the Draft Bill by just one vote. He believed more in Hitlerism than he did in Abraham Lincoln and Franklin Delano Roosevelt. On January 8, 1945, he issued a statement saying my election was a "disgrace" and that he would not "let Adam C. Powell sit by me."

The aisle down the center of the House divides the Republicans from the Democrats, although House members cross this aisle whenever they want to and sit wherever they desire. But unlike the Senate, no one seat is assigned to anyone. On hearing Rankin's remarks, I immediately stated that his presence was "distasteful" to me and that the only people "fit for him to sit by are Hitler and Mussolini." On January 10 The *Philadelphia Record* editorially agreed with me and concluded: "Let's put Rankin in a section by himself and mark it 'Contagious Disease.' "

Whenever Rankin entered the Chamber, I followed after him, sitting next to him or as close as I could. One day the press reported that he moved five times. Finally, on January 15 after a Party caucus, he had to shut up. The newspaper *P.M.*, now defunct, reported: "In order to inherit the un-American power that Martin Dies had previously, Rankin would have to accept Powell and his appointment to the Committee on Education and the Committee on Labor."

One day early in my first term, as I rolled down to Washington on the Congressional Limited, the incessant click-clacking of the wheels seemed to be drumming out the thought in my mind: "What should I do? What could I do? What would I do?". . . over and over. I faced the knowledge that I was only one of four hundred and thirty-five members in the House and ninty-six in the Senate. Yet millions were depending on me to do a task for them, and not just the people in my District.

As soon as I was elected to Congress my mail, involving cases for me to handle, people for me to see, came in such large quantities from behind the color curtain of America that the work of my own constituents had to suffer. Millions of Negro people in the South had no Congressman to speak for them, no one to whom they could turn with their basic problems of discrimination and segregation, no one who would even handle their simple cases. They were the disenfranchised, the ostracized, the exploited, and when they pressed upon me their many problems of many years, I could not refuse them because I love all people.

Then there were the problems of the people of the District of Columbia, with a population which was then close to being half Negro. They too had no vote and no one to speak for them. The District of Columbia Committee was then ruled by men who came from areas that were against the Negroes' dreams and hopes. They too I had to serve.

So there I was, minister of one of the largest Protestant churches in our country, elected Congressman from one of the largest ghettos in the world, and drafted as the Congressman-at-Large for half of the District of Columbia and millions of people across the Mason-Dixon Line. . . . "What should I do? What could I do? What would I do?"

When Clarence Darrow was a member of the Illinois Legislature, he said, "I soon discovered that no independent man who fights for what he thinks is right can succeed in passing legislation. He can kill bad bills by a vigorous fight and publicity, but he can get nothing passed." There was only one thing I could do—hammer relentlessly, continually crying aloud even if in a wilderness, and force open, by sheer muscle power, every closed door. Once inside, I had to pierce the consciences of men so that somewhere someone would have to answer; somewhere something would have to be done . . . for there is no way for an independent man who fights for what he thinks is right to succeed in passing legislation.

The mechanism of legislation in the United States Congress is a wondrous labyrinth of frustration. Numerous devices, each hallowed by tradition, enable a willful minority to frustrate the majority's program. The filibuster in the Senate, the gag rule in the House; the tremendous powers of committee chairmen; the enormous influence of such key committees as Rules, Ways and Means, and Appropriations; the ability of committee conferees to "sell out" the positions of their respective Houses—all these and more are powers for good or for evil. In either case, however, Congressmen without extreme seniority are seldom able to accomplish much of their legislative program.

There are many annoyances and abuses of the rules. For example, when one rises to make a speech after receiving a special order to do so, no one is there to listen, for the special orders come at the close of all business when weary men are returning to their homes and offices, and only the Speaker or his appointed Temporary Speaker is present. The galleries have emptied. You stand there with a document on which you have labored and you look around and no one is there to hear you except two or three members of the press. This is usual at all times for all members. So, when you read about an important speech on foreign policy or some other earth-shaking matter of grave concern to the nation, frequently no one has heard it. Oftimes it is not even delivered. Under the rules of Congress, by a curious device called "extension of remarks," one needs only to read two or three words of his opening remarks and can insert the rest into the *Congressional Record* as if the full text had actually been delivered orally.

In the course of debate men can say vile and ridiculous things, and when the copy is sent from the Official Reporters of Debates to a member's office that evening to be corrected, he can delete every single word he has said and substitute the Bible if he desires—and only this will appear in the *Congressional Record.* In short, what men have actually said in Congress need never be a matter of public record.

In the majority of cases the many quorum calls that abruptly summon one across Independence Avenue to answer on the Floor are instituted by the whims and caprices of a single member. When the bell rings once, it signifies that a teller vote is being taken. Two men stand in the middle aisle —the opponent and the proponent. The members pass up the aisle and are counted one by one: first those who are in favor of the amendments, then those opposed. It is impossible for a man in his office to rush over to the Floor and be there in time to be counted. So the first bell, the teller bell, is of no value. When two bells are rung, it means that a record vote is taking place.

Three bells are often the bells of caprice and whim. There are men in Congress who have never contributed anything to the advancement of our nation, but sit all day on the Floor of Congress, just to look around and see whether two hundred and eighteen members are present. If not, they question the presence of a quorum. Then the Speaker makes a count, finds there is no quorum, and three bells are rung. One must then scurry over to answer the roll call. This I refused to do. What is needed is an electrical system similar to that now in operation in many state legislatures: by pressing a button in his office, each legislator could let the Speaker know that he is in his office and available in the event a vote is taken. Sometimes three bells is an automatic vote when a member objects to the passage of a bill on the grounds of "no quorum."

When the bells ring four times, it's the end of the day.

In order to answer roll calls on present or not-present, to vote on various bills, and now with the new rule that requires recording of voting on amendments—which used to be unrecorded—all a legislator's time could be consumed going back and forth. When there is a roll call it takes twenty-two minutes to go from an office in the Rayburn Building, where my office was; and voting and coming back would consume—unless one has a car and chauffeur ready—almost an hour. This is absolutely antediluvian and I am against it. Thus I always picked only those votes that were important. Proof of this is that the AFL-CIO always rated me as one of the best Congressmen on voting, as did the NAACP and the ADA.

Half the people who are in Congress think that Washington is the biggest city in the world, and of course their wives have never been exposed to the kind of social life you get there—embassy parties, White House invitations, and so on. They're just so happy to come to the big town of Washington that they're carried away with it. They love to live there. To those from urban areas, Washington is nothing but a hick town, and it means nothing for them to parade up and down aisles to vote. Urban legislators frequently feel that they have more serious work to do in their offices. My casework, for example, was often more important to me than casting a vote. That casework load usually averaged five to seven thousand a year, often even involving people whose lives were in danger. To my mind it is also vitally important for a Congressman to spend time in his own bailiwick. When Congressmen live within thirty-five or forty minutes by jet from Washington, their constitutents demand that they spend considerable time in their home area because they can see them there without any cost. And as I commented in an article that appeared in *Smiling Through the Apocalypse, Esquire's History of the Sixties*, "The first duty of a Congressman, regardless of how crass it may appear to be, is to get reelected."

Late in January of 1945 the fading man in the White House sent over a message saying that we had to put through a labor-draft bill—men would either have to work or fight. The cause of democracy was suffering bitterly, but vicious men were still playing Hitler's game. They had taken the same oath of office I had, yet they resorted to every possible method to kill President Roosevelt's request. The strong isolationist bloc in the United

States Congress always held to the philosophy of "Let the whole world go to hell. America first!" With absolutely no sincerity, this group introduced an amendment to ban discrimination and segregation, the purpose being to kill Roosevelt's "work-or-fight" legislation.

I stood in the well on January 31, 1945, and said, "This is no time for anyone to use any method to stop full mobilization of the manpower of the United States of America. I brand this amendment as a cheap, partisan trick to play upon racial prejudice in order to defeat a bill which should stand or fall on its own merits. This amendment has erroneously been called an FEPC amendment. This it most emphatically is not. Passage of this amendment will not in the slightest help the Negro worker, or the worker of any minority, any more than he is being helped now. Under Executive Order No. 8802, administered by the Fair Employment Practices Commission, there can be no discrimination in industry during wartime. What we are interested in is a permanent FEPC—a permanent act of this Congress which will forever, in wartime and peacetime, rule out discrimination in public and private employment.

"It is the cheapest and lowest form of politics to play upon any subject as delicate as is the subject of race in connection with legislation which is distinctly of a non-racial character. This bill should stand upon its own merits. It should be passed on its own merits or rejected on its own merits."

Then I helped to lead my colleagues down the aisle past the tellers, and the so-called antidiscrimination amendment was defeated and the bill was passed. The Louisville *Courier-Journal* wrote that I had raised the debate to a "statesmanlike plane." With a note of prophecy, it concluded, "He showed himself a factor to reckon with in the future."

By this time I had introduced or co-authored whatever civil rights bills were before the United States Congress, including legislation for a permanent FEPC. Also, I was beginning to make friends. The bombs Mr. Sam had advised me against were beginning to drop, drop, drop upon the marble of men's conscience. I was able to start disturbing those who had been too long at ease. Thus, during the month of March, when the bill to draft nurses into the armed forces was passed, an amendment outlawing discrimination in the draft process became part of the historic action of the House of Representatives.

Soon the dream of a United Nations began to bear fruit. As the reality came closer, *The New York Times* reported, on March 11, my demand that a Negro sit at the first United Nations conference, and commented on what his presence would mean for the submerged peoples of Asia and Africa. As time went on the delegation of our government to the United Nations included names like Edith Sampson, Channing Tobias, Archibald Carey, Marian Anderson, Charles "Dawg" Anderson, Ralph Bunche, and Zelma George.

One day I was sitting in my massive old-fashioned offices in the Old House Office Building. Because of seniority I could have moved, as I later did, to the New Office Building, but I loved the old one: the ancient marble corridors that have been hallowed by the tread of the great, the high ceilings, the view . . . this was History. And the view was magnificent— the Capitol dome glistening under the spotlights that burn all night, making it a beacon for all to see and to symbolize the dream that one day what it stands for shall be a reality. I sat there in the polished black-leather chair and began to muse: black men were dying all over the world and yet the nation's two principal military academies, West Point and Annapolis, did not favor their admission. A scarce handful had been graduated from the former, but never in the history of the United States had a Negro been allowed to get beyond the first year at Annapolis. Each Congressman is permitted to appoint five young men to the U.S. Naval Academy at Annapolis, Maryland, and four to the U.S. Military Academy at West Point, New York.

I telephoned a Washington educator and asked, "Who is your outstanding Negro graduate this year?"

"Wesley Brown," he told me.

I phoned Wesley Brown and told him I wanted him to go to Annapolis. He was almost speechless. Finally, he said, "I'll go if you'll appoint me." And I did.

After Wesley Brown had been at Annapolis several months, I wrote a letter to the Secretary of the Navy, James V. Forrestal, one of the grandest men who ever breathed. In the letter I complained that there were "forces at work at Annapolis Naval Academy that are about to put Wesley Brown out." Jim Forrestal was so disturbed by my message that in the midst of that war period he personally went to Annapolis and investigated. He then wrote to me that he found no complaints being made by Cadet Midshipman Brown, nor by his family, and that everyone he talked with said Brown was getting along fine. This I knew. I had deliberately fabricated that letter in order to make sure nothing would happen to Wesley Brown. Sometime later at a cocktail party on Embassy Row I bumped into Forrestal and he asked, "Adam, why did you lie to me?"

"Jim," I said, "I had to lie in order to make sure that Wesley Brown would not be touched by anyone." And so Wesley was the first black man to be graduated from Annapolis and he has gone on to become a career man in the United States Navy.

The only concert hall we had in Washington was Constitution Hall— a national hall owned by the Daughters of the American Revolution but operating under a special charter of Congress and with a tax-exempt status. In October, 1945, my wife, Hazel Scott, had been scheduled for a concert there, but the DAR, under the presidency of Mrs. Julius Talmadge of Atlanta, refused to allow the impresario to have my wife perform. This followed upon the heels of their refusal to have the magnificent Marian Anderson perform and rapidly developed into a cause célèbre.

As a member of Congress I recoiled at the idea that a Congressman's wife, an American citizen, and a gifted artist would not be allowed to perform in a hall largely supported by tax-deductible contributions. I asked the President of the United States, Harry S Truman, to act, because Washington is controlled by Commissioners appointed by the President and subject to removal by him. These Commissioners could have put pressure on the DAR, but they refused. Representative Rankin, of course, immediately told the press, "This is all Communist-inspired." On Columbus Day I received a wire from President Truman agreeing with me. Yet on the same day his wife accepted an invitation to Constitution Hall as a guest of the DAR. Mrs. Eleanor Roosevelt, when she was First Lady, had resigned from the DAR because of the Marian Anderson episode, and I had expected Bess Truman to follow and to support her husband. I was marching up Fifth Avenue in New York City in the Italian's Columbus Day parade when newsmen stopped me and showed me an AP release: "Bess Truman goes to Constitution Hall to grace the DAR tea."

I said, "From now on there is only one First Lady, Mrs. Roosevelt; Mrs. Truman is the last."

The *Philadelphia Record*, on October 13, commented editorially: "Doesn't the DAR know that the Civil War is over?" The *San Francisco Chronicle*, on the same date, editorialized in similar vein. A few days later *The Christian Science Monitor* said, "This entire affair gives us 'cause for regret,'" and found the DAR's action "unwarranted." The *Washington*

Post condemned the DAR with sober, stern words and said, "They were misguided and unreasonable." Wherever Mrs. Talmadge, the DAR's president, went, pickets began to appear.

On October 18 Congresswoman Helen Gahagan Douglas introduced legislation to stop the DAR's tax exemption, and Congresswoman Clare Boothe Luce said she would resign from the DAR. I knew then that I would win my fight. The women in Congress are far superior to the men. Very few men have been more able during my years than Clare Luce or Helen Gahagan Douglas. Ours would be a much better nation if we had more women in Congress or more men with the character, ability, and the insight of the women who are there now.

The last great dean of the Roosevelt Administration, Senator Robert F. Wagner, Sr., and the Junior Senator from New York, James Mead, both supported my fight against the DAR. And on December 4 United States Federal Judge Phillip Forman banned all members of the DAR from his courtroom for their lack of Americanism.

Harry Truman could have ordered the District of Columbia Commissioners to give the DAR a certain period of time in which to join the Union or lose their tax-exempt status. Instead, in February, 1946, the Truman-appointed Commissioners upheld the DAR's lily-white policy. But the cause was not lost. The cries of outrage that the irritant provoked brought results, and on Sunday, February 17, 1952, Dorothy Maynor sang at Constitution Hall. Another fight had been won.

All during 1945 I had been in contact with the Secretary of War, Robert Patterson, stressing that we could not continue to fight wars to make the world safe for democracy while Negroes were being rigidly segregated in the Army, Navy, and Air Force. Most of the men in the Army were confined to the menial tasks of the Quartermaster Corps. In the Navy most Negroes were messmen. In the Air Force Negroes were practically nonexistent except for one Jim Crow squadron. In the Marines no Negroes were allowed, period. The first step toward integrating the armed forces was taken after my continuing conversations with the War Department, when on January 12, 1946, Secretary Patterson announced that studies were now "under way for integration."

Meanwhile, I was also making strides in the field of fair employment practices. New York State had passed an FEPC law and had established the State Commission Against Discrimination. As soon as I arrived in Washington I introduced the first Congressional legislation in this field, copying almost word for word New York's successful, bipartisan legislation. I began to get bipartisan support, and on January 18, when Harry Truman announced that he would support my legislation, five hundred peaceful demonstrators marched on the Capitol. Two months later Joe Martin, Republican Minority Leader in the House of Representatives, told me that when the FEPC legislation came up, he would marshal his forces to help me.

Secretary of State Dean Acheson also issued a statement calling for an FEPC, declaring that FEPC would be an "aid to the United States' foreign policy." In May of that year the *Chicago Defender* reported that I forced the Committe on Labor to bypass the Rules Committee and start the first FEPC Bill on its way to a vote. That was in 1946. It took four more years before FEPC reached the Floor for an actual vote.

In January of 1945, in an address at Charlotte, North Carolina, I had pleaded for real democracy, saying, "This nation can never return to pre-Pearl Harbor days of pseudo-democracy." What could I do, I wondered, to assure that this would be true. Was there some amendment that could be phrased in simple words which through the years might serve as a point upon which the isolated, backward, and reactionary thinking of men could be turned?

It was then that I decided to create the Powell Amendment, forbidding Federal funds to those who sought to preserve segregation, and wherever I thought there was an opportunity that it could be passed, or wherever the opportunity arose to defeat bad legislation, there I would introduce it. As I thought and as I prayed, the words came: "No funds under this Act shall be made available to or paid to any State or school. . . ."

The first test came with the school lunch program. Under legislation passed by the Congress, free school lunches were available to schoolchildren. This was of no importance to those in my district but of the utmost importance to millions of children living in those barren, benighted areas of the United States that are subcontinents of human misery. With the support of my colleagues, the first civil rights amendment, attached to the school lunch program, was passed. It is Public Law 396, enacted by the 79th Congress, June 4, 1946. From then on I was to use this important weapon with success, to bring about opportunities for the good of man and to stop those efforts that would harm democracy's forward progress. Sometimes I used it only as a deterrent against the undemocratic practices that would have resulted if that amendment had not been offered.

I was not successful when I introduced an amendment to abolish segregation in the District of Columbia. But within less than a decade Washington, by virtue of the light cast by the Supreme Court in 1954, had become a better place for minorities than even New York City.

My pledge to fight colonialism and imperialism began in July, 1946. It was at that time that the then Congressman, later Senator, Everett M. Dirksen moved to grant a recovery loan to Great Britain. I had not been to Britain nor had I yet witnessed the tremendous suffering, sacrifice, and courage of her people. But they were still in the stranglehold of Winston Churchill, the last of the imperialists. Therefore, I opposed that British loan, saying, "We cannot divorce this loan from imperialism. It could be used to show that the United States is supporting the colonialism of Africa and Asia."

When I returned to the 80th Congress in 1947, I reintroduced all my earlier bills and began my fight to give the citizens of the District of Columbia the right to vote. The Washington *Evening Star*, one of the few fair papers in this nation, reporting on January 10 that I had introduced the bill, noted that in my introduction I said we could not have "sterile hybrid citizens" at the heart of our government.

As I walked away from the well of Congress after introducing that bill, I happened to look up at the press gallery. The faces were all white, and I said to myself, "Where are the reporters of the Negro press—the daily papers from Atlanta, the weeklies from Chicago, the magazines—where are they?"

I began to investigate and found that the members of the press themselves were in charge of who should be admitted to the gallery. The chairman of the standing committee was a New York *Herald Tribune* reporter. When I pressed for the admission of Negroes to the press gallery, his standing committee voted four to one to continue barring Negroes. The excuse given was that Negroes did not serve on dailies, although the gallery did admit white journalists serving on weeklies. At last I took my fight to Speaker Rayburn, and on March 19, 1947, Louis Lautier of the *Afro-American* was admitted to the gallery. Today accredited black journalists no longer have problems in gaining admission to the House, the Senate, or the White House.

I determined that it was time to break down the prejudices within the Capitol itself. As soon as I came to Congress I began to take as many Negroes as I could into the hitherto exclusive restaurant of the House of

Representatives. Senator Theodore G. Bilbo of Mississippi was moved to comment that a certain Negro Congressman was a good Negro, but that "Mr. Powell is no good because he continues to use our facilities for Negroes." In March I introduced a resolution demanding that Negro employees of the Federal government, serving in the Capitol, be admitted to the Capitol cafeteria. Senator Wayland Brooks, key Republican leader, immediately called a full meeting of the Senate Committee on Rules and Administration. Although my resolution was never passed, it achieved its purpose because the order went down: "Stop Jim Crow in the United States Congressional facilities."

My father taught me that one should never answer his critics; your friends don't need to hear it and your critics won't believe it, he used to say. Nevertheless, I have never been able to understand how people with intelligence could say I have done nothing in Congress and that I have always been opposed to Federal aid to education, using the Powell Amendment to stop it. As early as May 29, 1948, the *Pittsburgh Courier* reported, "Powell asked the House of Representatives to proceed immediately to pass Federal aid to education."

One of the important days in my Congressional experience occurred in 1950. This was the sixth year of my fight for an FEPC bill. John Lesinski, Sr., of Michigan was the chairman of the Committee on Education and Labor. A great liberal, he appointed me with full power as chairman of the Special Subcommittee on FEPC. I was to select my own members. Rankin continued to rail at the FEPC, calling it Communist-inspired. Some members of the House were beginning to believe that perhaps it was. From California came a self-proclaimed Sir Galahad in the field of anti-Communism, young, pink-faced, fluid, and fluent. His name was Richard Nixon. I immediately went to him at the opening of the 81st Congress and said, "My name is Powell. I would like you to be a member of my five-man subcommittee on FEPC." He readily assented and because he was such a stern and uncompromising anti-Communist, this immediately shut Rankin's mouth, and the committee got down to work.

We held exhaustive hearings for weeks. I will never forget the testimony of Martin Quigley, prominent Roman Catholic layman and publisher of several trade journals in Hollywood, who told us: "Communism only succeeds when democracy fails." The leaders of the Railroad Brotherhood refused to testify, and I gave them notice that if they didn't, I would use the subpoena power and put them under oath. So they came and I castigated them before the committee for their constitution, which forbade membership to "anyone but Caucasians." Yet in that same year they endorsed and supported me for reelection, and I have lived to see them change those bylaws and constitution.

Finally, the FEPC Bill was ready for the Floor of Congress. In the subcommittee only one man voted against it, and that was Richard Nixon. In the full Committee on Education and Labor, Nixon again voted against the bill. At that point the Southerners, who formed the smartest bloc in Congress, used every method they could to stop FEPC from going to the Floor. The Rules Committee refused to give it a rule. But guided by John Lesinski and others, we resorted to what is called Calendar Wednesday. By the rules of the House, the Rules Committee can be bypassed and a bill presented directly to the House on Calendar Wednesday. Since each committee must wait its turn alphabetically, however, the Committees on Agriculture, Appropriations, Armed Services, Banking and Currency, and District of Columbia were in line to be called ahead of Education and Labor. Knowing of our intention to use this means for securing debate on my FEPC bill, the opposition committee chairmen invoked their powers to exhaust the full time of each Calendar Wednesday for their own bills, thereby forestalling the presentation of our bill. However, only one Calendar Wednesday is allotted to each committee and finally our day came. My FEPC bill was called up, and debate began at last. We did not adjourn until close to four o'clock in the morning, when Republican McConnell, with the support of Richard Nixon, killed the Powell FEPC bill. A toothless substitute that killed the FEPC drive prevailed.

8

Stevenson and Eisenhower

Early in 1952, after spending four and a half months all over Europe, in Israel, and in part of the Arab world, I came home with just one thought burning in my mind: the United States was rapidly becoming the most hated nation in the world.

As I walked through the bazaars in Acre, Israel, just across the border from Lebanon, Israeli Arabs sitting on their haunches with rags on their backs and no hope in their eyes spat upon me as I passed. "Why?" I asked the United States Embassy guide.

"Because we are Americans," came the answer. We Americans were beginning to reap what we had been sowing. Congressmen talked too much and too long about the problems of starving people. By the time we got around to doing something about them, ill will had been created.

The most disturbing message I brought back from abroad was given me by the United States Alternate Delegate to the United Nations, Dr. Channing Tobias. As I was leaving the Embassy in Paris, Dr. Tobias told me, "When you return to America, tell them that every dollar we have spent on the Marshall Plan here in Europe has been wiped out by the bombings in Florida—and, furthermore, I don't mind being quoted." Europe had been rocked by the news that one of the outstanding fighters for civil liberties in Florida, Harry Moore, had been bombed to death in his residence on Christmas night for the "crime" of holding the office of executive secretary of the Florida chapter of the NAACP. The Department of Justice, under Attorney General Howard McGrath, was so disturbed by this incident that as soon as I arrived in the States, I was asked to attend a top-level conference of national leaders in Mr. McGrath's office to discuss what could be done to heal this situation.

As I looked out upon my nation I knew that whoever won the Presidential nomination in the fall of 1952 would have the capacity to make us or break us in the intervening postwar years. The greatest single world figure, Dwight David Eisenhower, simply "did not have time" to answer any questions concerning the number-one domestic civil rights issue which was shaming us before the world. Yet he had time to answer in detail the highly technical questions of Jack Porter of Texas with regard to Tidelands oil.

This spirit of turn back the clock or do everything possible to make America a lily white "land of the free" was pointed up by the determination of Senator McCarran and Representative Walter to push through their immigration bill seeking to ban from the United States the colored people of the West Indies. Over a hundred and fifty thousand people of West Indian descent resided in my district in Harlem and they had brought to America a fresh viewpoint, great enthusiasm, and an ability to dig in and lift themselves up by their bootstraps. But as the result of a deal with Congressman Walter H. Judd, immigration of this group was henceforth to be limited to only a hundred per year. Under the proposed bill it would take fifty years for those who were already in the United States to bring their closest of kin to our land. In return for this Judd was to receive the realization of his long-cherished dream of admitting Orientals to American citizenship, though even they were to be limited to only a hundred per country per year.

In the House of Assembly in Barbados, by unanimous vote, a memorandum was sent to the Governor General: "The House of Assembly desires to place on record its appreciation of the efforts being made by Congressman Powell and his committee to act against the McCarran Bill and respectfully requests Your Excellency to have conveyed through the usual channels to Powell and his committee an expression of its heartful gratitude for their value and endeavors on behalf of our people." But nothing could be done, and on April 23, 1952, in spite of my efforts, that odious bill became law. The bill was aimed not only at colored people but also against the peoples of the Mediterranean, against Jews, against East Europeans, and against other minorities. It increased the quotas for the pure "Anglo-Saxon," even though those quotas had rarely been fully used, in order to decrease the quotas for the unwanted peoples.

Even in the church segregation began to flex its strengthening muscles. Toward the end of March, by a vote of twenty-seven to fifteen, the National Council of Churches of Christ in the United States of America postponed action on a proposed denunciation of racial segregation. As the minister of one of the nation's largest churches, I charged, in a sermon, that such an action was "ungodly, un-Christlike, and undemocratic." I asked, "How can we expect the legislators of America to be more Christlike than their clergymen? For two thousand years the Christian church has been waiting to abolish segregation within its own practices, within its own borders. After two thousand years the Council felt that it was still not the time to take a stand. The Council cannot continue to serve the God that has made all people of one blood and the mammon of second-class citizenship."

Threatening to resign from the Council, the issue was pointed up by Dr. Samuel Cavert, general secretary of the church body, who declared: "Many members of the General Board shared Dr. Powell's view that the issue of segregation is the most acute question facing the world today." When Board members met in Chicago in June, they finally rescinded their vote and came out with a strong denunciation of segregation.

Who was the person fit to be the standard-bearer of either party in this hour of America's weakening at home and waning abroad? Eisenhower was out of the question. Stevenson was still indecisive about whether he would be a candidate. I decided to work for the candidacy of Averell Harriman, a man who had distinguished himself in the service of President Franklin D. Roosevelt. I recalled an occasion when we were protesting the segregation then practiced at the National Airport located across the Potomac in Virginia. "The great liberal," Henry Wallace, then Secretary of Commerce, refused to change this policy, although he had the power to do so. One day he kept Mary McLeod Bethune, the great Negro educator, and myself sitting outside his office for more than an hour and then abruptly dismissed us, saying, "I don't have time." Yet all over America Communists and everyone in the extreme liberal groups were praising him as the

number-one independent. In contrast, when Averell Harriman succeeded
Wallace as Secretary of Commerce in the Truman Administration, he
changed the segregation picture at the National Airport in just one week,
simply by doing what Wallace had had the authority to do all along—he
ordered segregation to cease. This was the kind of man I could support for
the Presidency.

A committee was formed to promote Averell Harriman for the Presidential nomination. United States Senator Herbert Lehman was elected head
of the committee; Franklin D. Roosevelt, Jr., was named chairman, and I
was made the national vice-chairman.

Meanwhile my fight against racism continued. Murray Marder, writing
in the *Washington Post* on May 5, said, "A new move to enact a group
libel law making it a Federal offense to defame maliciously anyone because
of race, religion or class, was made today by New York Congressmen."
Along with Congressmen Jacob Javits, Arthur G. Klein, and Eugene
Keogh, I introduced that bill. It was for "the effective protection of freedom of speech" but not aimed at honest people regardless of how misguided. Bombings in Florida, desecration of churches and synagogues in
Pennsylvania and elsewhere are latter-day evidence of what racial or religious bigots are capable of bringing on American communities. The bill we
introduced would ban from interstate commerce or the mails any material
reproduced in multiple form which had the effect of "designating, identify-
ing, or characterizing him or them, directly or indirectly, by reference with
his or their race or religion, which exposes or tends to expose him or them
to hatred, contempt or obliquely causes them to be shunned, avoided or
to be injured in their business."

I discovered around this time that Secretary of the Treasury John W.
Snyder was allowing deductions in the computation of income taxes for
expenses incurred in pressing civil rights suits. Deputy Commissioner of
Internal Revenue E. I. McLarney admitted that "some proprietors feel that
they may deduct such damages and costs as business expenses in computing
their net income." I charged that this practice, in effect, meant that the
American taxpayers were paying businessmen for the "privilege of being
undemocratic." I demanded that the Internal Revenue Service henceforth
not allow any more payments for damages from civil rights suits to be
deducted, and this practice finally ceased.

That same year the House Committee on Education and Labor was
preparing to report out legislation to aid school construction. This, of

course, was before the historic 1954 Supreme Court decision on school desegregation. Nevertheless, I sensed the immoral and illegal injustice of appropriating funds from the Federal Treasury to support discriminatory educational practices. I wrote Representative Cleveland M. Bailey of West Virginia, chairman of the subcommittee: "I know how important such legislation is but I cannot as a citizen of New York State, which paid $9 billion to the Federal Treasury last year, vote in favor of legislation which allows New Yorkers and other Northerners to support anti-democratic legislation." Consequently, I demanded that the impending legislation contain safeguards against racial discrimination in the allocation of funds. This was the beginning of my long and ultimately successful fight against such practices.

The continued onslaughts against democracy increasingly aroused me until the moment came when I could no longer hold my peace. I simply could not abide the decadence in America's political picture. Addressing the annual meeting of the New York County Democratic Committee in June, I said, "The Democratic Party must stand up like a man for the rights of man." I called for the following planks to be included in the 1952 platform of the National Convention: abolition of Federal election poll taxes, abolition of segregation in interstate transportation, abolition of segregation in all branches of the armed forces, abolition of segregation in the nation's capital, the enactment of an FEPC law, and making lynching a Federal crime. "Unless this is done," I concluded, "Negroes will bolt the Democratic Party." The entire New York delegation supported me and Senator Lehman proclaimed that the "Democratic Party shall not be a party of compromise, a party of retreat, a party of surrender."

Even within the ranks of the Republican Party resentment began to rise against Eisenhower's say-nothing, do-nothing, think-nothing attitude on civil rights. Leading Republican delegates to the National Convention agreed with the statement made by the dean of the New York Republican leaders, Harold G. Burton, who commented, "Eisenhower's reply to Congressman Powell's questions in regard to segregation was quite disappointing." Nevertheless, Ike swept the convention and received the nomination. As the Republicans moved out of Chicago, the Democrats moved in for their convention.

On July 21 I traveled to Chicago on the chartered convention train as delegate-at-large. After a talk in the lounge car with Tammany leader Carmine DeSapio, W. Averell Harriman, Franklin D. Roosevelt, Jr., Senator Lehman, and others, I went back to my bedroom and began to think: Eisenhower was a world hero, and no one by himself or his own personality, regardless of how great his record, was going to be able to stand up against the magic of his name. The only opportunity for the Democrats to win, for this nation to have a real leader, would be to have a man of courage stand upon a platform that would spell out in detail the necessities of democracy. I decided, therefore, that the platform would be far more important than the man. Eisenhower's great weakness was his ignorance in the political field. This could be brought into sharp relief if we were to spell out in detail all the important issues on which Eisenhower had failed to take a stand. I turned out the lights and dropped off to sleep. The last picture that flashed across the screen of memory was of the immense crowd of people in Grand Central Station waving goodbye and carrying signs: "Don't retreat on civil rights!"

The Platform Committee of the Democratic National Convention was large and the membership was varied, representing the many interests of the many sections of our nation. Among those who sat on that committee were Senator Lehman, Senator Hubert H. Humphrey, and one Negro, Congressman William Dawson of Chicago. As the committee got down to work, we knew that there was considerable friction behind the scenes. There were those who stood forthright for the kind of civil rights platform I knew would save the nation and our party, and others who wanted no civil rights plank whatsoever, who were interested in the triumph of sectionalism rather than the salvation of America. Late one night, soon after the convention began, while the galleries were still packed with people breathlessly awaiting the final decisions of the Platform Committee, Senator Humphrey came to me, pale and haggard, his collar rumpled. "Adam," he said in disgust, "we didn't get the victory we wanted."

Amazed, I asked, "But Hubert, you said you had the votes—what happened?"

"I'm ashamed to tell you," he replied, and turned and walked away from me. At first my anger boiled over against Humphrey because I thought he meant by his statement that he had sold us out. But incredible as it may seem, rumors began to spread that the sole Negro committee member and the head of the big black Second Ward of Chicago, Bill Dawson, was the one who compromised the issue. Every single witness before that committee, as recorded in the Chicago *Defender* on Saturday, July 26, asked for "a Democratic civil rights platform with even stronger provisions than the

1948 platform." Even a white Southern farmer from Montgomery called for a complusory FEPC, saying, "When you commit discrimination on the job, it's the same as stealing a man's property."

I threatened to bolt the ticket and declared, "My position on civil rights is much more important than my seat in Congress." George W. Della, president of the Maryland Senate, demanded that the New York delegation take the loyalty pledge to support the Democratic slate. The *Washington Post* on Thursday, July 31, reported that Della's action "was prompted by the announcement of Representative Powell declaring that Negroes could not campaign for the Democratic ticket."

As we left Chicago the press reported that the platform was so weak, that even Senator John Sparkman of Alabama said that he and Senator Spessard Holland of Florida had agreed to accept a stronger wording of the plank, but that "Congressman Dawson killed it." Dawson at first denied this, but he later issued a statement carried by the Associated Negro Press on August 2: "I am very proud of the civil rights plank as a whole."

For me the convention came to an end as Harriman's strength waned on the third ballot. I refused to cast my vote for Adlai Stevenson and left Chicago, disgusted with my party. The Negro had been sold down the river at both conventions when eager Uncle Toms sabotaged the civil rights planks of the two major parties.

One by one, throughout the nation, rubber-stamped, handkerchief-headed Negroes began to desert my position. Even in my own district civic leaders began to say I was wrong for being so adamant on a strong civil rights platform. Nevertheless, I refused to abandon my convictions. I kept repeating that regardless of what political reprisals might be taken against me, I was not going to campaign for the ticket unless a change was made by Adlai Stevenson in his own civil rights pronouncements, I wanted pronouncements that would strengthen the weak-kneed in the party's platform.

In this light I sent messages directly to Governor Adlai Stevenson in Springfield, Illinois, pointing out the dangers arising from the weakness of the party platform and requesting an appointment with him. Hearing that I was to be in Springfield on the last Sunday in August to speak at the annual state convention of the NAACP, Governor Stevenson contacted me and said he would be glad to see me then.

When I arrived at the Governor's Mansion, I was greeted by William Blair, his lifelong friend and assistant. We walked through the historic main room, turned right into the small study where Governor Stevenson was waiting for me. That afternoon and evening we discussed the platform. I pointed out that I was not merely representing my personal views, that he and the platform were being patted on the back by a lot of old-time Democrats who did not mean much any more in the post-World War Two era, and that those who really represented the rank and file of the masses —the new, thinking voters—were backing me up. They included such people as the Commissioner of City Property in Philadelphia, Charles Baker; the Director of Civil Rights, IVE-CIO of New England, James Brown; the Director of Civil Rights of the New Jersey CIO, Arthur Chapin; the head of the New Jersey Young Democrats, Odell Clark of the CIO laundry workers; Luther Cunningham, Commissioner of Civil Service of Philadelphia; Austin Norris, Tax Revision Commissioner of Pennsylvania, Lloyal Randolph, advisor to the Mayor of Baltimore; Bishop James Robinson of the St. Thomas Liberal Catholic Church; Reverend Marshall Shephard, Recorder of Deeds, Washington, D.C.; Parole Commissioner of Massachusetts Silas Taylor, and others.

The Governor asked me, "What shall I do?"

I said, "Take the weak civil rights plank that came out of the Chicago, strengthen it, and undergird it."

When he came to New York the next week, Adlai Stevenson was a different man and we had a different party platform. Speaking on successive nights at public meetings of the Liberal and the Democratic Parties, he came forth with a fighting civil rights platform. My long efforts had not been in vain. Stevenson had included all the points for which I had been fighting and which are now the law of the land. He repeated this kind of speech in Richmond, Virginia, and in Houston, Texas, saying, "I cannot say one thing up North and another in the South." While he was in New York he arranged a conference in his suite at the Hotel Biltmore. To this conference came the very people I had told him about in Springfield, from their various states and cities. Also present were the chairman of the New York State Democratic Committee, Paul Fitzpatrick; the County Leader, Carmine DeSapio, Averell Harriman, and Lloyd K. Garrison.

After our meeting I issued the following statement: "I consider Stevenson's newly announced support of compulsory FEPC and majority cloture (against Senate filibusters) a personal victory. We have been urging since the convention that he take the stand he now has taken. I am immensely pleased to be able to announce my one-hundred-percent support of Stevenson."

I was gratified when on September 6 the *Amsterdam News* the largest weekly in New York editoralized that Congressman Powell,

> more than any other individual, brought the presidential candidates into realization that civil rights is a major rather than a lesser consideration in the campaign and that large numbers of people, not only Negroes, would measure the candidates by their position on civil rights. The record must show that in 1952 civil rights received top ruling because the New York Congressman demonstratively and colorfully refused to "go along" with his party without a fight.

After making speeches for the Democratic Party, I left for the second conference of the World Association of Parliamentarians for World Government in London. When I spoke at historic Kinsway Hall, the auditorium was jammed and people were sitting in the aisles. I said then:

> The modern horsemen of the Apocalypse—Lutherism, racism, and poverty—can only be defeated by the united impact of the peoples of the world who do not want war, poverty, and hunger and who are against any division on the basis of race or creed. We who are the elected representatives of the peoples of the earth must assume the mantle of leadership, and through our fight within the United Nations bring to pass in this immediate future what despairing millions feel can only come in the far-off future.

Because it was already apparent to me that the United States had degenerated from a lofty ideal as a positive force for world peace to a negative organization capable of preventing war, I called for

> a tyranny-proof United Nations peace force controlled by and responsible to the United Nations only, and the establishment of an International Court of Justice with compulsory jurisdiction to decide all legal disputes between nations, provided such disputes are capable of decision by recognized legal principles.

On the Friday preceding the November Presidential election Governor Stevenson and I walked side by side through the streets of Harlem. I introduced him at a gigantic open-air rally to a crowd estimated by the Police Department and various newspapers to be anywhere from sixty-five thousand to two hundred thousand. As reported by the press, he drew a larger crowd than either President Truman or General Eisenhower. At that rally Governor Stevenson called forthrightly for full employment and equal rights. But the magic of the Eisenhower name was too much and, on November 4, after twenty years of Democratic control of the White House, Dwight David Eisenhower was elected thirty-fourth President of the United States.

At the same time old John E. Rankin of Mississippi was defeated for reelection to the 83rd Congress. The *Jackson* (Mississippi) *Advocate* called him "The leader of the white trash bloc," and also "the number-one race-baiter in Congress." Rankin was defeated by Representative Thomas Abernethy and, indirectly, because of Negroes. In the decade between 1940 and 1950 the colored population of Mississippi had dwindled by about one hundred thousand persons. Reapportionment threw Rankin into a new district and his thirty-year Congressional career, noted almost solely for its hatred of colored people, Jews, and Italians, was brought to an end. As chairman of the House Veterans' Affairs Committee, he had tried to block all moves to change the segregated pattern. The *Washington Post* called his "forced retirement a happy accident," while the *Washington Daily News* cheered the fact that "the sassy little irritant from Mississippi with the long white hair and ferocious words was beaten. . . . Rankin had planned to stay around until at least 1971 so that he could round out fifty years in Congress and save the country, he said, 'from skullduggery.' Now Congress at least has been saved from that."

As the 83rd Congress convened on Friday, January 3, 1953, I pondered whether it was worthwhile to continue the fight. We now had a man in the White House who refused to open his mouth to say one word concerning civil rights while our nation was being shamed throughout the world. And we had as Vice President Richard Nixon—who, on June 22, 1949, had been the only member of the Powell Subcommittee on FEPC to vote against FEPC; who on July 29 led the opposition in the full committee against FEPC; and on February 22, 1950, helped the Northern Republicans defeat my FEPC bill when it went to the Floor of the House.

Even after election to the Senate, Nixon had not changed his views. He and Senator Robert A. Taft were the only two members of the Senate Labor and Public Welfare Committee to vote against FEPC. In 1952, when we tried to change the rules of the House of Representatives so that civil rights bills could get to the Floor, it was again Richard Nixon who voted against the change and prevented even a parliamentary discussion of bills pertaining to anti-lynching, anti-poll tax, anti-segregation in railroad transportation and in the armed forces. On June 27, 1952, it was again Nixon who voted against the brown people of the West Indies, the black people of Africa, the yellow of Asia, other minorities of the Mediterranean and Europe, and Jews from everywhere when he supported the McCarran-Walter Immigration Act, which cut down the already inadequate quotas of these peoples. When Harry S Truman vetoed that immigration bill, Richard Nixon voted to override that veto. He had voted against low-rent housing six times; he had voted many times against slum clearance and middle-income housing. From March, 1948, to June, 1952, he voted against rent control four times. From February, 1947, to June, 1952, he voted against price control nine times, as well as against extension of Social Security and Unemployment Compensation.

I had worked hard with Senator Robert A. Taft as one of the conferees from the House to raise the minimum hourly wage from fifty cents to seventy-five, and even when Senator Taft voted in favor of it, Nixon voted against it.

He had just bought a $40,000 house in Washington, putting up $20,000 in cash. At that time he signed an agreement with the former owner never to sell or lease his house to any Oriental, Jew, or Negro. Money had come to him in a back-door way that would have caused the indictment of any member of Congress who did the same thing. Yet he "cleared" himself in the famous "Checkers" TV speech, using every trick in the actor's closet of TV hocus-pocus.

With these two in the White House, I felt at first there was little hope for Negro legislative progress, and I ceased introducing bills of a civil rights nature. Then that same still voice came to me and said, "Do not give up. Maybe their high positions will make these men into the kind of human beings they should be." So again I introduced civil rights bills guaranteeing full and equal privileges in all public places in the District of Columbia, prohibiting discrimination in employment, making unlawful the require-ment of the payment of a poll tax, amending the U.S. Code to make unlawful the transportation of libeling groups, outlawing lynching as a Federal crime, prohibiting the segregation of passengers in interstate com-merce.

I also set out to establish a contact at the White House. Sherman Adams of New Hampshire had sat with me in the House of Representatives. He was now the number-one man next to the President. We began to work together. The secretary to the United States Cabinet was Maxwell Rabb of Boston. We became especially close. Things began to change. At a White House luncheon early in the Eisenhower Administration I met the President for the first time and we immediately got along well. In the words of Max Rabb, we were "a team."

In less than two years from the date of his election, Eisenhower had brought about significant changes in the Federal picture which had not been accomplished by Roosevelt or by Truman. No Negro, for example, had ever been employed at the White House except as a messenger or janitor; President Eisenhower appointed Mrs. Lois Lippman as the first Negro secretary. He also appointed forty-seven Negroes to important posts; twenty-seven of these positions had never before been held by Negroes. Since the time of President Taft, no Negro had been appointed to a position in the "Little Cabinet" until Eisenhower appointed J. Ernest Wilkins, a prominent Chicago attorney, as the Assistant Secretary of Labor. In the same way Scovel Richardson, former Lincoln University Dean of Law, became the first black Federal Parole Commissioner.

Under President Truman, Navy shipyards in the South had been segregated despite repeated protests by myself and other civic leaders. Soon after his inauguration President Eisenhower, at my request, ordered an inquiry toward the elimination of this segregation. With a minimum of friction in all Southern naval bases and installations, a silent revolution took place overnight. The "White Only" and "Colored" signs were removed from drinking fountains. Doors painted with these repulsive words were painted over. Cafeterias were opened to both races. Within only a few months segregation was thus completely eliminated from Norfolk, Virginia, to Houston, Texas, in twenty-one naval installations employing seventy thousand whites and Negroes.

On February 5, 1953, I contacted the White House regarding segregated Veterans Administration hospitals. While on concert tour in the South my wife had agreed to perform without a fee at the veterans' hospitals in Nashville and Murfreesboro, Tennessee. She had never played to a segregated audience and was shocked when she arrived at the Nashville Hospital to find Negroes and whites rigidly divided. The manager assured her that this was voluntary, but the Negro servicemen told her they were forced to do this. Therefore, before going on to the Murfreesboro Hospital for her concert there on February 4, she called in advance. A Mr. Dietrich, in charge of special events, told her, "We enforce segregation in the wards and in all the public events."

Gen. Wilton Persons, Special Assistant to the President, replied immediately to my request: "I assure you the President is interested in this matter and it will be looked into." The White House went to work. Formerly there had been racial segregation in forty-seven hospitals in the Veterans Administration, ranging all the way from separate waiting rooms to total exclusion from some institutions. This was immediately changed upon orders from Eisenhower to the Veterans Administration. Segregated libraries were integrated; partitions separating the races in the snack bars were torn down, and integrated recreational facilities were opened. Negroes were treated at previously all-white hospitals and whites were treated at a former Negro-only hospital in Tuskegee, Alabama.

Along the way it was not an easy fight. On May 18, 1953, Vice-Admiral J. T. Boone, Chief Medical Director of the Veterans Administration, wrote me suggesting that VA hospitals "be guided by the local customs of the areas in which they are located." My memorandum to the President on May 21 stated, "Admiral Boone is saying that Federal hospitals for veterans operated by Federal funds must be guided by local customs. I do not believe you personally condone such segregation and I ask you for a directive as quickly as possible on this question."

One of the most significant victories was the desegregation of Washington, D.C. Because of segregation in the capital's movie houses, General and Mrs. Eisenhower refused to go to a single motion picture after he was elected President. The only one he attended was *The Life of Mahatma Gandhi,* which was shown in the then only nonsegregated motion picture house in Washington, the Dupont, managed by my good friend Gerald Wagner. Using the power of the Executive, as Truman and Roosevelt had never done, Eisenhower had the Attorney General move in on local restaurants with vigorous action: "All segregation has to stop!" The officials of the Restaurant Association of Washington reported that not one single case of serious friction arose. The Board of Commissioners of the District of Columbia appointed by the President could have moved on many previous occasions to eliminate segregation, not only in Constitution Hall but elsewhere. But the Commissioners did not move until they were urged by Eisenhower's newly appointed chairman to seek voluntary cooperation from the bars and restaurants in hotels of the city. This barrier, too, was dissolved. Jim Crowism was wiped out in Washington, except for discriminatory newspaper ads and some segregated housing. It was done with such an absence of publicity that in the summer of 1954 a large group of Negroes arrived to picket a theater. They were so surprised when tickets were sold to them that they turned around and went home.

Segregation in recreational areas—golf courses, swimming pools, tennis courts, and so on—vanished overnight without a single reported case of friction. The District of Columbia Public Housing Agency ceased to display "White Only" and "Colored Only" signs on public buildings. As I wrote in the October, 1954, *Reader's Digest*, "Washington at last is becoming the capital of our democracy in fact as well as in name. Today, when foreigners come to study our democratic institutions, Americans, instead of apologizing, can point with pride to their national capital."

By Executive Order, President Truman had initiated integration of Negro and white soldiers in the armed services; nevertheless, four and a half years later, when Eisenhower took over, 40 percent of the Army's all-Negro units were still intact and 75 percent of the Negroes in the Navy were still serving in the segregated messmen's branch. One by one these were eliminated and integrated. While on an official visit to the Military Academy at West Point, I noticed Negroes serving as servants to the cadets. As soon as I reported to President Eisenhower the existence of this segregated Negro unit, the practice was wiped out. The outstanding American weekly of Chicago, *The Defender*, which had always supported Roosevelt, Truman, and Stevenson, commented with "delighted astonishment" on President Eisenhower's record.

How did all this come about so quickly? In the early months of the Eisenhower Administration, after we had formed "the team," news came to me that Mrs. Oveta Culp Hobby, Secretary of Health, Education and Welfare, would deliberately countermand President Eisenhower's orders on civil rights. I sent a telegram to the President on June 3, 1953:

> The hour has arrived for you to decisively assert your integrity. You cannot continue to stand between two opposite moral poles. You stated publicly to the White House press and the news rang around the world in the hearts of freedom-loving people everywhere, "I find no moral or legal justification for the use of Federal funds in the support of segregation."
>
> You abolished, by Executive Order, segregated schools on Army posts. Your White House secretariat has assured me for months that they are working on the abolition of segregation in veterans hospitals. Through

your Assistant, Major General Wilton Persons, I was assured that the White House would look into the question of segregation of Negro workers on Federal property, working on a Federal project, getting paid entirely with Federal funds in the Norfolk, Virginia, and Charleston, South Carolina, Navy yards.

Your official family in the past five days has completely undermined your stated position on segregation. The hour has definitely arrived for you to speak out. You must assert the leadership the people vested in you and of which you are so capable.

First, Admiral Boone, Chief Medical Officer of the Veterans Administration, has reaffirmed within the past days in a letter to me that he will not change the practices in veterans hospitals because he insists on maintaining "local customs" on Federal property.

Second, the Secretary of the Navy, Anderson, has informed you over the weekend that the Navy is going to continue to maintain segregation in the Charleston, South Carolina, and Norfolk, Virginia, naval shipyards and the Navy is not going to deal with this social poblem.

Third, word has reached me that the Secretary of Welfare, Mrs. Hobby, has virtually contermanded your order abolishing segregated schools on Army posts by issuing a memorandum to the Secretary of Defense, Wilson, telling Mr. Wilson not to follow your directive.

This is insubordination. This is not support of you as the Commander-in-Chief and the President of the United States. This detracts from the dignity, integrity and power of your office.

I have faith in you as a man of good insights, decent instincts and strong moral character. I beg of you to assert these noble qualities. The free world is looking to you as its last hope. Strong leadership is imperative now, tomorrow may be too late. For fear that this might not reach you, may I have the courtesy of a personal reply.

Robert Donovan, in the only authoritative book on Eisenhower, *The Inside Story,* devoted a whole chapter to this incident. He pointed out that no single event caused more disturbance in the White House than when President Eisenhower read the headlines that night in the Washington *Evening Star.* He instructed Max Rabb to call a special Cabinet meeting. Max Rabb came running to my office to complain, "Adam, you have made a great mistake. Things are in an uproar in the White House. Why didn't you get in touch with me first?"

"Max, maybe I did make a mistake in the manner in which I handled this, but I am sick and tired of the White House under every administration saying one thing and the people who work under the White House doing the opposite."

"Well, Adam, all hell has broken loose. I tell you what you do: the President is going to write you a letter and I want you to reply in a complimentary way and from here on we walk together. We have received orders to do everything within reason to wipe out segregation and discrimination in the Federal government."

On Tuesday, June 6, I received the following letter from the President:

I have your telegram and I want you to know that I appreciate your kind expression of confidence that I will carry out every pledge I have made with regard to segregation. I shall continue to devote my earnest efforts to advance both the spirit as well as the fact of equality. I believe that the fight to achieve tangible results will be increasingly successful.

In your communication you have indicated that there is some evidence that the policy I am pursuing against the impairment of equality through segregation has been obstructed in some agencies of the government. I have made inquiries of the officials to whom you refer and learn that they are pursuing the purpose of eliminating segregation in Federally controlled and supported institutions.

We have not taken and we shall not take a single backward step. There must be no second-class citizens in this country.

As you are so well aware, this problem cannot be solved wholly with either laws or directives. The spirit of these objectives cannot be achieved as a result of the action of any one person, no matter with how much authority and forthrightness he acts. To achieve our purpose we must plan and work together to win the victories one by one, and not to be content until we have gained our goal.

And so I replied:

Your letter of June 6, in reply to my telegram of June 3, completely justified my confidence in you. Heretofore, this confidence has been on a personal basis, but, because of your pledges, as contained in your communication, my confidence in you is now more than faith in an individual. My confidence is now in you as the President of the United States, and as the leader of the American people. . . .

The most significant statement in your letter, and the one which makes it a Magna Carta for minorities and a second Emancipation Proclamation is "we have not taken and we shall not take a single backward step. There must be no second-class citizens in this country."

This is the reassurance that people need in these troubled hours—the

reassurance that nothing that has been gained will be lost, and, more than
that, that we will press on to the goal of complete equality, of first-class
citizens.

Many enemies were made by this liaison. There were people close to the
President at that time who resented my intrusion upon the palace guard.
But let it be said that there were two Texans who cooperated fully in this
teamwork: Robert Anderson, the Secretary of the Navy, and Mrs. Oveta
Culp Hobby, Secretary of Health, Education and Welfare. After the President laid down the law, no two people worked harder than these two to
bring about the realization of our dream.

The memorandum that had been issued in January, 1952, under the
direction of Truman's Under Secretary of the Navy, Francis P. Whitehair
of Florida, officially sanctioning segregated facilities in the South, was
countermanded by Robert Anderson. And when he did this, as reported
by Lee Nichols in his book *Breaking Through the Color Barrier,* Anderson
stated, "I have no bias or prejudices of any kind." Moreover, he cooperated
fully when, a year before the 1954 Supreme Court decision, President
Eisenhower ordered all schools on defense bases to be integrated.

9

The Bandung Conference

In 1955 the Department of State deliberately and calculatedly imperiled the future of the United States of America for perhaps the rest of our lives. It did so despite advice from me which every subsequent event of history has more than supported.

On April 19, 1955, for the first time in the history of the world, twenty-nine nations of Asia and Africa met together in Bandung, Indonesia. Since then, the number of independent nations in that area of the world has climbed to form the largest bloc in the United Nations. The United States deliberately boycotted the Bandung meeting. The Administration did everything possible to prevent any American from going. Finally, when I decided to go at my own expense, they used every method to dissuade me, but I went. I went in the face of organized resistance from the Department of State.

On January 26, 1955, I rose on the Floor of the United States Congress and spoke of the importance of our participation at Bandung:

We need to let the peoples of Asia and Africa know that we do not consider them second-class nations. Therefore, I think it very important when this conference is held in Indonesia in April, of the twenty-nine colored nations of the world led by Pakistan, India, Ceylon, Burma, and Indonesia, that our Department of State send to the Conference, not as delegates, because we are not invited, but as observers, not an all-white Department of State team, but a team composed of Negroes and whites, Jews and Gentiles, Protestants and Catholics. We need to let the two billion colored peoples on the earth, without whom we cannot continue much longer as a first-class power, know that America is a democracy of the people.

I then wired President Eisenhower suggesting that such a good-will mission be sent. On February 16, I was shocked to receive as my reply a copy of a memorandum to the White House from the Department of State: "The United States will not be a participant, we have no plans to send observers, and Congressman Powell should not be encouraged in his apparent hope to attend the conference as an observer." Until this moment I had not decided to attend, but when I realized that our government's stupidity would not allow them to send an observer to this, one of the most significant conferences in our times, I then informed the White House that I was going to Bandung anyway and that I was going to pay my own way.

Immediately all hell broke loose. Top-level conferences were held in the State Department. Efforts were begun to prevent my going. And finally a deal was suggested to me by a State Department emissary: if I did not go to Bandung, the State Department would send me, at its expense, on one or two red-carpet missions to Asia and to Africa—but after the Bandung Conference. The Assistant Secretary of State, Thruston Morton, later Republican National Chairman, came to dissuade me, but before he could open his mouth I told him that I was going and that there was nothing he or anyone else could do to stop me. The chairmen of the two Congressional committees on which I was serving, Representative Graham Barden of North Carolina and Representative Clair Engle of California, gave me letters that forced the Department of Defense to furnish transportation for me on the Military Air Transport Service from Washington to Manila and back.

Bandung was a pilgrimage to a new Mecca. I was one of the pilgrims and I went because I had to. Divine compulsion had been lain upon me. I did not know what I could do. I had no idea that I would be more than an

interested bystander rubbing elbows with history and breathing in the
ferment of a new world. I went to Bandung knowing it could be one of the
most important events of the twentieth century. I left Bandung knowing
that it had been.

It was the first such conference in the world, drawing together twenty-
nine nations that spilled across half the earth—from Liberia in far western
Africa and on in an unbroken array to Red China and Japan in the East.
The delegates represented 1.4 billion people. Present were every color,
creed, belief, and disbelief. Bandung was a revolution with the power of
moral violence welded into one vast striking force against all the evils that
the peoples of the Far East have suffered since time immemorial—colonialism, racialism, discrimination, and second-class nationhood. No force in the
world could stop Bandung.

Why did the Department of State not want an American to go to what
has now become the most important conference in modern times? Simply
because we did not have an adequate foreign policy for Asia and Africa. The
foreign policy of our government for too long has been arrived at through
evaluations given to us by the existing colonial powers. We have too many
leaders in our nation who are color-blind, who see only white. Three-fifths
of the free peoples of the world are colored, and this means that the United
States is in danger of becoming a second-class power by letting history pass
it by.

The two individuals upon whom the Department of State relied for an
evaluation of the Bandung Conference were George V. Allen, former
Ambassador to India, and William Lacy, former Indonesian desk officer in
the State Department. George V. Allen had just returned from India,
lacking a complete understanding of the Indian people, and William Lacy
was considered by the leaders of the Indonesian government as one of their
enemies. President Sukarno told me that he blamed Lacy for allowing the
Dutch to stage their second armed attempt to destroy Indonesia. Sukarno
told me that the Indonesians knew that the Dutch were massing troops and
he conveyed this information to Lacy, who deliberately buried it without
bringing it to the attention of our government or the United Nations.
These, then, were the two men the White House and the State Department relied on to evaluate the Bandung Conference.

William Lacy told me in my office in the presence of Thruston Morton
that our government had an attitude of "benevolent indifference." How
could any nation, including the United States, afford to be indifferent to

1.4 billion people? Lacy and Morton told me that they had stopped Chester Bowles, our great Ambassador to India, from attending and they did not want me to go because I would be "persona non grata." I told them they were wrong, that the Indonesian government was arranging my commercial transportation from Manila to Bandung and back; that while there I would be their guest and that furthermore the Indonesian Ambassador to the United States, Mr. Moekarto Notowidigdo, was giving a dinner in honor of myself and those who were attending the conference as representatives of the American press.

The Administration virtually ordered me, a member of the United States Congress, to stay away from the United States Embassy, the United States Ambassador, and all the United States employees in Indonesia. I assured Assistant Secretary of State Morton, "I will be more than glad to do this because I am ashamed of the Department of State's and the White House's attitude toward the Bandung Conference."

Harold Stassen, then director of the Foreign Operations Administration, and Theodore C. Streibert, head of the United States Information Service, came to see me. "We disagree with the Department of State. They are completely wrong, and we need you at Bandung. Please go." So, on March 29, 1955, I addressed the Congress prior to my departure: "I am going to this conference at my own expense, entirely unofficially. I hope that my presence there will be of some value for the peace, understanding, and strengthening of the brotherhood of our world. Greetings should be sent from the President of the United States," I urged, greetings of good will. Somewhere at that conference there should be a member of the United States government, showing by his presence that this country is sympathetic to the aims for peace of the peoples of Asia and Africa." At the conclusion of my speech, members of Congress—Northerners, Southerners, Republicans, and Democrats—rose to their feet, praised me, and wished me Godspeed. Then, and only then, did the Department of State offer to give me some assistance, and the only reason was, and I quote their representative, "If we do not give you complete cooperation and if our Embassy ignores you while you are there, then the Communists will say that we are doing this to you because you represent a minority."

I took off for Bandung on April 8, with the promise that the Department of State was behind me. In *The New York Times* that day Dana Adams Schmidt wrote, "Congressman Powell was to receive 'complete cooperation' from all the Embassies of our Government." In fact, this was another

Department of State lie. The only individual who was cordial to me was former Senator Homer Ferguson, who had just arrived in Manila as the American Ambassador to the Philippines. He twice cabled the exact time of my arrival and the number of my flight from Manila to the Ambassador from the United States to Indonesia, Hugh S. Cumming.

I arrived at Djakarta, the capital of Indonesia, with General Carlos P. Romulo and the Philippine delegation. The airport was packed with tens of thousands of people, the flags of twenty-nine nations were unfurled to the winds, Indonesia's Army national band was playing, a guard of honor was drawn up, and Foreign Minister Sunarjo of Indonesia headed the welcoming committee—but not a single person from the United States Embassy was there to meet me. I stood there on that airstrip completely alone. I had come twelve thousand miles to see history made. I had come to show the people of Asia and Africa that the United States cared. I had come to tell the truth so that the Communists could not use racialism for their own propaganda. Yet not a single person from my government was there to meet me, not just a citizen but a Congressman, a senior Congressman of twelve years' standing, a ranking member of the Committee on Education and Labor, and a member of the Committee on Interior and Insular Affairs. Never to my knowledge has the United States government let down a member of the United States Congress more completely than it let me down and, in so doing, let down all the American people, on Friday afternoon, April 15, 1955, in Indonesia.

Some of the American newspapermen spotted me and came over. The more than seventy American journalists who were there were a dedicated group of hard-working men and women. While I was being interviewed by them, an individual approached me, furtively, and told me he worked for the United States Information Agency but that he was not there officially. He was a good fellow, Jerry Donahue. I asked him, "Where is the United States Ambassador?" Donahue finally admitted that the United States Embassy had received official orders from Washington to stay away from me—and this they did. Not a single person connected with Washington in any capacity came to see me in Djakarta. But the Indonesian government took excellent care of me.

I went immediately to Bandung, where a lovely apartment had been provided for me.

I had asked President Eisenhower, just as a matter of good will, to send a wire to the Conference, not an endorsement. On Monday, April 18, the

Department of State wired me: "We do not believe relationship of this government at the Bandung Conference would warrant such a message from the President." Every single delegate I met criticized our government sharply for this utterly unwarranted action and, naturally, messages of good will began to pour in officially from the Soviet orbit. The Indonesian newspaper *The Observer* the next day featured two headlines: "UNITED STATES REFUSES TO SEND MESSAGE TO ASIAN-AFRICAN CONFERENCE," and "BEST WISHES FOR ASIAN-AFRICAN CONFERENCE FROM THE UNION OF SOVIET SOCIALIST REPUBLICS."

Nevertheless, the United States did win a victory at Bandung which it did not deserve to win, which it did nothing toward winning and deliberately tried to lose. We *won* at Bandung only because the idea of democracy triumphed over the idea of Communism. I played a small part in this but only because God willed that I should be there.

Make no mistake about it, the Soviet Union, through Red China, had deliberately planned in advance to take over the Bandung Conference and to make it the greatest propaganda victory to be won by any nation in modern times. The Asian-African Conference was going to become a weapon of twenty-nine nations aimed directly at the United States. Not one of the nations present, including those committed to us by military alliances, could have stemmed the tide, because they were united—Communists, Christians, Hindus, Moslems, democracies, and theocracies—on one ideal: "Down with racialism, down with colonialism."

The Soviet Union knew this and sent in advance of the opening of the Conference two agents—a very attractive dark-brown girl from India, and a man from Ceylon who was almost black. They arrived as two of the some four hundred working journalists who attended the Conference. Obviously, they had been deliberately picked because of their color.

When the Union of South Africa's unofficial delegates called their press conference on Sunday morning, April 17, at the Savoy-Homan Hotel, the maneuverings of Khrushchev and Chou En-lai became apparent. The leader of the the the all-colored Congress of the Union of South Africa rose to state the case of the natives of that country. His name was Moses Kotani.

He stated simply and factually the unbelievable story of segregation and discrimination in that dismal land of brutality and murder. He asked in Bandung, Indonesia, that the United States intercede and use its power to bring justice. This was the moment for which the Red propaganda machine had been waiting. Immediately, the Indian girl rose and asked a question that was pretyped on a card: "How can you expect help from the United States of America in the Union of South Africa when the United States practices the same kind of doctrine toward the American Negro?"

From that moment on the United States could have been finished. The Red propaganda machine would have rolled. More than fifty correspondents from Soviet Russia, Red China, North Vietnam, countries behind the Iron Curtain, and the *Daily Worker* of London had assembled for the press conference. This was what they had been waiting for. They were waiting to smear the United States of America on the race question before the twenty-nine colored nations of the world. And when Chou En-lai arrived on Monday, he planned to press immediately for a resolution condemning the United States for racialism within its borders. Such a move would have been a tremendous defeat for our country, for Western civilization, and for democracy. This was the master plan of Khruschchev and Chou En-lai.

I knew before I left the United States that they were going to do this. I told members of the State Department in my office that the Soviet Union would use the Asian-African Conference as a means of attacking the United States on the Negro problem. It was a natural. But this was what I had come to Bandung for, not knowing I would have the opportunity, and I went into action. I went up to the young lady from India and asked her to come to a press conference that I would hold that afternoon just so that she could ask me questions, which I would answer on the spot. She never showed up.

But more than a hundred newsmen and newswomen from all over the world, including every representative of the Communist press, were there. And I told them the truth. As the Hearst papers reported in the United States: "At a press conference Adam Powell shot straight from the shoulder at Communist correspondents who tried to trot out the Red charge that the Negro is horribly treated in America. With the oratory for which he is noted, Powell told them that it just isn't so. He said racism and second-class citizenship are on their way out in the United States and pointed pridefully to the number of Negroes who are holding public office."

The New York *Herald Tribune*'s ace correspondent, Homer Bigart, hit the front page with the story: "The Communist correspondents put away their notebooks in sneering disgust."

The Hearst papers then wrote a nationwide editorial: "Now in our opinion, Representative Powell's unofficial trip will pay off in a great deal of official and unofficial good will for our country and its ideals. We offer a rousing, 'Atta boy, Adam!'

"P.S. Another thing we do not quite understand is why the State Department coldly turned down Representative Powell's suggestion that President Eisenhower send greetings to the Asian-African Conference. What harm could there be in that?"

Democracy had won. It had won despite the fact that the State Department had fought me every step of the way, refused me minimum courtesy, and snubbed me. Nevertheless, from the moment of my press conference on, the question of racialism in the United States was never again raised in public, although Chou En-lai definitely raised it in Executive Session behind closed doors. He tried desperately to get the Conference to adopt a resolution likening racial discrimination in Africa with that of the United States. But I had laid the basis in public for resistance to this. When a resolution did come out of the Executive Committee, a member of that committee told me that they unanimously voted down Chou En-lai's and that the new resolution read, "We are against racial discrimination in Africa and *in all other parts of the world.*"

I was amazed to learn of the tremendous discrimination and segregation practiced by the colored peoples in Southeast Asia, Jim Crow American style, anti-Semitism Oriental style. Delegate after delegate told me behind the scenes how much they hated the Chinese in their country. In Thailand, Chinese are forced to live in ghettos called compounds, with special extra taxation. The same prejudice was revealed in a book given to me by the Minister of Information concerning the population of Bandung. It cited: "Indonesians, 698,073; Indonesian Citizens of Chinese origin, 62,792; and Chinese, 32,183." In other words, they were separating all Indonesian citizens from the Chinese, just as the United States separates Negro and white.

There isn't much difference between the Union of South Africa and the union of South Carolina, but as I said to a journalist from behind the Iron Curtain in Poland, "Let's not judge the United States by what is happening in its worst states, but let's judge it by what is happening in most of its states and use this as a goal to clean up the rest of our country."

And another journalist said, "But what about the Negroes from the South who cannot go to restaurants, hotels, and lunch counters?"

"Yes, that's true," I replied. "That's one of the changes to be made. But in the meantime, what about 50 million brown-skinned Indians in your all-colored country who cannot associate with anyone because they are 'untouchables'?" He shut up.

An Indonesian said, "You have Negroes who can't ride on some trains." I said, "That's not true. But what about the 120,000 Indonesians in this all-colored country who are behind barbed wire starving to death at the rate of one hundred per week, only because they are Christians and this is a Moslem country?" He shut up.

A journalist from Red China stood up and said, "You are not a Negro. Your skin is white." I pointed to an Oriental standing nearby whom the journalist did not know, and asked, "What is he? Chinese?"

The journalist looked and said, "I do not know."

"Well, then, how can you say what I am?"

"But," he replied to me, "he is an Asian."

And I said, "Yes, and I am an American." He shut up.

Frankly, at Bandung I wished my skin had been black, for it was a mark of distinction. The distinguished writer Vincent Sheehan told me he was so tired of walking around the streets of Bandung alone that he was going to hang a sign around his neck saying, "Me colored too," so the people would speak to him.

My picture was in the newspapers and as I was walking up Freedom Road, the day after my press conference, hundreds of children besieged me with their autograph books. When I wrote "A. C. Powell, U.S.A.," a ten-year-old moppet looked at me and in perfect English said, "You are the Congressman the United States didn't want to come here. You paid your own way. Thank you for being so kind." A ten-year-old child on the streets of Indonesia had more insight, courtesy, and vision than our State Department.

Not a single journalist at Bandung could understand why our government had been so blind. James Michener of *South Pacific* fame, when we first met, grabbed my hand and said, "Powell, it's good to meet a man of courage and vision."

Even after my press conference, when I defended the United States of America and silenced the Communist journalists from *Pravda* in Moscow, the Tass news agency, and the New China News Agency of Peking, still no word from the Embassy. Raymond Gram Swing said to me, "I told Ambassador Cumming you were worth $5 million today for our government." But for them I was not worth a penny, although my colleagues in the House of Representatives were overgenerous in their praise. Resolutions were introduced by Representative Eugene J. Keogh of New York and Representative John D. Dingell of Michigan:

84th Congress
1st Session

IN THE HOUSE OF REPRESENTATIVES
May 9, 1956

Mr. Keogh submitted the following resolution; which was referred to the Committee on Foreign Affairs.

RESOLUTION

Resolved, That the Member of Congress from the Eighteenth District of the State of New York, Adam Clayton Powell, is hereby commended for the statesmanship, patriotism, and forthright courage displayed by him at the recent Afro-Asian Conference at Bandung, where, as a delegate at his own expense, he forcefully and eloquently voiced the opinion of millions of Americans who not only advocate democracy but condemn and disavow communism and colonialism wherever and in whatever form it exists.

The day following my meeting with the press, which was the opening day of the Asian-African Conference, I deliberately sought out Ambassador Cumming and told him I expected at least minimum courtesy from him. He replied, "I have been instructed by Washington to be discreet in my dealings with you."

After the news of my press conference had hit the front pages of the United States press, however, and editorials had been written in scores of papers, North and South, praising me and criticizing the Department of State, then, and only then, did Ambassador Cumming come to me and ask me to be his house guest while I was in Indonesia. I would rather have slept in a gutter in Bandung than to have accepted any hospitality from the Department of State at that time.

In the year 1215 at Runnymede the common people of England received their first emancipation—the Magna Carta. On April 18, 1955, at Bandung, twenty-nine Asian and African nations gave the white man his second emancipation—they relieved him of the traditional white man's burden. They took a block-long building, citadel of white superiority under the Dutch, and renamed it Merdeka, which means the Freedom Building.

Here the Conference was held. Another building, once for whites only, they called the Bi-Color Building. The name of one of the main streets was changed to Freedom Road, and the main highway, which had been called the Eastern Road, was renamed the Asian-African Road.

I will never forget one line that President Sukarno spoke in his opening speech, after which Ernest K. Lindley of *Newsweek* turned to me and said, "Thrills ran up and down my back." For Sukarno had said:

> The battle against colonialism has been a long one, and do you know that today is a famous anniversary in that battle? The eighteenth day of April, one thousand seven hundred and seventy-five, just a hundred and eighty years ago, Paul Revere rode at midnight through the New England countryside, warning of the approach of the British troops and of the opening of the American War of Independence, the first successful anticolonial war in history. And about this midnight ride the poet Longfellow wrote:
>
> > A cry of defiance and not of fear,
> > A voice in the darkness, a knock at the door,
> > And the word that shall echo forevermore.
>
> And let us remember that for the sake of all of the world, we Asians and Africans must be united: I declare the Asian-African Conference open. Bismillah! Godspeed!

Any individual from any part of the world who had a grievance was allowed to come to the Conference and air it. And they came—from Turkestan, the South African Congress, the Indian Congress, the African National Congress. The Archbishop of the Greek Orthodox Church on the Island of Cyprus came to ask free colored people to hear a white man whose people were still in a colony. The question of the Mau-Mau in Kenya and other colonial questions of the Belgian Congo and French Equatorial Africa were all raised behind the scenes.

President Sukarno was correct in his opening speech. "Let us not be deceived, colonialism is not dead." One night I was talking with my good friend Kojo Botsio, Minister of State of the Gold Coast, an Oxford University graduate, and I asked, "Why is it, Botsio, that none of you who is here representing the submerged countries of British colonialism in Africa has opened your mouth?"

He looked around, took me out on the balcony of his room, shut the door behind us, and said, "The British Foreign Office has agents on the scene here in Bandung and these agents have bluntly told me and other chiefs of the Sudan and the Gold Coast that if we opened our mouths and said anything more than just the perfunctory word of greeting, the British government would not allow the Sudan nor the Gold Coast to achieve the Commonwealth status which they have been promised." So he kept his mouth shut, as did others, and today Sudan and Ghana are parts of the Asian-African Conference and are free.

One evening during dinner Marvin Stone, chief of the International News Service in the Far East, rushed to my table and handed me a cable from London: "Editor Glen Neville, *New York Daily Mirror,* ask Powell directly, urging him to deal personally with Chou on behalf of the imprisoned flyers."

We immediately left the dining room and Stone said, "Now let's get to work."

"I am not going to crawl," I said. "I am not going with my hat in my hand. I am not going to throw my weight around as a Congressman. I am going to approach him as a human being approaching another human being. I am going to appeal to him, and see if he has any decent instincts at all."

At that time eleven men, American flyers, had been downed in China and were imprisoned. Their loved ones had not heard from them and no one in the States knew what their future would be. It was the cause célèbre in early 1955. On April 21, in Bandung, I wrote to Prime Minister Chou En-lai, crossing off the word "official" on my stationery, saying, "I am referring to the imprisonment of the eleven American flyers on charges of subversion. I cannot stress too emphatically the importance of this problem to all people of the United States of America. The discussion of such a problem could go far toward easing world tension. Would it not therefore be of mutual value to both our countries to discuss this matter? I am prepared at any time within the next twenty-four hours to meet with you."
At five o'clock we sent it off by messenger, who returned and said that Chou had received the letter. We waited to see if there was a grain of humanity in Chou's makeup.

While we were waiting Stewart Hensley of United Press told me that word had gotten to the United States by way of their London office that Peking was discussing releasing the eleven flyers. Early the next morning the French News Agency reported that the flyers would soon be released. But thirty-six hours had passed since my letter was delivered, so I penciled a brief note reminding Chou that the twenty-four-hour period was over, and asking if we could have some word immediately. That Saturday evening, April 23, at the close of the last Executive Session, Chou first announced publicly that he was ready to sit down and talk to the United States about Formosa, and also that he was considering announcing the release of the flyers at the closing session on Sunday. Now, with the reports trickling in from London, Paris, and the United Nations, plus the fact that Chou had made an open-door statement on Formosa, I felt that another mission had been accomplished.

That same night my friends from Liberia, led by Acting Secretary of State Momolu Dukuly, gave a very small cocktail party. It was only for the chiefs of state attending the Conference, and I was the only non-chief invited. When I arrived, the cocktail room was pitch dark; a motion picture about Liberia was being shown. Chou En-lai was ushered in and seated by me, and I said to him, "I am the American who wrote to you about the flyers."

In perfect English, he said, "Oh, yes. You can understand that I have been rather busy this week." As he left, his secretary, Mr. Pu, a graduate of Harvard, said to me, "You will hear from him very, very soon." News then came to me that on the next day, Sunday, when the final speeches were made, Chou would announce that Red China would release the American flyers.

During that Saturday night our State Department again did the unbelievable. John Foster Dulles was at his island retreat in Canada, which had no telephone. President Eisenhower was at his Gettysburg farm, not to be disturbed. And somebody in the State Department—we never learned who—sent a cable to the Asian-African Conference which was posted on the bulletin board at 9 A.M. Sunday, stating that the United States "doubted Chou's sincerity"!

Every American newsman there was shocked that this ill-advised, hastily prepared, ill-timed cable from the State Department could have arrived at the Asian-African Conference. Chou stood up and did the only thing he could do. He struck back at the United States, reemphasized Red China's claim to Formosa, and refused to say a word about the flyers.

I had to leave that evening and asked Prime Minister Mohammed Ali of Pakistan to talk with Chou for me. While I was in Singapore later that night, Mohammed Ali announced to the press that he had talked with Chou for two and a half hours and that Chou had told him that if America would just bend a little and stop its attitude of non-negotiation, he would consider releasing the eleven flyers.

One of the United States' best friends, Sir John Kotelawala of Ceylon, said in Singapore that day, "It is a pity that the United States replied to the offer without thinking." The great tragedy is that we had men in high places in our State Department who acted "without thinking." President Eisenhower finally, on April 28, said that the cable received at the Conference might have "overstated" the case or contained "an error in terminology."

The final communiqué of the Asian-African Conference was definitely pro-West, pro-American, pro-democracy, and pro-United Nations. The United Nations was referred to eighteen times in one way or another as a basis upon which to shape the future of the Asian and African nations and of the world. The communiqué praised the contributions of the United States to their countries. Because of the unanimity rule, Red China had to sign the communiqué, which meant that it joined in praising the United States. President Eisenhower's proposal for an International Atomic Energy Agency was specifically approved, and under Section F, entitled "Promotion of World Peace and Cooperation," Subsection 1, they specifically *excluded* Red China from membership in the United Nations.

We missed the boat at Bandung. But when I came wearily back to Washington, I came back to a hero's welcome, to top-level, off-the-record meetings with the key people of the State Department, to a classified security meeting of the heads of our Central Intelligence Agency under Allen Dulles, and to a meeting with the President of the United States on Wednesday.

I will not say much concerning the two-and-a-half-hour secret classified meeting with Allen Dulles and the chiefs of the CIA because that would violate the confidence placed in me. But I will tell a story that indicates that even this group didn't function at the Bandung Conference. Allen Dulles was a wonderful, dedicated man, usually in a tweed suit and always smoking a pipe. I was seated beside him with the top espionage leaders of our country ranged around the rest of the table. The soundproof room was guarded. I began to tell Allen Dulles about the final communiqué issued by the Asian-African powers. He became excited and asked, "Where did you get a copy of this?"

I said, "They were printed in English and stacked on the desk at the Information Center for anyone who wanted one."

He pounded the table and demanded, "Why didn't our men bring me some?"

And then, from the end of the table, one man spoke up: "Mr. Dulles, it was also on the Associated Press wire service in full."

"You mean we have a copy of that here and I haven't seen it?" They all looked shamefaced. Then Allen Dulles demanded, "Bring me that wire service copy now." And sure enough, within five minutes Mr. Dulles was furnished the complete communiqué as sent over the Associated Press wires to all the newspapers of America almost a week earlier. He, the head of the Central Intelligence Agency, hadn't been informed of its release.

At my meeting with the President at the White House, he complained to me of bursitis in his shoulder and said they had him on a diet of soybeans, of which he was sick and tired. He congratulated me on going to Bandung and on the success of the trip.

I reported to Mr. Eisenhower that I had been able to stop the Communist propaganda drive at Bandung by referring to the work he personally had done against racism and to the Supreme Court's civil rights decisions. I therefore believed that the leadership he had so ably projected should not be slowed for a moment but should be stepped up. "Regardless of the neutralism of its leaders, we should go ahead and help India," I told him, "not only because the Indian people desperately need help, but because it may be one way of keeping them on our side even though their leaders tend toward neutralism." I went on to say that in my opinion the area to be aware of was Africa. "This is the emerging continent for the immediate future."

I pointed out that Bandung had stepped up the timetable for freedom, and that it was absolutely impossible for the United States to continue to hope for further support from the peoples of Africa and Asia if we continued to abstain before the United Nations on the question of colonialism. "The cold, stark fact confronts us that whether we take a stand or not, imperialism is finished. The natives, country by country, are going to drive out the colonial powers."

Finally, I urged the President to make a meaningful gesture toward the people of Asia: "You are the only international symbol around which the free world can unite. You should take a trip to the Far East now." He agreed, and General Romulo made the same plea on television the following Sunday, but somewhere along the line somebody stopped Mr. Eisenhower from going on that trip. When he did go in 1960, it was only to have his trip destroyed by the riots in Tokyo.

I also told Mr. Eisenhower that by the following year Morocco and Tunisia would be free. He was amazed, and, in fact, the chiefs of the Department of State told me it was impossible. They were right. It was not the following year—it was September of that year!

We went to Africa centuries ago carrying a cross, but it's time to go back to Africa again carrying an offer of full equality, dignity, mutual respect, direct and adequate assistance for social change. Africa is the number-one problem of our world. That vast continent is shaped somewhat like an inverted question mark, and that is what it is—stretching from Cairo to Capetown, five thousand miles of questions.

And why not a summit conference with the peoples of Asia and Africa? Why not be bold and daring? And, in my own words to President Eisenhower, "An eight-power summit conference meeting in Manila would just about annihilate the propaganda of Red China." Such a meeting has never been held in our history and this alone proves the inadequacies of our foreign policy. The Presidents of the United States have for years been participating in Big Four, Big Five, Big Six meetings all over Europe, but in not a single meeting with the leaders of Asia and Africa.

There is not much time left in which to do this. The world is moving with a rapidity that transcends not only the vision but even the imagination. With our Yankee courage, our Madison Avenue knowhow, our religious heritage, and the bulwark of the Bill of Rights behind us, we can launch a drive for peace and for full equality now in Asia and Africa. Only through such a bold maneuver can we win, and history will pass us by if we do not. Bandung was a punctuation mark in history. Whether it will be a period, comma, colon, exclamation mark, or question mark depends upon the United States of America.

10

Congress and Eisenhower

Bandung had completely changed my thinking. It made me over into an entirely new man. Before the Bandung Conference I could have been called, with some justification, a nationalist. Nearly everything I had done was aimed at obtaining more rights for the Negro people. After the Bandung Conference I came back to find the America of 1955 hungrily desiring a partnership with this new Afro-Asian bloc, and to find that such a union was blocked by the crass stupidity and ignorance of our State Department. I knew then that something drastic had to be done, and a great change took place in my own thinking; my perspective changed.

Whereas previously I had thought of civil rights in terms of rights for Negroes only, I now thought of civil rights as the sole method by which we could save the entire United States of America. Throughout the land, I began to speak on the subject "The Fight To Save the United States." I called on Negro people to take the leadership in this fight and urged them to get out of the rut of thinking that I had once been in: that the fight for civil rights was their fight alone; they must realize that it was also America's fight. They were the yardstick by which not only black Africa and brown

Asia, but also white Europe were measuring our land.

In the House of Representatives I helped combat the unholy alliance of Dixiecrats and biased Republicans. A new civil rights bloc was formed, led by people such as Emanuel Celler, James Roosevelt, and Charles Diggs on the Democratic side, and Jacob Javits, Kenneth Keating, and Hugh Scott, all later to become Senators, on the Republican side. The Supreme Court decision of May 17, 1954, had changed the tide of American thinking. The pendulum began to swing back toward the dreams of the Founding Fathers.

As my personal tide in thinking and perspective began to change, members of Congress asked that I help them in their political campaigns. These colleagues came not just from the North, but also from the South—Al Thomas of Houston; J. Howard Edmondson, candidate for the Governorship of Oklahoma, and his brother, Ed, running for Congress from Muskogee; Tom Morris from New Mexico. How the times had changed!

I called upon the White House to institute a crash program to catch up with the Soviet Union's tremendous strides in education. Dr. Benjamin Fine, Education Editor of *The New York Times*, had pointed out astounding facts in a series of front-page articles. Our country had definitely become a second-class power in terms of educating physicists, engineers, scientists, and technicians. Out of my proposal there was later developed the National Defense Education Act of 1958 which, however, was inadequate to meet the challenges of Soviet Russia's educational system.

Next I plunged into the fight to abolish segregation in the National Guard. Drew Pearson wrote, "It is not often that Representative Carl Vinson of Georgia, the astute chairman of the House Armed Services Committee, suffers a defeat. He is a tough legislative battler and most colleagues are afraid to tangle with him. Vinson took a drubbing on the Universal Military Training and Service Act, however. The man who defeated him was New York's brainy Congressman Powell. Powell outmaneuvered and out-talked his powerful Georgia colleague for two hectic days." My amendment to bar segregation in the military reserve program carried 126 to 87. By this time the new civil rights bloc was really moving —15 Congressmen from both sides of the aisle served as regional leaders, with a signed-up following of 201 Democratic and Republican legislators.

On January 5, 1956, I introduced at the new session a proposed constitutional amendment to give the District of Columbia the vote for President and Vice President, a long-overdue step that I knew the President would call for in his State of the Union message that week. This, too, finally became a reality. On April 3, 1961, the last of the required number of States ratified the amendment, based on a Resolution offered by Senator Estes Kefauver. The amendment passed both bodies of Congress in June of 1960.

In May, 1956, after I had presented many complaints to the White House, the Civil Aeronautics Administration issued a new directive abolishing all segregation in airports. The press recorded: "Congressman Powell revealed today that the CAA had released a memorandum denying federal funds to airports for construction or remodeling for any segregated facility."

The Veterans of Foreign Wars gave me its 1956 Award of the Year, citing my fight against Communism. We were turning away from the darkness of 1953, when in those early months I thought all was lost and there was no hope for liberalism in the land, and that a man who believed in it could not proclaim it without being pilloried. The tide had definitely turned, the crest of the wave was mounting, and now was the moment to hit with all the power I could summon up. The Dixiecrat-GOP alliance had been temporarily dissolved; there was a new civil rights bloc; I had stepped away from my racist thinking; I saw the true perspective of America before the congress of the world. I had formed front-door alliances with the White House; had achieved rapport with the leadership on both sides of the Congressional aisle; and, at Bandung, I had proven that I was right and the foreign-policy experts in our State Department were wrong. Remembering what I had been able to accomplish with the Civil Aeronautics Administration, I wondered what could be done to make the 1954 Supreme Court decision more effective. Congress had not yet spoken out in support of this decision. Large numbers of states were still in defiance of it but were receiving Federal funds. I remembered the Powell Amendment, which had been enacted into legislation years ago in the Federal school lunch program, and the fact that the White House had indicated that it had the power to withhold funds from airports. Now was definitely the time to act.

When Congress came back to session in January, 1955, I announced that I would attach my amendment to all new legislation in the field of education. The *Washington Post* reported, "He has got the votes to attach the Powell Amendment to proposed federal aid to school construction legislation." The *Amsterdam News* of New York editorialized on February 4: "If the South wants good schools, let them get them in the right way. We stand with Mr. Powell on his amendment. We hope he stands fast."

The Powell Amendment as used in the Federal aid to school construction bills would have been totally unnecessary if the Executive branch of the government had lived up to its oath of office and had done what it had the power to do. The government of the United States is divided into three sections, and all represent the supreme law of the land, whether it is an act of Congress, an order of the Executive, or a decision of the Supreme Court. In 1953 President Eisenhower had promised me that he would not "take a single step backward," he would not "allow second-class citizenship," and we would "go forward together step by step." But something had happened to Eisenhower. Some influences had begun to pressure him into changing his views. Maybe it was the defeat that his appointees in the State Department had suffered because of the Bandung Conference. At any rate, while I was at Bandung, a letter came from a member of his staff indicating that his position had changed. During the years following the Supreme Court decision, no Federal aid bill for school construction passed in Congress. This was due to the complete failure of the President of the United States to assume the moral and legal leadership with which he was charged. If President Eisenhower had implemented his philosophy, as laid down to me in writing in 1953, this nation would be years ahead in school construction. The facts of the historical background are these:

In a letter to the President on June 3, 1955, I stated:

> I am forced to write this letter because during my absence at the Bandung Conference, a letter came from a member of your staff indicating that your position on the use of federal funds in support of segregation had been modified. I am sure that this does not represent your thinking and, in view of the recent Supreme Court decision, I am positive that you would not countenance the allocation of federal funds to any state which openly through its governor and/or state legislature has announced that it will defy the decrees of the United States Supreme Court.

Other parts of that letter read:

> Now that the Supreme Court has handed down the implementation decree on the question of desegregating our public school system, certain developments have resulted which force me to write this letter.
>
> You are aware of the statements made by the Governors of several states saying that they will not abide by the final decree of the Supreme Court. . . .
>
> Also, the school authorities of Prince Edward County, Virginia, . . . refused to appropriate money for a new building which was to be used for an integrated public school system.

Now in view of these actions and attitudes, do you not think, therefore, that my amendment to the bill is more necessary than ever? . . . I take the position that you have always announced, that not one cent of federal funds should be used to support segregation; and I further take the position that no federal funds shall be used to support any state which refused to abide by the law of the land.

At a White House press conference, the President said that the Powell Amendments (he called them "riders") that had been passed by the House of Representatives on two successive days were "against the national interest." (He was completely in error in calling them riders, since a rider is attached only in the Senate to an appropriation bill. My motions were amendments and, once passed, were not riders but were then part of the actual bill. These are the rules of Congress.) As for Eisenhower's saying that my amendments were "against the national interest," that was patently ridiculous. Nevertheless, I asked him in a telegram of June 19: "If they are against the national interest, why is it that someone from the Department of Defense has not contacted my by telephone, by mail, or in person? Therefore, I request an appointment."

On June 21 the President replied. He erred seriously in his personally signed letter. Three years later he would eat the very words he wrote on June 21, 1955:

From your own experience in Congress, you realize that progress in ending segregation is difficult if not impossible if we are to depend upon incorporating non-segregation clauses in legislation that the Senate will not favorably consider and that hence will never become law. And it is a fact of history that no legislation, however meritorious, containing such a provision has ever passed the Senate. So we must find other means of dealing with the problem.

Across the nation the news swept. Headlines appeared on the front pages of the American press, similar to the ones of *The New York Times* of June 24: "PRESIDENT APPEALS TO POWELL." Within the same issue of *The New York Times* I pointed out that the President had placed the Legislative branch of the government in a secondary role, and as a member of that branch, I personally resented his saying it would be "difficult, if not impossible." Eisenhower was allowing the minority in the Senate to dictate to the nation. When he said that "no bill containing civil rights has ever passed the Senate," I immediately pointed out that on August 28, 1940, the Senate, by a vote of fifty-eight to thirty-one, had banned discrimination in the Draft Act. In my final statement I said that the tone of the President's letter definitely indicated that he condoned the use of Federal funds, in defiance of the Supreme Court decision, to build segregated schools.

The very next day, June 25, Vice President Nixon visited my Congressional District, proclaiming everywhere that he was against antisegregation amendments.

By this time the President was so angered because I refused to bow to his wishes and, furthermore, had the votes in the House of Representatives to defeat him, that he did the unprecedented. Eight Departments of his Administration were ordered not to testify on civil rights bills before a special subcommittee of the House Committee on the Judiciary. I wired him on July 14:

> The President of the United States, The White House, Washington, D. C., My dear Mr. President:
>
> You have stated that civil rights legislation in the form of amendments against segregation should not be attached to bills, but that the matter of segregation should be considered separately.
>
> Today, for the first time during this First Session of the 84th Congress, the matter of civil rights was formally brought before the Congress through a special subcommittee of the House Committee on the Judiciary. The following agencies of government, each of which could make a vital contribution to the success of the proposed legislation, were invited to testify but declined—Government Services Administration, Labor, Justice, Interstate Commerce Commission, Defense, Health, Education and Welfare, and Civil Service Commission.
>
> Since this is the sole opportunity in this session to consider civil rights bills on their merit, may I inquire of you why these agencies have refused to testify?

Two days later, behind closed doors in executive session of the Committee on Education and Labor, sixty-nine-year-old Cleveland M. Bailey, Democrat of West Virginia, supporter of other civil rights measures, tried to hit me because I refused to yield on the Powell Amendment. Bailey declared that I was really against Federal aid to school construction.

All over the nation strong forces began to be marshaled against me. The Washington *Evening Star* of January 11, 1956, editorialized, "Powell Amendment is the biggest threat to school aid." The AFL-CIO released a statement, printed in the *Washington Post* of January 30, saying that my amendment was "unnecessary." From California on February 5 Earl Mazo, political analyst, reported to the New York *Herald Tribune* that Stevenson "was opposed to the Powell Amendment" since there was "no need for it," and his position "now paralleled that of Ike." In his syndicated column, "Inside Washington," Robert Allen reported to the nation on February 28 that "quietly 21 Southern Senators, under the leadership of McClellan, were ganging up on Powell, due to his amendment." But in addition to the Negro, one force stood firm throughout the nation, and that was the church. No representative body of the three faiths ever differed with my position on the Powell Amendment. During this period from November, 1955, until the first of April, 1956, great spiritual forces began to build up support for the honesty and justice of that position. By 1956, with the 1954 Supreme Court decision, Negroes should have been integrated in all aspects of our American way of life.

I was invited to Montgomery to speak to a Negro citizens organization in the fieldhouse of the Alabama College for Negroes. As my plane taxied up the apron at Montgomery, an air-conditioned black Cadillac limousine, license plate "Alabama–1, the Heart of Dixie," drew up to the plane and out of it sprang two State Troopers. I said to myself, "This is trouble!"

As I walked down the steps, they came forward and surprised me with, "Congressman Powell? Governor Folsom has asked us to put the Governor's limousine at your disposal and we are your escort officers." As I was being whisked to town, members of the Negro delegation who met and rode with me in the car could not believe their eyes.

Soon after I arrived at the home of my host, I received a phone call from the Governor, "Kissing Jim." He asked me to drop by the State Mansion that evening before the rally: "Now, I don't want you to go in the back door . . . that's for Negroes. And I don't want you to go in the side door . . . that's for politicians. I want you to come in the front door . . . if we can get the damn thing open."

That evening, in the small den off the foyer, we sat and talked. The Governor had a beer, which he drank out of the can, and I had a Scotch. The next day Alabama newspapers reported that the Baptists had censored me for having a drink with the Governor. That night when I spoke in Birmingham, I replied, "If having a drink with the Governor of Alabama is going to make things easier for Negro people, then you are looking at a confirmed alcoholic."

Speaking to four thousand people at Montgomery, I outlined the various direct-action nonviolent resistance programs that I had led in New York, mentioning, among others, the successful rent boycott in Harlem. After it was over a group of the leaders of Montgomery met in the home of a Mr. Nixon. They asked me to detail how such a boycott was started and how it worked. Sitting in that room was an unknown newcomer to Montgomery named Martin Luther King, Jr., and a member of the committee named Rosa Parks. Exactly three weeks later, on December 5, they started the Montgomery bus boycott. It ended with the most successful massive resistance movement for civil rights that the South and this nation had ever witnessed.

The police authorities of Montgomery struck back with power. Clergymen were arrested and jailed. But the boycott increased in power. In early March two leading New York citizens, attorney Cornelius McDougal and Dr. George Cannon, asked me to dramatize the Montgomery fight nationally and suggested that I do it through a national prayer meeting. I organized the committee, and established March 28 as National Day of Deliverance, and from California to Massachusetts the spiritual voices of the nation rose up in massive, prayerful cooperation. Governor Goodwin Knight of California proclaimed that day as the official day of prayer. In Boston the great Archbishop Cushing also cooperated. On March 28, in the language of the press, "Millions all over the world prayed for victory in Montgomery." Seventy-four men and women of the Massachusetts State Legislature, including the Judges of the General Court, walked out of the historic Capitol at noon, and Catholic, Protestant, and Jew prayed together. The Old North Church on Boston Common pealed its ancient bells, summoning people for prayer. The spiritual forces of this nation had truly supported the cause. Thousands of dollars flowed to the Montgomery Improvement Association for its God-inspired strike against wrong.

What mattered, then, the opposition to the Powell Amendment when I had these forces of right on my side? And the words of an old Protestant hymn kept pounding through my brain: "There is a God who rules above, with a hand of power and a heart of love, and if you are right, he will fight your battle, and you will be free some day."

But all this power of right did not move the President of the United States. It became apparent to me that Eisenhower did not approve of the Supreme Court decision, although he stated that not even his wife knew his opinions concerning it. He refused to undergird it with his massive power. He refused to say clearly that it was a moral as well as a legal

decision. On March 14, 1956, just before the National Day of Deliverance,
I wrote him again:

My dear Mr. President:

. . . there is no denying that the number-one problem facing our
country, and more than that, our relations to the world, is the problem
of civil rights. . . .

Firstly, there has been considerable discussion for and against the
so-called Powell Amendment to the pending Kelley Bill and McConnell
Substitute on federal aid to school construction. I have received statements from your official family—Comptroller General, General Counsel
for the Department of Health, Education and Welfare, and from your
Administrative Assistant—indicating that no action is contemplated in
reference to withholding funds from the five defiant states (Alabama,
Georgia, Mississippi, South Carolina, Virginia) in the event that the
Kelley Bill does become the law of the land. It is the feeling expressed
by many people that such funds would be withheld through your executive power because of the Supreme Court decision. Now, Mr. President,
I wish to ask you specifically, if this is true, why have you not instructed
the Comptroller General to withhold roughly $100,000,000 which is
now being appropriated from the federal treasury to these five states
which by legislative action, not public opinion, are defying the law of the
land?

Unless you issue such a directive to the Comptroller General, what
recourse have the American people to prevent federal funds from defying
federal law? I await specific reply to this issue. We need not contemplate
what shall be done if the Kelley Bill or McConnell Substitute become law.
Right now more money is being appropriated than would be if the Kelley
or McConnell Bills became the law of the land.

Secondly, do you think it is fair to Negro people and to the fundamen-
tal precepts of our government and to the peoples of the world, especially
to those in Asia and Africa, to continue to refuse to call a White House
Conference of Negro and white leaders from the tension areas of the
South to try to ameliorate the situation in our southlands? . . .

I believe this is a time for you with your great prestige name to act.
You have made great contributions in the field of civil rights during the
first two years of your office and I am aware of the fact that you are
eliminating as many conferences as possible; but in your own words they
are conferences involving ceremony. This is not a conference involving
ceremony. This cannot be passed to Congress; only you, the President of
the United States, can do it. Where would our nation be today if Lincoln

had waited for Congress; or if President Roosevelt in enacting the war-time FEPC had waited for Congress; or if President Truman when the Communists invaded North Korea had waited for Congress; or where would we be today in our daily leadership of the free world if you had waited for Congress to approve your conference at Geneva? You have a conference set up now between the President of Mexico and the Prime Minister of Canada—a very worthwhile one I am sure, but I can assure you that more important than that conference is a conference aimed at healing the wounds of our country and bringing our country back to a sense of decency.

Negro people are being murdered in the South and the murderers are going free. States are in open defiance of the law of our land. In an hour such as this only the Chief Executive can speak and bring the leaders of these tension areas together.

As pointed out in my previous communication, I believe that in this moment we need all the powers available to help us, and the greatest power available is the power of things of the spirit. I think it would symbolize the grave concern that you and our country have if you would call together at the White House for prayer spiritual leaders of the three faiths. . . .

The Palace Guard had captured him. He was being insulated from all direct contacts. No more letters came from him; they were signed by either of two assistants, Bryce Harlow or Gerald Morgan. Writing for the President on May 11, 1956, Morgan indicated very definitely that the President was *not* going to do anything to support the Supreme Court. He even went so far as to say, "The President does not assume that the Judicial branch lacks the capacity to implement its own decree." How could the Judicial branch of any government, lacking police power, implement its decrees?

The moment of truth came on the Fourth of July Weekend in 1956. In the course of the proceedings of the House on the Kelley (Federal aid for school construction) Bill, I introduced the Powell Amendment:

Amendment offered by Mr. Powell: On page 6, line 15, after the period, insert: "(8) Provide that school facilities of the State are open to all children without regard to race, in conformity with the requirements of the United States Supreme Court decisions; except that if a State plan does not so provide, it shall not prevent payment of funds authorized under this act to such State for use in counties or other political subdivisions within the States that are operating their schools in conformity with the said Supreme Court decisions."

In reply to the objection that the Powell Amendment would kill the bill, I stated on the Floor of Congress: "The only objection that we hear is that this will kill the bill. This bill is going to pass the House if the Powell Amendment is in it. How will it kill the bill? We are told there will be a filibuster conducted against it in the other body. That is impossible. The other body does not have the Kelley Bill before it. The other body has Senator Lister Hill's bill before it and the Powell Amendment will not be in that bill. So there will be no occasion for a filibuster there unless some member of the Senate does introduce a Powell type of amendment. . . ."

And in reply to the stand that "we should not implement the Supreme Court decision by legislative action," I stated: "I am sure that we all agree that whenever there is a constitutional executive order, judicial decision, or legislative action, immediately it is encumbent upon all other branches of the government to yield to whatever that decision, order, or law may be. We implemented the Supreme Court decision for fifty-seven years in Plessy against Ferguson, which was the doctrine of separate but equal. We in this House and in the other body passed amendments to the draft bill, the Hill-Burton Act, the Federal school lunch program, implementing the Supreme Court decisions. Now we come to a new decision, a decision of integration, and this is the first test of whether we are going to abide by the Supreme Court decision as a legislative body. This is not a racial amendment. . . ."

I concluded my remarks with: ". . . We have before us the American dream. It is a dream of one nation, indivisible, with liberty and justice for all, and I believe that you should vote according to that American dream."

The *Congressional Record* reported: "The Committee divided; and the tellers reported that there were Ayes, 164, Nays, 116, so the amendments were agreed to."

One of my most severe critics and still my most illogical one, *The New York Times*, was forced to editorialize on July 4, 1956, "The fighter for civil rights, Adam Clayton Powell, Jr., the country's most vocal crusader for Negro rights, is a Protestant minister who is making his voice heard these days on every aspect of the controversy over racial segregation. He averages a telegram to President Eisenhower every week or two. On the floor of Congress, in articles, statements and numerous public speeches, he denounces public segregation in all its works. His language seldom is mild. Nowadays, Mr. Powell is taken seriously indeed, by his colleagues in the

House of Representatives. Mr. Powell is not a partisan Democrat on the question of Negro rights."

The *Denver Post* editorialized approvingly, "Powell is the nation's full-time battler against racial bias."

Nevertheless, in September of that year, when the time came for the Presidential nominating conventions, the parties had already chosen their nominees: Stevenson and Eisenhower. "Regardless of my seniority," I thought, "regardless of the fact that what I might do would endanger my eligibility for eventual chairmanship of the Committee on Education and Labor, nevertheless, for the good of my country, realizing the peril facing us, I am going to see objectively what can be done to get one of the candidates to stand four-square on the number-one domestic issue of our time, civil rights."

Stevenson in 1956 was not the Stevenson of 1952. Columnist Murray Kempton said, "The civil rights platform of 1956 was so deplorable because Stevenson could not find the will to fight for a better one." Meeting with Carmine DeSapio and other leaders of Tammany Hall, I pointed out that I could not campaign for Stevenson in 1956 unless he reassured me and the American people that his stand on civil rights was as forthright as it had been in 1952. City Councilman Earl Brown, always one of my stern critics, agreed. "Adam is right. He should see Stevenson." DeSapio said he would arrange it. Next day, when Stevenson came to New York, DeSapio went to see him with a simple statement he and I had worked out, recommending what Mr. Stevenson should say from then on. Stevenson refused to see DeSapio. He was taking his civil rights advice from Harry Ashmore, the editor of the Little Rock *Gazette*. DeSapio came back: "Adam, he won't talk to you."

I did not believe it. I called my friend Congressman William Green, the Democratic boss of Philadelphia. "Bill, it is imperative that I see Stevenson," I said, and explained why.

"Adam, you're exactly correct, and I will see that you do. Stevenson's campaign manager is one of my men, James A. Finnegan." The next day I called Bill Green again, only to learn, "Adam, he won't see you. I don't know what in the hell is wrong."

That day I was visiting my old friend Lionel Hampton. One of his buddies, Charlie Willis, who was chief of patronage at the White House and married to one of Harvey Firestone's daughters, dropped by. He said, "Reverend Powell, if you want to see President Eisenhower, I will arrange it." Somehow the news leaked out. New York politics got busy, and on the eve of the appointment with President Eisenhower, Federal marshals were sent to serve me with a subpoena to appear as a witness in the income-tax trial of one of my staff. This summons, of course, was totally unnecessary, as proven by the fact that I later went to court voluntarily and did appear as a witness.

I was ushered into the presence of President Eisenhower at the White House on October 11, 1956. I brought up our differences over the Powell Amendment and expressed the hope that something could be worked out whereby there would be an agreement on that at the forthcoming session. He then assigned Sherman Adams and Maxwell Rabb to discuss the matter with me. But I asked him, specifically, for commitments on the following: Would he call for an omnibus civil rights bill in his State of the Union message? Would he direct Attorney General Herbert Brownell to draw it up? Would he see that his lieutenants, Senator William Knowland and Congressman Joseph Martin, personally threw all their power behind it to help make it Congress' first order of business?

He indicated that he would and so I said, "I will support you for President of the United States." And I did. I campaigned for him from coast to coast. After Eisenhower won, he lived up to each of the pledges and the nation received its first civil rights law in eighty-two years.

One month after Eisenhower was reelected a Grand Jury was convened in New York to consider an indictment against me for alleged income-tax evasion. My two patronage appointments in the House of Representatives were fired by the Democratic leadership. My prior claim for a new office was ignored and given to Frank Chelf of Kentucky. And with every single Republican voting against me despite my support of Eisenhower, I was stripped of my seniority on the Committee on Education and Labor—instead of receiving the subcommittee chairmanship I was entitled to by virtue of seniority, I received only an assignment to an insignificant subcommittee. The seniority of every other member was rigidly respected. Siding with the entire Republican membership were six Northern Democrats.

Southern Democrats had repeatedly committed worse offenses than I. I had refused to campaign against any Democrat—local, state, or national —except Stevenson. Dixiecrats had left the party, even formed a new one —States' Rights—and yet returned to the fold with a hero's welcome. I alone had been singled out for punishment.

Even the Republicans broke their word and various promises made to my workers were not kept. After waiting almost one year, on September 27, I detailed all this in writing to Sherman Adams:

> My dear Governor:
> October 11, 1957, will mark the first year since my announced support of President Eisenhower. As you well know, I asked for nothing. Nor indeed would I have accepted anything. The President has lived up to my trust and expectations.
> However, the following facts, which I have not yet made public, leave me wondering what has happened to the word of the Republican leaders. I have waited patiently . . . I can wait no longer. I am not complaining about my loss of seniority, and related benefits, in the House Education and Labor Committee, or anything else that has happened to me personally. That was a calculated risk. But I am most definitely complaining to you for the last time concerning your broken word to me. . . ."

I referred, first, to the money owed members of my staff for overtime and unused vacations; second, to jobs for my patronage appointees who had been fired; and third, to money promised workers who had worked for Eisenhower's election. Not one penny of this had been paid. Only when Sherman Adams moved were these details taken care of.

There was a definite resistance on the part of Republican leaders because they resented the fact that I had come out for Eisenhower. Basically, I think it was a combination of the Democratic and Republican leadership in New York City, which often worked hand-in-glove on many things, deciding that there was no place in their program for anyone who was an independent, even if that independence favored one of them. I have no proof of this but I do not think all of these things occurred without a bipartisan coalition, emanating from New York or from the South. One must never forget that the major recipient of Republican patronage in Mississippi was Senator James Eastland.

The simple fact was that they had used me and now wanted nothing more than perhaps to destroy me. The local Harlem leaders of the Republican Party did not forget, however, and despite bitter objections by County Leader Thomas Curran, insisted I receive the Republican nomination.

Further, I lost the friendship of Mrs. Roosevelt, who wrote to me on November 6, criticizing me for supporting Eisenhower: "There is no chance of passing any bill through the Senate on Civil Rights without changing Rule 22." (This rule, in effect, makes defeat of a filibuster on debate exceedingly difficult.) Passage of the 1957 Civil Rights Bill and the 1959 Right-to-Vote Bill were, of course, to prove her wrong. I replied, "Once again I want to say that I will always consider you America's greatest lady and that you stand before all the world as our Ambassador of human decency."

With everyone now against me, all seemed lost. Stripped of my seniority and patronage, with Republican leaders out to knife me, Carmine DeSapio whispering that a purge was coming, Mrs. Roosevelt becoming a blindly unreconstructed enemy, I felt like giving up. But the still, small voice bade me, "Fight on!"

11

Little Rock
Brush-Off

It was a beautiful September day in Paris in 1957. I had come to the end of my European trip and was taking my last walk down the Champs Élysées. Before going to my hotel, I stopped at a sidewalk café to sip a tiny cup of bitter, black French café filtre. A friend from the Embassy passed by and said, "Kelly of the Paris edition of the New York *Herald Tribune* is looking for you. He wants to see you about the Little Rock mess." I returned to my hotel immediately and called Kelly.

Little Rock had roared across Europe, a misguided missile, leaving in its wake considerable anti-Americanism. The Arkansas Senators, visiting in London, had made light of the incident to the British press, which only hurt our rapidly dwindling supply of good will. In my conference with Frank Kelly, I said what I could to try to rebuild in the European press some of the image of America which Arkansas and its Senators had torn down.

Eisenhower was in the Summer White House at Newport, Rhode Island, where he had already conferred with Senator Richard Russell of Georgia and Arkansas Governor Orval Faubus. When I arrived back in New York on September 17, I was greeted by scores of people begging me to get through to the President immediately on the matter of Little Rock. Leaders from all over the nation had been trying to arrange appointments with him, but had been turned down. I immediately sent a wire to President Eisenhower asking for an appointment to discuss the Little Rock situation.

The next afternoon the President replied by telegram: "I shall arrange a meeting with you and have directed my staff in Washington to confer with you for this purpose."

I then wired Jim Hagerty at Newport: "I would personally like to talk with you before the conference so that you can help me to make it as successful as possible. Am I to make arrangements through Max Rabb or Sherman Adams?"

There was no further word from anyone for a week. Then on the morning of September 25 I heard on an NBC broadcast that a group of Southern governors was arranging a conference with Eisenhower.

Here begins an amazing series of events. On September 25 I wired Max Rabb: "Note Southern governors desiring conference. May I remind that our appointment was granted first. Suggest that this be expedited as quickly as possible for the total good."

Someone somewhere along the line deliberately struck the second sentence from the wire before passing it on to President Eisenhower!

On September 26 Charles Von Fremd, broadcasting for CBS news from the Summer White House at Newport, reported that I had approved the Southern governors' conference with Eisenhower and had suggested that the President see them immediately. My Washington administrative chief, Maxine Dargans, called Von Fremd at Newport, and the monitored conversation was as follows:

DARGANS: I'd like to get from you the exact quote concerning Mr. Powell on the 9 A.M. CBS News this morning.

VON FREMD: I just couldn't give it to you word for word now, but I could give you the general sense of what I had to say. I mentioned, first of all, that the President had agreed to meet with the five Southern governors. Hagerty also announced that New York Democratic Congressman Powell, a strong, ardent supporter of complete school integration, had told the White House that he approves of the meeting between the President and the governors. Powell, in a telegram to White House minority expert Maxwell Rabb, said that he thought

the meeting would be productive and should be held as soon
as possible. Powell is scheduled to meet with the President
at some future date. I believe that is not exactly word for
word, but that's almost it.

DARGANS: That's the essence. That's the gist. I heard it. That is entirely an error. The wire he sent Rabb reads. . . .

Then she read him the original wire, including the sentence that had
been deleted, and Von Fremd replied, "That sure is not what Hagerty told
us. This afternoon when we see Hagerty again at 4:30, we will tell him that
CBS News has been told by Powell that what Hagerty said this morning
was not true."

Meanwhile M. H. Paine, acting superintendent of the Western Union
Telegraph Company, Washington, D.C., wrote, "I must be frank to admit
that there is no reasonable explanation I can make for the delivery of an
incomplete copy of your telegram of September 25 addressed to Mr. Maxwell Rabb."

Mrs. Dargans then called Max Rabb at the White House, person-to-
person. Excerpts of this monitored conversation follow:

DARGANS: Mr. Powell asked me to call. He heard on CBS News this
A.M. at 9 a statement that is totally untrue.

RABB: What is this totally, wholly untrue?

DARGANS: Let me read you the telegram. . . . Someone left out that
particular line. . . .

RABB: I thought it was a little strange, but this makes him look a
lot better.

DARGANS: According to what side you are looking at it from.

RABB: . . . .

DARGANS: Let me give you the feeling on the part of the Negro. They
are anxious. . . .

RABB: . . . We have marched in troops over there. We have done
something that we have to go all the way back to the Whisky
Rebellion in Washington's time to get any kind of justification for. . . . Well, whatever he wants to do, all right, but
he is not going to get the meeting right away. That, I can
assure you. The way the deletion reads does him credit.
. . . I'll tell you what my thinking was—and I didn't mean

to say it before this, and what I had to tell him was—we
don't want it [the conference] this time. We want it when
it is divorced from this particular issue.

Despite Von Fremd's report to Hagerty on September 26 that his release
was wrong, despite the phone call to the White House to Rabb telling him
that it was wrong, and despite the original copy's being redelivered to the
White House by Western Union—all on September 26—no one bothered
to tell President Eisenhower of the error. On the next day Eisenhower,
uncorrected and still believing in the erroneous wire, wrote, "I thank you
for your wire and for your favorable reaction to the present course of
events."

A month passed by and still no word from Mr. Eisenhower. On October
27, I again wired the President, reminding him, "While the date for the
meeting is being delayed, the situation is deteriorating hourly. This is giving
aid and comfort to the enemies of democracy abroad, and the elements of
lawlessness at home. Once again your leadership is needed to demonstrate
the conscience and moral decency of America. I urge that you immediately
hold the meeting in order to give assurance that the voices of Negro
Americans may be heard as well as those from other areas."

On October 31 the White House replied, "I can fully assure you that
the meeting you mentioned is going to be held. Further, it will be held
at the earliest date deemed advisable by the President. I share your hope
that the meeting will take place before too many additional days have
elapsed." But no conference was scheduled and the entire civil rights thrust
of the White House began to crumble.

On January 28, 1958, I again wrote the President: "A rapidly rising tide
of criticism is mounting against your administration, not only from your
enemies but from your friends, not only from Democrats but also from
Republicans. It will be extremely regrettable that your administration,
which spearheaded giving to this country its first civil rights law in eighty-
two years, should find itself branded by its friends as being anti-civil rights
because of the present seeming indifference, if not procrastination, by the
administration."

In the letter I cited three specific examples of what I considered procrastination by the Administration. First, in Ghana in March, 1957, I had
introduced Martin Luther King, Jr., to Vice President Nixon. Nixon invited the Reverend Dr. King to come to see him. At a meeting in June,

Nixon promised King he would bring the Government Contract Compliance Committee to the South at an early date. Just before writing the letter of January 28, I spoke with King in Atlanta and he told me he had not heard a single word further from Nixon concerning his promise, but that it "definitely was a promise." So I wrote to the President, "Seven months have gone by since that conference, and the Government Contract Compliance Committee has not even crossed the Potomac River."

The second item I raised in that letter was that four months had gone by since he had agreed to a conference with me on Little Rock. Since the subject had recently been raised at a White House press conference, I reminded him, "Many conferences have been held by you at the White House and in Paris. Little Rock has not quieted down. Negro churches of God have been destroyed and the perpetrators have gone free. Two murders have taken place within thirty days by law enforcement officers. I can assure you, Mr. President, that if you think a conference is no longer necessary, then you are the recipient of some very bad briefing and advice by your aides. Russia can sweep Asia and Africa on the basis of the dilatory tactics of our government in the field of equality and time is not on our side."

The last item in that letter was criticism of Attorney General William Rogers, who had announced on December 9, 1957, that there would be no call for civil rights legislation at that session of Congress but instead asked for a "cooling-off" period. I wrote the President, "I was able to speak to the Deputy Attorney General of the United States, Mr. [Lawrence C.] Walsh, last week. There was placed before him the views of the NAACP through Mr. Clarence Mitchell, who accompanied me," and that "the Department of Justice attitude was harmful to our government and could be disastrous."

Maxwell Rabb answered for the President on February 3, with the view that the questions I raised represented matters that could not be answered immediately. I rejected Rabb's letter as an answer to my letter to the President, and insisted that some kind of reply that could be made public should come directly from the White House.

In March the Grand Jury was called back in on my tax case, and in May I was indicted. It was at about this time that the President made plans to hold the White House Conference that I had arranged the preceding year —except that I was excluded. Those invited were the Reverend Dr. Martin

Luther King, Jr., A. Philip Randolph of the AFL-CIO, Lester Granger of the National Urban League, and Roy Wilkins of the NAACP.

On June 20, upon learning that they were going to meet with the President, I sent each of them a wire urging that they take up several items: "In no unmistakable terms, the President should see that the Department of Justice and the Civil Rights Commission immediately spend more time and vigor on these glaring un-American activities." I was referring to the bombing of synagogues and Negro churches in the South, and the continual brutality and killings by law enforcement officers. Moreover, I felt that "The President should demand that the State Department respect and follow through his executive desires, as stated to me in the presence of Mr. Maxwell Rabb on May 6, 1955, that there should be utilization of Negroes in overseas embassies and consulates."

And so, the meeting I had fought to arrange was held without my presence. I could only conclude that the Administration feared that I would take too militant a stand. If so, the fear was justified.

12

My Home Town

On December 7, 1950, John Derrick, a serviceman in uniform, minding his own business, was killed on Eighth Avenue in Harlem by two policemen. The incident was whitewashed by the New York City Grand Jury. I protested and got nowhere. After years of dealing with the city fathers and receiving no justice, I thought of asking the FBI to come in on the case. I was also aware that innocent people—some whom I knew personally, some of whom were members of my church—were routinely being killed and beaten by policemen. I could take this intolerable situation no longer. So in June, 1951, I requested that the FBI investigate the Derrick case. This was the first time they had ever been brought into a situation of police brutality in New York City.

While the FBI was investigating the case, a curtain of silence dropped overnight. Neither in Washington nor in New York could I get any specific replies. I simply could not find out what had happened to the Derrick case. On February 11, 1953, the darkness of this mystery was cracked when Frederick Woltman, ace reporter for the *New York World-Telegram & Sun*, published the shocking truth. Woltman unearthed an agreement between the Department of Justice and the New York City Police Department, under which J. Edgar Hoover was to keep the FBI from investigating New York City's sordid record of police brutality. On February 18 *The New York Times* editorially called for an investigation:

> The public will not stand for police brutality. There cannot be one code of treatment of Negroes and another code for other people. The police are not a law unto themselves. Their actions must stand unashamed before public scrutiny, just as the actions of other citizens. Finally, there cannot be one law for the rest of the United States and another for New York City.
>
> But our Police Department has long had a habit of the closed door, the tight lip, as if it were a military establishment.
>
> But light is needed on the whole past relationship between the Police Department and the Justice Department on this question of who shall investigate civil rights complaints in New York when the policeman is accused. There are discrepancies and contradictions still unexplained by official statements.

On that same day I addressed the Congress by special permission and gave them the unbelievable details that Woltman had unearthed. The Congress was shocked. Representative Kenneth B. Keating, later the Junior Senator from New York, rose and asked me if I would give the facts to a special committee. The committee was organized with Keating as chairman, and on February 19 we met together for the first time. Congressman Keating assigned committee counsel Robert A. Collier to confer with New York's Mayor Vincent R. Impelliteri and obtain all the documentary evidence.

Immediately, denials broke out all over. The man accused by Woltman of making the agreement, James N. McInerney, former head of the Justice Department's Criminal Division and later Special Assistant to the Attorney General, denied there was such an "agreement." Representative Jacob K. Javits, now Senior Senator from New York, countered by saying, "There was corruption beyond corruption." Any plan for making the FBI keep its hands off investigations, he testified, struck at the moral foundations of society.

I charged before the committee, "New York City today is a city of terror for minorities."

Later that week Police Commissioner George P. Monaghan denied any such agreement on behalf of himself, First Deputy Commissioner Frank

Fristensky, Jr., and Chief Inspector Conrad H. Rothengast. He charged, in a television statement, that I had lied. I demanded equal television time and NBC granted me this opportunity.

In my broadcast I charged that the Police Commissioner and his two assistants would perjure themselves if they gave the same testimony under oath that they had given to the public thus far; and that Commissioner Monaghan was, consciously or unconsciously, being used as cover-up for the top brass of the Police Department. "Your talk last Sunday was a half-truth, therefore a half-lie," I said. I had seen a report sent by Monaghan to the Justice Department and signed by Chief Inspector Rothengast concerning the case of Jacob Jackson. In that report the Police Department of New York City had deliberately suppressed important evidence of brutality, including the fact that following the station-house beatings, Jackson was hospitalized and twice had to undergo brain surgery and the placing of a steel plate in his head. It was this report that called to the attention of the Attorney General of the United States, James P. McGranery, the fact that there was an agreement between the FBI and the New York City Police Department. As soon as McGranery learned of the agreement he canceled it.

In my television speech I also pointed out that Monaghan had refused to allow Leland Boardman, the Special Agent in charge of the FBI office in New York, to interview policemen in regard to the Jackson case. Addressing myself directly to Monaghan, I said:

> And when you flew to Washington to see the Deputy Attorney General of the United States, William Rogers, did you or did you not in any way mention that former memorandum? Did you or did you not in any way ask that it be continued in the new administration? And were you not told that it was absolutely impossible? Even while you were piously stating on television Sunday, and I quote you, "The Police Department is unalterably opposed to the use of force by anyone," a white citizen of New York, Pace, had just been beaten by members of the police force.
>
> You requested the FBI, which is directed by the laws of the Congress, not to investigate your policemen. But there is a law of this land which no individual, even you as a police commissioner or any of your deputies, has the right to abrogate.
>
> Here we Northerners have been charging violations of civil rights in Miami, in Birmingham, through the South, while behind our backs in New York City efforts were being made by our own officials to keep the

citizens of New York from appealing to the Federal government. This is fantastic. Southern members of the United States Congress are mad and justifiably so. . . .

How dare any police commissioner of any city, including New York, tell the FBI when to start and when to stop? You, Mr. Commissioner, and the tarnished brass of the Police Department, by allowing corruption and brutality to flourish, have destroyed the morale of our town's finest.

The Institute of Public Management was hired by the Mayor to survey your Police Department. Mr. Bruce Smith, last Sunday, two hours before you spoke, said that as a result of their investigation [they discovered that] police brutality in the city of New York has gone unchallenged for fifteen years.

I'll tell you why this happened. This tarnished brass of the Police Department got mad in the Spring of 1951 when I, for the first time, invoked the civil rights statute and got the FBI to move into New York and investigate the killers of John Derrick.

I went on to point out that in the preceding year juries in New York City had awarded almost $200,000 to victims of police brutality; and that the *World-Telegram & Sun* had remarked, "This was enough money to vaccinate every child in New York City against tuberculosis." I then made several constructive proposals: one, that police recruits be psychologically tested so that the Civil Service would stop sending misfits into the Police Department; two, that the training-school tactics of the Police Academy be changed so that a man would be trained to use his brains and his heart as well as a stick and a gun; and three, that the salaries paid rookie policemen be raised.

The next morning the Congressional committee opened its hearing in the Federal Court House in Foley Square, and the same one that was to be used for my trial seven years later. Witnesses followed each other swiftly, testifying that Monaghan, Fristensky, and Rothengast had not told the truth. The Attorney General of the United States testified that he had found the agreement in his files and had promptly torn it up. Robert F. Wagner, then Manhattan Borough President, said, "It seems almost incredible to me that this could have been done with full consideration of all the factors involved apart from purely police administration problems."

FBI Special Agent Leland Boardman said Monaghan had told him not only that there was an "agreement" but also that "civil rights laws were only for people south of the Mason-Dixon Line." He testified that Monaghan then called in the top police officials of New York and in Boardman's presence told them, "I have decided to make the police officers accused of brutality available to no Federal law enforcement agencies for questioning."

Mr. Boardman further charged that even after Attorney General McGranery learned on January 12 of the hands-off agreement and had "hit the roof," Monaghan maintained this policy. Boardman's assistants, Vernon T. Smith and John P. Foley, testified with official reports and memoranda that Monaghan had met their "courtesy" request with a "flat and square-cut 'no.' "

When the committee left New York following the hearing, Chairman Keating announced that there were serious indications of perjury on the part of the Police Commissioner and his assistants.

Finally, on February 23, the *World-Telegram & Sun* reported: "Commissioner Monaghan, now for the first time, conceded that he had not always cooperated with the F.B.I." The Republican and Democratic members of the subcommittee unanimously sent their report to the full Committee on the Judiciary. We all sat back and waited for the official report to the Department of Justice.

Meanwhile, I received anonymous telephone calls and letters saying that one day the Police Department and the career and Civil Service men in the Department of Justice would get me for what I had done. But I knew I was right and Representative Keating knew he was right and we waited for official action.

But the long arm of sinister political power reached out and began to work. For an entire year nothing was heard from the Judiciary Committee. Finally, on March 5, after many fruitless telephone calls, I wrote a formal letter to the Chairman of the House Judiciary Committee, Chauncey W. Reed, Republican of Illinois: "I have been patiently waiting for the Judiciary Committee to issue the Keating subcommittee report on the deal between the former Assistant Attorney General and the Police Department of New York City.

"As you will recall the Keating subcommittee took action after I had personally made the charge on the Floor of the House. I am personally, therefore, responsible to my constituents and to the citizens of New York City for an explanation as to why the Keating subcommittee report has not been released."

Chairman Reed promptly replied: "The matter of disposition of the reports of the subcommittee was brought up at a meeting about two weeks ago and was deferred until later in the session."

On April 15, I called the committee, and Representative Reed replied, that the committee's schedule was still heavy and no meetings were to be scheduled until April 26. On May 10 I called again. This time I spoke to a staff member on the House Judiciary Committee, who told me that the matter was still on the agenda, but that no meeting was scheduled for that week.

Finally, on June 11, Frederick Woltman, the reporter who had originally unearthed the story, reported on the disgraceful use of political power to stop justice in the United States: "A Dewey Republican and a Bronx Democrat had joined forces in the House Judiciary Committee to suppress an eleven-month-old subcommittee report criticizing former New York Police Commissioner, Mr. George P. Monaghan, since named the state trotting race czar by Governor Thomas E. Dewey." Monaghan, Rothengast, and Fristensky had resigned the night that Manhattan Borough President Robert F. Wagner was elected Mayor of the City of New York. New York's Governor Thomas E. Dewey immediately offered them all jobs. Monaghan had been a Dewey protégé when Dewey was New York's District Attorney, and in setting him up as the trotting track czar, the Governor said Monaghan was "the best Police Commissioner New York City had ever had." Woltman continued in his article: "The report was unanimously approved by both Democrats and Republicans on the Congressional subcommittee following a series of hearings in New York and Washington in February of 1953." Mayor Wagner indicated that the report's findings were the major reason he would not reappoint Commissioner Monaghan.

Democratic Congressman Sid Fein moved on June 15 that the report be tabled. It is absolutely impossible for anyone to get hold of that report today. Whether it has vanished from the files or not, I do not know.

When Nelson Rockefeller took over the gubernatorial reins of New York, he fired Monaghan. Later, at a café table in Paris one day, Monaghan's lawyer friend Victor Hurwitz was overhead to say that one of the reasons I was being investigated for income-tax evasion was that Monaghan's old political friends were trying to "get even" with me. I have no idea whether this is true or not, because the information was sent to me anonymously.

But this I do know: our country is in mortal danger as long as the FBI can, by the machinations of corrupt politicians, be kept out of areas where it is sorely needed; and when investigations by committees of Congress can be silenced by those same politicians.

In 1959 and 1960 I turned my attention to the numbers racket and other criminally run activities that were preying on the poor of Harlem.

"Nobody, not even Thomas E. Dewey, has hit the business as hard as it is hit now. Dewey was asked to get Tammany leader Jimmy Hines, and he got him. But nothing like this has happened in the forty years that I have known this business. It's through all the way down." So began, on April 18, 1960, the first article of a series—"A Second Look at a Racket-Numbers Game Hard Hit"—in the *New York Post*.

On January 13, 1960, I was granted permission to address the Congress for one hour on the New York City numbers racket. Single-handed, using nothing more than the sounding board of the House of Representatives, I was able to begin what the *New York Post* finished off. In these articles, written by a staff headed by Ted Poston, the *Post* further stated:

> The lush city-wide numbers racket grossing an estimated 250 million dollars a year just three months ago, has plummeted to new low depths, a re-survey of the racket by the *Post* disclosed today. At least sixty percent of the bars, stationery stores, groceries, luncheonettes, newsstands, pool rooms and other protected locations have gone out of the numbers business altogether, at least for now. The remaining forty percent of the numbers spots are doing less than half of their former business. The Pad itself under which crooked cops systematically collected an average of two thousand five hundred dollars per month for each protected spot (even if only an agreed-upon tenement hallway) has been suspended, temporarily at least, by the racketeering police officials who directed it.

In 1959 I had held a conference with Police Commissioner Stephen B. Kennedy in his headquarters. I met him in the same room in that gloomy building on Spring Street where my father had gone almost fifty years before to complain about prostitution in front of his church on 40th Street. I came to complain about the discrimination of the Police Department in its dealings with numbers racketeers in front of that same church, now on 138th Street. Mr. Kennedy assigned a confidential inspector to work with my forces and to report directly to him. J. Raymond Jones was appointed by me to work with this inspector, whose name I hold in confidence. Every single thing that Mr. Jones asked him to do regarding complaints on prostitution, narcotics, crap games this inspector did. But every single thing he was asked to do in connection with numbers he did *not* do. Place by place, the Police Department raided mainly those spots that were owned by Negro numbers bankers.

On January 10, 1960, Emanuel Perlmutter wrote in the editorial section of the Sunday *New York Times:* "The charge made by Representative Powell that more Negro than white men had been arrested in Harlem is true. . . . It is also true that the Negro bankers who once controlled numbers gambling there have either been driven out by the white racketeers or are now working for them."

What touched off this fight of mine against the Mafia, the Syndicate, and the Combine? Quoting from my speech as printed in the *Congressional Record,* where I had also published a number of revelations dealing with the rackets: "A former police sergeant by the name of [Joseph] Luberda was arrested for drunken driving in a nearby county to New York City. In his car was not only discovered $19,495 in cash but also a sheet listing the names of the major numbers bankers and their addresses and the amount of money they were paying off each week. These sheets have never been made public. I hold in my hand photostatic copies of them. I would like to read these addresses and names and the amount of the payoff into the record." When I did this, the police closed down many numbers drops in my Congressional District within thirty-six hours, and arrested a hundred and five people. So they knew the names and places all along. But they did this only in my District.

My fight was against the criminalization of Harlem by the white underworld, and the pauperization of those who could least afford it—a quarter of a billion dollars a year was being taken out of their pockets. I requested that the Library of Congress obtain information regarding criminal arrests and convictions, according to race, in New York City. On January 14 the Police Commissioner replied to the request of Dr. Hugh L. Elsbree, director of the Legislative Reference Service, by refusing this information: "It is not my policy to release such information." This was a total untruth because on January 6, before the assembled press, Deputy Chief Burns, in reply to the same question, had said, "Eighty-two percent of those arrested were Negroes." At that same press conference I turned to Mr. Burns, "Every name and every address that I have you know?" He nodded his head in assent.

When Judge Mullen sentenced Sergeant Luberda to prison for failing to speak, he charged that Luberda was the "bag man" for the payoffs. The Assistant District Attorney of New York County in presenting the case against Luberda identified Luberda's list as "the payoff list." Deputy Police Commissioner Walter Arm made the damaging admission to the press that the list I had put in the *Congressional Record* "was five years old." Sergeant Luberda was arrested in March of 1959. If that list was five years old, it meant Luberda was a "bag man" while on the force. And if that list was five years old, why hadn't the police done something about it, and why did they obstruct justice by not informing District Attorney Frank Hogan that such a list existed? The very first name on it, Louie the Gimp, was known to the police as one of the biggest payoff men, operating his numbers bank virtually in front of my church. Yet he was not arrested until the day after I held the press conference revealing what the police had known for five years.

I asked Governor Rockefeller for a conference; he telegraphed his refusal. I asked the Mayor of New York to appoint a special commission with subpoena power to investigate the numbers. Nothing happened. The Director of the Intelligence Division of the Internal Revenue Service, H. Alan Long, wrote to me on January 18: "Our New York office is already alert to this situation and I am sure they will take all steps necessary to enforce the laws within our jurisdiction." However, the New York State Crime Commission invited me to an off-the-record meeting. I also met with District Attorney Hogan, who showed me a chart that he had had his staff draw up, indicating that almost 90 percent of the forty-five hundred defendents who had been tried during the previous year in the gamblers' courts of New York were represented by the same lawyers. The bail bond business also was operated by virtually one firm. The chart indicated clearly that the overlords of the underworld could be tracked down by a Grand Jury through these lawyers and bail bondsmen.

Information began to pour in. Of all the tips that I had placed in the *Congressional Record*, only two were in error—because of incorrect addresses. One particular tip turned over to the District Attorney traced the legitimizing of the millions of dollars from policy rackets right out into the normal channels of trade and finance. This was an important step since one of the most difficult problems for a large illegal business is getting the money clean—that is, getting it moved somehow into legitimate companies so that the rulers of the crime empire can prove a right to the money and make use of it. The tip I turned over to the District Attorney gave his office the information needed to uncover and destroy this money pipeline.

Early in February I revealed to Congress that one of the numbers bankers was formerly Deputy Collector of Internal Revenue for Manhattan. "New information has reached me within the past few minutes," I stated. "I now have the name and address of a former member of the Bureau of Internal Revenue who was the Deputy Collector for Manhattan and who resigned in 1952 to become the numbers boss of lower Harlem." I then proceeded to list the various addresses from which he was operating. "Mr. Speaker, it is absolutely shocking that a former official of the Bureau of Internal Revenue who was in charge of an area in my Congressional District resigned to become the numbers boss of the same area."

The Speaker of the Assembly of the New York State Legislature, Joseph Carlino, pointed out on television that what I was saying was correct, but went on to make the serious charge that all I was revealing was just the beginning of this unholy alliance between top public officials in New York City and the Mafia, the Syndicate, and the Combine.

John Cassesse, president of the Patrolmen's Benevolent Association, representing the twenty-four thousand New York policemen, charged that Police Commissioner Stephen Kennedy was "lowering the morale" of the New York Police. Mr. Kennedy declined comment on these accusations but John Cassesse was reelected by a unanimous vote.

The New York Times ran an editorial lambasting me for daring to criticize the Police Commissioner and saying I was trying to "push him around." But I had the facts, and even though the *Times* ignored them I continued putting them into the *Congressional Record.* Things began to happen. I began looking for the new "bag man" of the Police Department since Luberda had been jailed. On February 25 I placed in the *Congressional Record* the account of a citizen who on August 17 of the previous year and again on September 9 complained to John Walsh, the supervising Assistant Chief Inspector of the Police Department, that a woman named Esther James was extorting money from gamblers and those operating numbers in the uptown area for the purpose of transmitting this money to police officers. I charged that the Police Department had not stopped this practice and that no investigation had been made. I also placed in the *Congressional Record* a letter that had been sent to the New York State Crime Commission, making accusations against Police Sgt. Steve DeRosa.

That night Sergeant DeRosa resigned from the Police Department in

The Adam Clayton Powell, Sr., family. Adam, Jr., is three months old.

Josephine, the Powell's household factotum, with Mrs. Powell's cat, 1921.

Mrs. Adam Clayton Powell, Sr., 1921.

Adam Clayton Powell, Jr., and his mother.

The nation's only black Congressmen for many years were Representative William
L. Dawson, Democrat, of Illinois, and Representative Adam Clayton Powell, Jr.,
Democrat, of New York, seen here in 1949.

The winner, Powell, surrounded by jubilant supporters, beams after winning the race for the Democratic nomination in the Sixteenth Congressional District, New York, August, 1958.

New York delegates consult during the 1952 Democratic National Convention, Chicago. With Representative Powell are, left to right, Leon M. Martin, W. Averill Harriman, New York's "favorite son" Presidential candidate, and Representative Emanuel Cellar.

While heading the House Education and Labor Committee, Representative Powell guided to passage legislation increasing the minimum-hourly wage to $1.25 for 3,600,000 workers. Here President Kennedy signs the bill as Powell and others, including Representative John W. McCormack, Representative James Roosevelt, and Secretary of Labor Arthur J. Goldberg look on.

Congressman Adam Clayton Powell, Jr.

such haste that he left behind $700 in salary due him. When asked by the press why he didn't go back to pick it up, he said that was "his prerogative." When Sergeant DeRosa went before the Grand Jury he left after only ten minutes, pleading "exhaustion."

High police officials suddenly began to resign. Commissioner Kennedy, who had scoffed at everything in the beginning, fired his entire confidential squad and installed a new one. He redistricted the divisions in Manhattan so the possibilities of graft would be lessened.

This was my greatest single-handed victory. The *New York Post*, bringing its series to a close on April 24, wrote, "Just what happens to The Pad in the future depends on Steve Kennedy. If he does nothing about the brass in his department who have been getting rich from The Pad for years, then you can be sure they will revive the system any minute."

During all this time that I had been warring on the numbers racket I received many grave threats and had been offered a round-the-clock bodyguard by the Police Department, all of which I ignored or spurned. Ironically, when the rackets establishment finally did make its attempt to silence me, the weapon was not a pistol or a bomb, but the New York courts.

During a television interview I had repeated the same charges that I had made in Congress and to the Police Department. Among them was the allegation that Esther James was a "bag woman." The next day I received word that I was going to be sued by Mrs. James for defamation of character and slander, and that she was going to ask $1 million in damages.

At this point I made a grave mistake, one that would eventually cost me a large sum of money. I did not take the threatened lawsuit seriously. I thought it was just another of the smear tactics that were being employed against me. Later, in Washington, I was notified that the suit had actually been started. At that point I realized that I was already late—it would take time to gather evidence that could prove my statement. And by now the investigation had generated enough publicity so that many of the people who had spoken up earlier would be hard to find and harder to persuade to testify. In addition my work load in Washington was very heavy and I did not have sufficient time to devote to the case.

The jury that heard the case finally decided—I assume because I was ill in Washington and unable to appear—that Mrs. James was innocent of any wrongdoing and that I was guilty. Mrs. James was awarded $46,500.

My lawyers immediately began a long series of appeals, but through the years the courts added penalty after penalty until the total judgment reached almost $200,000. The matter did not end until December of 1968. By that time the New York State Court of Appeals had reversed some earlier decisions and reduced the judgment to near its original figure. Since we had exhausted every possible legal method of reversing the original decision, there was nothing left to do but to pay Mrs. James.

13

The United States vs. Powell

"I ask you if they were conducting an investigation into his taxes, or if they were waging a political vendetta designed to destroy him?"

That was the question posed by Edward Bennett Williams to the jury sitting on *United States vs. Adam Clayton Powell* in Foley Square, New York City. It was immediately objected to by the government's prosecuting attorney, Morton Robson. Judge Frederick Van Pelt Bryan stared Robson straight in the eye until he sat down and never ruled on his objection. Mr. Williams proceeded.

Edward Bennett Williams is one of the greatest trial lawyers ever to stand in any courthouse. He is dedicated to the now outmoded proposition that all men are innocent until proven guilty. He is a great man, a great heart, a great soul, and a man greatly feared by the Department of Justice. And by virtue of his ability he may yet be able to bring the Justice Department back to that now outmoded concept of holding a man innocent until guilt is proven. He is a thing of beauty to watch in a courtroom, where he stands like a Jesuit priest ticking off the facts, propagating the faith, and trying to convert all within earshot. He is a number-one fighter for civil liberties, a member of the Board of Directors of the American Civil Liberties Union. A staunch Roman Catholic, he is a believer in "the majestic vengeance of God," and he said to me, "This is it at work, and if we fail, there will be a better justice."

Men like Williams are desperately needed to change the tide of injustice and reaction that is infiltrating the judicial system of our land. Today any man who is accused of a crime and goes into a Federal courthouse to be tried has only one chance in ten of being acquitted.

When he was only thirty-five, Ed Williams beat a case that the government had spent over a quarter of a million dollars on and eleven years preparing. This was the case of the former Office of Strategic Services officer, Lt. Aldo Icardi, charged with perjury for having denied the murder of a fellow worker, Major Holochan, behind the enemy line in Italy. Williams also represented Senator Joseph McCarthy of Wisconsin before a Select Committee of the Senate hearing arguments over whether McCarthy should be censured by the Senate. He has defended Robert Rossen, a Hollywood director blacklisted during the McCarthy era; Robert Harrison, editor of *Confidential* magazine; and the underworld figure Frank Costello. Another of his clients was the Boston industrialist Bernard Goldfine.

One of his most dramatic acquittals was that of Jimmy Hoffa of the Teamsters Union in 1957. When he won that case, the press asked him for a comment and he said, "I am going to buy Bobby Kennedy a parachute."

Robert Kennedy was the counsel for the McClellan Committee investigating rackets. He had the "goods" on Jimmy Hoffa so wrapped up, the case so well constructed, that he openly stated he would "jump off the Capitol Dome if Hoffa was not convicted."

It was Ed Williams who led for many years the successful fight with the Bar Association of Washington, D.C., to force them to admit Negro lawyers as members. Within a few months in 1959 he went through two great tragedies—the loss of the mother of his children and the sudden death of his best friend. During this period I spent some time with him and grew to know him better and increase my respect for him.

Tall, handsome, with a lower lip that makes girls swoon, and curly brown hair that's always falling over his forehead, here stands a man with a horizon unlimited, the reincarnation of Clarence Darrow. This was the man I needed.

Thirty days after Eisenhower had been reelected, all the records of the Abyssinian Baptist Church were subpoenaed and a Grand Jury began, on December 17, 1958—eight years after the period in question—a study of whether or not there had been any tax evasion. Not one single agent of the United States government, the Internal Revenue Service, or the Department of Justice had given me the courtesy extended to criminals, gangsters, and underworld figures—namely, to allow me or my representatives to go over the records for the years in question. Each year prior to those years and every single year since then such courtesy had been extended, but this time, for the first time, the usual courtesy was not extended to me, not only a member of Congress but minister of one of the largest and oldest churches in our nation. The chief of the task force set up to go after me was Morris Emanuel, who as the chief of the Internal Revenue's group testified on the stand under cross-examination by Williams that the procedure in this case was "not the usual." When Williams pressed him as to why they had not given the usual treatment to me, the same treatment that was accorded to criminals and thugs, he said he was acting under orders from the Department of Justice.

Prior to the Little Rock, Arkansas, episode, the Grand Jury on my case had discontinued its meetings. The lawyer assigned to the case, Boland, then resigned and became associated with the extreme-right-wing Republican periodical the *National Review,* which is owned by the old McCarthy crowd and is headed by William Buckley. Two other interesting points must be noted. The publisher of the *National Review* was William Rusher, who was the former Assistant Counsel to Senator Eastland of Mississippi. Also on the periodical's advisory board was Senator Byrd of Virginia, whose personal recommendation for head of the Internal Revenue Service of the United States, T. Coleman Andrews, was accepted by President Eisenhower.

While T. Coleman Andrews was the chief of the Internal Revenue Service, the investigation was begun on my case. Andrews subsequently resigned to run for President of the United States against Eisenhower on a 100-percent anti-segregationist ticket and a platform to abolish the income tax. This group then, using the *National Review,* circulated copies of an issue of the magazine directly to the homes of the grand jurors. The names and addresses of the grand jurors were furnished the *National Review* by Boland, the former Federal attorney, who also gave the *National Review* supposedly confidential information that had been presented to the Grand Jury. The magazine's editors took what they desired from this material and printed it in their McCarthy smear sheet.

Edward Bennett Williams moved that the case be dismissed because the jury had been tampered with. The case was presented to Judge William Herlands, who ruled that the indictment was valid. Just fifteen years before that I had led the fight in the City Council of New York, where by a vote of eighteen to five we investigated William Herlands because of the way he had conducted the investigation of a case in which an individual had tried to buy off a member of the City Council. Now Herlands was the judge who ruled on Ed Williams' motion.

I was tried in the very room in which I had caused a special committee of the United States Congress to come to New York and investigate that same Department of Justice and the Police Department of New York for their infamous agreement to keep the FBI out of the investigation of police brutality in New York City.

The Grand Jury reconvened for the first time in seventeen months. In a few short days it handed down an indictment that it had not been able to arrive at for many months in the latter part of 1956 and early 1957. Eisenhower then held the conference at the White House that had been arranged for me over the Little Rock incident and, of course, I was not invited.

From the time I was indicted and on through the trial, there came a unanimous cry from all media of public opinion that I be lynched. Edward Bennett Williams told me, "Adam, I thought they were vicious concerning Jimmy Hoffa, but what they are doing to you is twice as bad as what they did to Hoffa." Not a single newspaper in the United States of America said one word about fair play, except the Negro press and the Washington *Evening Star*, which reminded the American people that an indictment did not mean proof of guilt. All the white newspapers—liberal, conservative, North, South—cried for a lynching. Mrs. Eleanor Roosevelt in one of her columns implied that I was guilty when she said that I should not be chairman of the Committee on Education and Labor because of my impending trial. Even before the trial had begun, she was presuming guilt. Drew Pearson wrote column after column of vilification. Senator Williams,

Republican of Delaware, made a speech on the Floor of the Senate during the trial, demanding that the Senate investigate me, although it was totally unheard of that one House should investigate the other; totally unheard of that while a man is on trial this kind of atmosphere should be created. *Confidential* sent out a smear article about me and mailed copies of it to all members of the United States Congress. The leading liberal radio show of New York, the Barry Gray show, gave its time free to a representative of *Confidential* to air the filth of that magazine while the jury was still sitting. When one considers that the newspapers, radio, television, magazines, columnists, commentators, Senators, all openly attacked me while I was being tried, it is a wonder that the members of the jury in the midst of this atmosphere remained as objective as they did. And their objectivity was indicated when they voted ten to two that I be acquitted.

In the midst of all this, strong political forces, both Republican and Democratic, were wielding political power not only in New York City and New York State but throughout the nation. Senator Maurine Neuberger of Oregon called me one day and said, "Adam, it is being freely talked about around the Hill that Senator Eastland has asked Bill Rogers [the Attorney General] to give you the works. As you know, Adam, all of the appointments of the Department of Justice—not only the judges but also the attorneys—must go through Senator Eastland for his approval, and if he, as chairman of the Senate Judiciary Committee, does not approve them, they are not appointed. Things look mighty bad for you, if what I hear on the Hill is true—and I have every reason to believe it—that Eastland has virtually ordered your indictment and conviction."

In this rule-by-mob, get-Powell-damn-the-cost, lynch atmosphere one man stood like a rock—Judge Frederick Van Pelt Bryan. I did not know him, had never seen him before, had never talked to him, but he was the first official in the United States government in all the years they were trying to get me who used the words "fair play." The public opinion media to which the jury might be exposed were of great concern to him, and these words which I now present come for the first time to the American public and are from the official minutes of an executive session of my trial in the Judge's chamber. Present were the Judge (referred to as "The Court"); Ed Williams; Harrison Jackson, my lawyer-of-record; Morton Robson, prosecuting attorney; and Morris Emanuel of the Internal Revenue Service.

UNITED STATES OF AMERICA vs. ADAM CLAYTON
POWELL, JR.

New York City
March 29, 1960
10:30 o'clock A.M.

Trial resumed

(*The following took place in the robing room*)

THE COURT: In the first place, gentlemen, I say this for the record so that
everybody should be informed. At quarter past seven this
morning at my home, I got a call from a reporter of the *New
York Post*—I answered the phone myself, incidentally, because my family is away—who said in substance, "Judge, do
you know of a publication concerning the defendant which
goes into a good many details about him, which is on the
newsstands?"—I think he said today. I don't know whether
it was he or she. He said, "I refer to *Confidential* magazine."
I said, "I am aware of it." Then he said, "Well, how did you
become aware of it?" And, designedly, I said it was called to
my attention by counsel, at which point the reporter said,
"Well, there is some rumor that there will be a mistrial on
that account, and what have you to say?" I said, "Of course,
I have no comments whatsoever." This, as I see it, is of no
significance except that I think it is only fair to counsel that
they should be informed of such call and my replies to the
press. Any comments, gentlemen?

MR. ROBSON: None. We have already covered it. . . .

THE COURT: Yes.

MR. WILLIAMS: I know that it does come onto the newsstand today. At least,
that is the information I have.

MR. ROBSON: That was the date I have been told it would be on the stand.

THE COURT: We are informed it was on the newsstands yesterday.

MR. JACKSON: I would like to notify the Court, through Mr. Williams, that
my home was called this morning at 6:15 by the *New York
Post*, and when it was reported, I refused to answer the phone.

THE COURT: Good, that is as well.

MR. WILLIAMS: Judge, last night—I didn't hear this myself, but I am told—
on a radio show over station WMCA here, Barry Gray had
the author of this *Confidential* piece on his show, the author
being one Fred Weaver. Weaver repeated in substance all the

things that he said in the *Confidential* piece and went into
detail in response to questions that Gray propounded to him
with respect to the transactions, which are detailed in the
piece.

That disturbed me a great deal when I heard it this morning, for this reason, that while the jury may very well be able
to guard against newspaper matters, it is a little more difficult to guard against things that are inflicted on you over the
air when your radio is on, and I don't, frankly, know how to
cope with that kind of thing.

I would like Your Honor particularly to ask them if they
heard Barry Gray on the air last night. . . .

THE COURT: I think this is very dangerous. I think that is almost. . . .

MR. WILLIAMS: I am very surprised about this because I had indicated to you
before that—incidentally, as to all this publicity throughout
the trial—I had been asked to go on the radio show, and it
was Gray himself who called me several times and asked me
to go on his radio show and promised that he would not
discuss this case or the defendant or anything in relation to
it, but he was interested in some law subjects, he said, on
wiretapping and things of that nature, constitutional questions.

I refused to go on his show because I saw that it had a
potential danger, it could be misconstrued that I was on the
air during a trial, and I told him I wouldn't do it, and I told
him, as I indicated to you, that I felt the spirit of my understanding with counsel on the other side, which was arrived at
the first day, prevented this kind of thing even though the
letter of it I don't think did.

Gray then said to me, "Look, I am the greatest believer of
anyone you know in the English concept of a trial, that nothing should take place during a trial that would in any way
affect its course."

Now you see what happens. He puts a man on the air
who comes out with a diatribe on the defendant right in
midstream of the trial, and it is pretty disillusioning and
also. . . .

THE COURT: It is very distressing, and I may say on the record that, to me,
it shows a surprising and distressing lack of public responsibility on the part of this particular medium of public expression.

MR. ROBSON: I might suggest, Your Honor, I don't know whether you want to do it or not, but there have been so many newspaper accounts and radio accounts and magazine accounts of the trial, some favorable and some adverse, etc., it might be possible to simply ask the jurors a general question indicating there has been a great deal of publicity involving the trial, with opinions rendered of all sorts and colors, and have any members of the jury seen anything or heard anything about the trial?

THE COURT: I think as a matter of precaution at the conclusion of the trial this afternoon, not this morning, as we start, because I don't think that it is the most favorable atmosphere to begin a trial today, I can do this at the end of the day, at the same time as I deliver my usual warning to the jury, and go into the thing a little more in detail and say I assume that the jurors have been following my strictures very carefully, but I want to know whether inadvertently anybody has any such matter which has come to their attention, and, if so, they should inform me.

In that case I would take each juror individually, not in the presence of the other jurors, and inquire as to what he had heard, and keep counsel thoroughly informed of anything of that nature, so that counsel could take whatever position, if that unfortunate event occurred, he saw fit with respect to the matter.

If, for example, some juror listened, let's say, to the Barry Gray broadcast, then I would certainly want to hear counsel fully on the subject.

I would doubt—perhaps I am overly optimistic, but I would doubt if any such thing occurred, because my impression is we have very conscientious jurors who take their task very seriously. But I will do that at the end of the day, in view of all that has gone on, and make what I consider to be appropriate inquiries at that time designed to elicit whether there has been strict compliance with my instructions to them.

MR. WILLIAMS: I don't know what the fact is, but I am told this man has a very wide radio audience every night.

THE COURT: He has a wide radio audience, I know that, because some years ago, before I went on the bench, I appeared on his program in connection with political subjects. This was five, six, seven years ago, but even at that time he had a very broad audience.

What is his station?

MR. EMANUEL: WMCA. He goes on at midnight.

THE COURT: It is a midnight show and used to be given from a restaurant.

MR. WILLIAMS: It is now given from the studio.

THE COURT: We will handle that that way and that is the soundest way to handle it for everybody's protection.

MR. JACKSON: The defendant has been heard on the Barry Gray program at least ten times heretofore, last year and through the years.

THE COURT: The last thing that I have to talk to you about this morning, there is a story in the *Post*, which I am going to mark, which appeared yesterday afternoon and which says, among other things:

"Bryan will outline for a jury of nine women and three men the scope to be permitted the testimony of Morris J. Emanuel, special agent in the intelligence unit of the Internal Revenue Service.

"Emanuel, who probably knows more about the Powell case than any other person, came to Court Friday ready to testify from large charts and extensive documents which have been accumulated in his personal investigations halfway around the world.

"But Edward Bennett Williams, Powell's Washington attorney, challenged some of the exhibits, and questioned the scope that Emanuel may use in amplifying testimony already given by witnesses from London, Scandinavia, France and Israel on an extensive European concert tour by Powell's pianist wife, Hazel Scott, in 1951."

Then there is some further discussion of the indictment and so forth along the usual lines. Then it goes on to say:

"And the defense had hinted that it planned to show additional errors in favor of the government when Louis Marshall, the certified public accountant who prepared the 1952 joint returns, took the stand as a prosecution witness.

"But United States Assistant Attorney Robson did not immediately call Marshall as the expected witness. He summoned Emanuel instead.

"The jury was sent home Friday for the third time so that defense and prosecution could argue the legal points involved 'in executive session' in the judge's chambers, etc."

The reason I call that to your attention is that it does seem to be based on some knowledge of what went on in the executive sessions with the Court. It is rather difficult to tell whether this is just normal inferences the reporter had raised or not.

My recollection is that there had been reference in open court to the possible testimony of Mr. Marshall, and, in fact, I think Mr. Robson at one time stated that he anticipated calling Mr. Marshall toward the end of his case. So there is nothing here definitely to indicate that there is any leak in our discussions in executive session, and I am not implying that there is.

I merely say this to you gentlemen as indicating the utmost caution with respect to all this subject matter, because this trial is being covered by very able reporters who can build stories merely by reciting how somebody coughed or blew his nose.

I am sure all of you have observed the rules we laid down here very carefully, indeed. But I ask you to exercise the utmost caution all along so that in view of all this publicity that is going on we shan't get anything that will prejudice the defendant particularly. Any comments, gentlemen?

MR. ROBSON: Nothing, except to say I haven't discussed the matter at all. I don't think anybody did.

Someone evidently did. All during the Grand Jury investigation the weekly New York *Amsterdam News,* which was printed on Tuesdays, would carry information regarding Wednesday's actions.

Through the years my relationships with the Internal Revenue Service have been good and I had always used the normal procedure—the returns of Hazel Scott and myself were gone over each year with our accountants and representatives from Internal Revenue. Sometimes we got a refund and sometimes we had to pay more. As a matter of fact, my wife had just settled for $10,000 a United States Government claim of $19,000 for the year 1945. Not a single year had gone by without this standard procedure of the Service, which was extended to all citizens, including the non-law-abiding.

However, after a two- or three-year lapse in this procedure of yearly tax conferences I began to ask what was happening. The accountants kept telling me "normal procedure will be followed." In those years my enemies were increasing, and they were powerful, so I asked the Service to check with my accountants. The Collector of Internal Revenue was then T. Coleman Andrews.

Meanwhile two members of my staff, Acy Lennon and Hattie Dodson, were convicted for claiming dependents they could not prove. I had absolutely nothing to do with their cases, but did voluntarily appear at their trials as a character witness and to answer freely any questions that the government was disposed to ask. Boland, who prosecuted them, implied that Mrs. Dodson had kicked back her salary to me and tried to prove it. Judge Kaufman threw out this part of her case and so instructed the jury. Despite this, many papers frequently refer to it as a fact, even though the Judge ordered it out of the case.

Then in December of 1958, during a vacation in Jamaica, I was breakfasting one morning with my friend Dick DeLisser, who owned the Bay Roc Hotel in Montego Bay, and read on the front page of the *New York Times* that the United States government had seized all the records of the Abyssinian Baptist Church and that a Grand Jury was about to begin looking into possible tax evasion on my part. I received phone calls from friends in New York City, advising me to stay in Jamaica until Congress reconvened in January and then the Grand Jury could not subpoena me to appear in court because of my immunity. This I immediately rejected and, canceling all plans, flew back to New York so that I could be available before Congress opened and the Grand Jury could call me or serve me with a summons. Getting off the plane at Idlewild, I met the press and announced that I was available for the Grand Jury. Nevertheless, at no time was I ever invited to appear before it nor was a summons ever served upon me.

I knew I was innocent and at that time had faith in the American system of justice. Consequently, it came as no surprise when I learned, early in 1957, that the Grand Jury had stopped activity. My accountants were ready to sit down and discuss with the government the years in question. But seventeen months later the previously mentioned McCarthy crowd moved in. The Grand Jury was then reconvened and in a matter of a few days I was indicted on three counts, two of which pertained to aiding my wife to file a fraudulent return. She was not indicted.

The day I came before Judge Weinstein to be arraigned, the steps of the Federal courthouse were packed and clergymen dressed in their garb crowded the corridors. I was the first person from any outstanding church to be indicted for income-tax evasion. These men, many of whom had known me since I was a child, placed their faith in me. The venerable Reverend Dr. O. Clay Maxwell, national president of the National Baptist Sunday School, said to me with tears in his eyes, "Adam, they are out to get you. But there is a God who is in His Heaven and He has more power than all the forces of this government and all governments. My prayers are with you. I know you are going to win because you are right."

Judge Weinstein slumped down in his chair, obviously undertaking an unpleasant task. He was extremely cooperative—no fingerprinting, no bail, no limit to my travel. From then on my future was in the hands of Edward Bennett Williams. Wherever I went, radio, television, and the press always wanted to speak to me concerning the case, and I always said, "Talk to Edward Williams; that's what I'm paying him for."

During this same period I underwent a series of tremendous physical setbacks. On June 1, 1957, they carried me out of the pulpit of the Abyssinian Baptist Church to Cornell University Medical Center suffering from a heart attack. I was transferred from there to the United States Naval Medical Center at Bethesda, Maryland. On June 11 I was ordered to take a rest and get away from it all for two or three months or face a breakdown. Again, during the end of July 1959, the physician of the United States Congress, Dr. Calvert, sent me back to the Naval Medical Center to have a growth examined. It was diagnosed as a hernia, and I was set for an operation the following week. But on July 30, after suffering agony and pain on the Floor of Congress, I was rushed to the Naval Medical Center, not for the hernia but for an emergency appendectomy.

I was discharged on August 8 with the admonition to come back in six weeks for the hernia operation. So on September 28 I did go back. The preliminary X-rays were taken and, as I was being prepared for surgery, the nurse rushed in and exclaimed, "Stop! We need to have him X-rayed again." On that day, October 5, and for the next five days I went through every type of X-ray examination known. Experts were called in for conferences from nearby hospitals, universities, and the National Institutes of Public Health across the street from the hospital. They discovered a two-inch growth at the bottom of my esophagus, next to my heart and against my lung. Using bronchoscopy, they pushed down to the base of my esophagus to see whether the growth was inside or outside. It was on the outside. The tumor staff of the Naval Medical Center under the Chief, Admiral Robert Brown, sat down and talked with me. He said, "This has suddenly come forward in the X-rays. We didn't find it before. We don't know what it is. It might be cancer. You should have it out immediately."

I replied, "Let me talk to my friend Dr. John R. Heller, Director of the National Cancer Institute, at the National Institutes of Public Health."

I did. Dr. Heller told me, "I will send across the street to the Naval

Medical Center the best men I have and they will go over everything, and confer with Admiral Brown."

Finally, it was agreed by all who had sat in on the case that an emergency operation of the most serious type had to be performed immediately.

I had complete trust in Admiral Brown, who is one of the finest human beings I have ever met and a most brilliant surgeon. This country ought to be extremely grateful that a man of his skill and learning is willing to forego a private practice, which would bring to him many, many times the salary he is now receiving as an admiral. When the decision to operate had been made, I said to him, "Now tell me the truth. What is this operation?"

"We'll have to cut you in half," he said, "beginning just in the middle of your chest and going around the entire right side and then up your back. We'll have to spread the ribs if we're lucky and, if not, I would like you to give me permission to cut them away. We've got to go deep down into the center of you."

I asked, "How long will it keep me out of work?"

He said, "If it is malignant, it might be the end. If it isn't malignant, you still will be out several months."

"Okay, give me two weeks to get things in order at the church and get my personal life straightened out."

Back to New York I went, and for the next two weeks I moved around among the people of Harlem and New York, making them aware of the situation I faced. On the last Sunday before I went back to the hospital, I said during my sermon, "After thirty years of standing in this pulpit and proclaiming and exhorting you to have faith in God, after thirty years of being a minister and a clergyman, there now comes this great crisis in my own life, but don't you know that if I haven't got the faith to go through with this without whimpering, then all my preaching has been in vain? I want you to know that I am totally prepared."

At my request the great choir of the Abyssinian Baptist Church, under the direction of Howard Dodson, sang the Negro spiritual, "I Ain't Got Time To Die."

I returned to Bethesda, calm in the faith that there was a Great God whom I had tried to follow all my life, that he was the Supreme Physician, and that not my will nor anyone else's but His would prevail.

On the eve of the operation Jimmy Booker, one of our great New York reporters, telephoned to ask Admiral Brown how I was feeling. The Admiral replied, "Powell has nerves of steel." I gave absolutely no indication in any of the preoperative tests they performed that I was in the slightest way tense or nervous. I slept like a baby the night before the operation, and when they awakened me in the morning, there were my loved ones.

Dr. Aaron Otis Wells, Professor of Internal Medicine at Cornell University Medical School and one of the doctors of our church, had received special permission to witness the operation. He stayed on in Washington for two days after the operation so that he could talk to me. When Dr. Wells was given permission to visit, he said, "Adam, I wanted to stay here for these two days so that I could tell you just one thing—I stood there looking over the shoulders of Dr. Brown and the other members of his excellent staff, and as they cut you in half—your lungs, your heart, everything exposed—all the time the instruments recording that there was no tenseness, I said to myself, 'This God that Adam has been preaching about is really a Great God, because only a man who had faith in Him could undergo such an operation without some kind of a reaction.'"

Yes, I had nerves of steel. I had a draining tube in my side with the motor pumping, tubes taped into my nose with another motor pumping; my arm in a splint with a needle in it dripping in the transfusion; I was sewn with stitches of steel wire, eighty-two of them; yet on the next morning I asked the orderlies to help—it took three of them to carry everything—and I got on my feet and took a couple of steps. I personally took myself, day by day, off of all forms of sedation: morphine, demerol, cocaine, and finally down to just plain old aspirin. In ten days, I walked out.

The date of the trial on the income-tax matter had been changed because of my health, and on March 7, 1960, it began. The Department of Justice set aside the largest courtroom at Foley Square. People stood in line day after day waiting to get in. The press was there in full. My old friend from the New York *Journal-American*, Jim Kilgallen, Dorothy Kilgallen's father, was the dean of all the reporters there. Murray Kempton covered as a columnist for the *Post*. There was even a journalist there dressed in a sari, representing the press of Southeast Asia.

We were shocked when they brought in the panel from which my jurors were selected. Something was wrong! Here in Manhattan, where half the population was Puerto Rican and Negro, there were only five of them on that panel of more than a hundred and twenty-five. When my lawyer challenged this, I was shocked to hear the Commissioner of Jurors say that he had chosen them from the real estate advertisements in the *New York Times*. His personal system of picking jurors was to select those apartments in the high-income areas, such as Sutton Place, Park Avenue, and Fifth Avenue, and then requisition jurors from those buildings. My lawyer asked him if he ever looked at the real estate section of the *New York Post*, a liberal newspaper; or the *Amsterdam News*, which is circulated in Harlem; or *El Diario*, the Spanish-language paper. The answer, of course, was no. A man is supposed to be tried by his peers and here I was to be tried before a panel which came mostly from those areas of Manhattan where no members of minorities were allowed to live despite the law to the contrary. In Ed Williams' words, this was "geographic and economic discrimination."

Finally, on March 9 the all-white jury was chosen—nine women, three men. The four alternates included an American of Cuban birth, an Oriental-American, and a Negro housewife, who later on in the trial, on March 22, filled the seat of a woman juror who became seriously ill. Then my eyes shifted to the table in front of me where sat the task force that had been selected to try to convict me: the chief, Morton Robson; his assistant, Gordon; the chief of the Internal Revenue, Morris Emanuel; and his assistant, Frischman. As I looked at these four members of a minority group, I wondered if this had been a deliberate effort by the Department of Justice. After all my years of fighting for all minorities, including theirs, here I was, faced with an entire task force of the Department of Justice composed of members of only one minority.

Except for that task force, everyone in the courtroom was sympathetic and cooperative—the court attendants, the stenographers, the judge's clerks. And there I sat for seven weeks, having no faith in justice, but having faith in the "majestic justice of God."

Before the trial had even begun, Morris Emanuel, who had dedicated his recent years to "getting" me, told Ed Williams how much he hated me. Members of the press told me, individually and collectively, that their newspapers had instructed them to slant their articles against me. But as the trial went on, one day Morris Emanuel came to Ed Williams and said, "I have always hated this guy, but now I am beginning to like him." One by one, members of the press admitted likewise.

All through the early days of the trial, when the government was presenting its case, every form of ridicule and vilification was printed on the front pages of the New York City press. But when Ed Williams began to turn events in our favor, the truths he brought out were buried on the back pages. A reporter for one of our top New York dailies told Ed Williams that he had personally gone to the editor and demanded that the Powell side of the story receive the same coverage that the anti-Powell had. And sure enough, the next morning the facts were on page one.

My lawyer-of-record was Harrison Jackson, lifelong friend and lawyer of the Abyssinian Baptist Church. Ed Williams' assistant was Vincent Fuller, young, dedicated, brilliant, who in three weeks of analyzing the government's records had unearthed more truths than had seven Internal Revenue agents and five lawyers working on these same records with their vast staffs over a period of years.

We lived and breathed that case. We did everything but sleep together on it. From early in the morning when I picked them up until late in the evening we were together. This was our life. The toll began to take its effect on Ed and Vince. Vince was taking bicarbonate of soda because his stomach was tied in knots. One of my doctors prescribed sleeping pills for them. One night as we were discussing the case in Ed's apartment, I saw him suddenly collapse and turn gray in the face. I rushed to him, helped him to his bedroom, made him go to bed, and said, "Vince and I will work on this. You go on and sleep now, and see if you can get yourself together for tomorrow morning." In ten minutes he was up, charging out of the door, yelling, "What are you guys talking about?" He had slept all of seven or eight minutes.

I kept people from disturbing them during lunch, which we had at a little café across Columbus Square behind the courthouse. I would permit neither friends nor the curious to interrupt them. Sometimes I had to make sure they went to bed. Suddenly it dawned on me that here I was standing the trial of my life, and I was taking care of them. We have had many laughs over this since then.

As for me, I was in the best shape. I went into training deliberately, as I had not done since my days of athletics in high school and college. I was in bed every single night at ten o'clock, sleeping the sleep of the just, knocking out around ten hours nightly. In the morning I would dress carefully in one of my dark suits, white shirt, white collar, black tie, black shoes, and black homburg. I gained eleven pounds during the seven weeks of the case.

The trial was a valuable experience in my personal life because I had never been in a courtroom before except as a character witness. As I sat there and objectively watched for the first time what is called "justice" in the United States of America, I did not believe it was possible for men to take the stand under oath and utter obvious untruths. John Reddington, a member of our Foreign Service, testified that all the time I was in London, even though I came to the American Embassy "every day," I was not there on official business. But when confronted with a bill for telegrams to Members of Parliament which he had paid and for which I had reimbursed him, he had to admit that perhaps I did conduct some business while there.

As I looked at the jurors one by one and tried to analyze them, I wondered how it was possible that any human being—in this prejudiced and lynch-murder atmosphere created by the metropolitan press and the knowledge of the years and money which had been spent by the United States government on trying to get evidence against me—could maintain any objectivity. But I raised my eyes and looked above them through the high windows to the blue sky and I knew that there was someone else in that courtroom—someone else in addition to the loyal and curious, the press, and the government . . . someone else above even Judge Bryan. Churches all over town began to hold prayer meetings for justice. In my own church a group of women met together every day at noon and prayed for one hour that God's will be done, not man's.

In keeping with the ethics involved, I shall not comment on the conduct of my trial except to say that my defense attorney, Edward Bennett Williams, performed a dedicated and masterful service for which I shall ever be grateful; that Judge Frederick Van Pelt Bryan was a symbol of the very best in American jurisprudence; and that the jury voted its convictions, as they saw them, ten to two for acquittal.

For the sake, however, of whatever history may be involved, I do present hereinafter my own Bill of Particulars, as extracted, as near verbatim as possible, from my attorney's summation. The following items were taken from the printed minutes of the trial. Many of these items never found their way into the newspapers and will be revealing to the reader.

BILL OF PARTICULARS
By Adam C. Powell

1. The indictment charged that true net income of Hazel Scott Powell was $9181.08, and that she reported $3815.31, for a difference of $5365.77 net deficiency. (Based on Emanuel's testimony to Grand Jury on May 6, 1958—see note 10.)

2. Emanuel told Grand Jury that Hazel received gross income of $54,000 in 1951. During trial, the government's total claim amounted to

$49,362.94, or over $200 more than the Grand Jury was told by the government that Hazel reported. (The return disclosed that $49,976.23 was reported—see note 6.)

3. Both of the above statements to Grand Jury were in error.

4. Emanuel told Grand Jury that due to errors the return showed a duplication of $5935.66. During trial (see notes 10, 11, and 12) government did not contradict revelations by Williams that the real amount of duplication was $12,222.11. This means that there were $6286.45 in duplications about which indicting Grand Jury was not told.

5. Seventeen months after investigation began six trained government accountants, five lawyers, with all records available to them, failed to report to the Grand Jury through the Internal Revenue Agent-in-Charge, Emanuel, about the $6286.45 worth of duplications of income, an amount greater than the total unreported net income charged in the indictment.

6. The Grand Jury was told, on April 16, 1956, that Adam C. Powell reported for Hazel Scott Powell only $45,800 for 1951, while the return itself, introduced as evidence at trial, showed a written declaration of $49,076.36 on the face of return (see note 2).

7. On April 22, 1956, the government told the Grand Jury that Hazel Scott Powell's gross income was about $60,000 (see notes 2 and 6).

8. On May 6, 1956, two days before the indictment, Emanuel told Grand Jury that Hazel Scott Powell's income from Israel was $7233.66. In trial, government never claimed more than $1000 was received by Hazel Scott Powell from Israel. This was an admitted error of $6233.66.

9. During trial, Emanuel, under oath, testified as follows on the above error:

MR. WILLIAMS: Then the Grand Jury did not have the benefit of complete and accurate investigation from you, is that right?

MR. EMANUEL: You make that sound a little difficult, Mr. Williams.

JUDGE: All right, that is a question and it requires an answer, Mr. Emanuel. Did it or did it not?

MR. EMANUEL: It received whatever information our investigation had developed up to that point.

MR. WILLIAMS: And you know now, do you not, Mr. Emanuel, on April Fool's Day, 1960, that that was not accurate information?

MR. EMANUEL: That's correct.

MR. WILLIAMS: You were wrong, weren't you?

MR. EMANUEL: I was wrong in a lot of things at that time. (*A murmur runs through the courtroom and it takes the judge a while to get order. Jurors are visibly disturbed.*)

10. In April of 1959 United States Attorney Christy filed memorandum in court in which his Bill of Particulars was based on:

"The government expects to prove that Hazel Scott Powell's total receipts from business or profession in 1951 exceeded the figure reflected on the tax return by the amount of net income alleged in the indictment."

In effect, he said, "We are going to prove that she made $5365.77 more in gross income than she reported." He said this despite the fact that records in his possession for over two years indicated that there was MORE than this amount nullified by duplication, or overstatement, in gross income (see note 4).

11. The $12,222.11 in duplicated income (see note 4) came about because of errors of Hattie Dodson, Adam C. Powell's secretary, and James Johnson, hired to work on 1951 return. Both reported the same income from engagements TWICE.

12. Despite errors of duplication that the government discovered, they never told either Dodson, Johnson, or Adam C. Powell of these errors —although there were several conferences with Dodson and Johnson prior to trial.

13. December, 1959, the government came into court and changed the nature of case from understatement of income to challenge of deductions, through an amended Bill of Particulars.

14. Elementary procedure of challenge of deductions is that person is called in and deductions are gone over. At worst, a civil suit is started by government.

15. AT NO TIME did the government call in either Adam C. Powell or Hazel Scott Powell to discuss collection on 1951 return, despite fact that every year prior to 1951 and every year since 1951 the Internal Revenue Department [sic] has held such discussions.

16. *National Review* group called in members of Grand Jury and held rump meeting in Commodore Hotel, urging them to reopen Powell Case. Paul Williams had said that, at best, government had "civil case."

17. United States charge against Adam C. Powell is that he violated Section 3793(b) of Title 26 of the Internal Revenue Code, a section which makes it a felony to assist, procure, counsel, or advise in the preparation of a false or fraudulent return, claim, or affidavit in connection with the Internal Revenue Code.

Adam C. Powell never "worked" return of 1951, but turned matter over to Dodson and hired Johnson, tax attorney, at cost of $500. Adam C. Powell's own return was never in question.

18. Testimony on April 22, 1958, by Morris Emanuel before the Grand Jury showed that the government did not challenge or consider any fraud in the deductions on Hazel Scott Powell's return of 1951. Before the Grand Jury:

MR. EMANUEL: Now actually the tax returns disclose a deduction of $9800 on Mrs. Powell's return and a deduction of $5400 on Mr. Powell's return for a total of $15,200. Now on our theory that need not be an overstatement of the deduction. However, in my recommendation I did not consider the item of $9800 on Mrs. Powell's return as a possible fraud item.

19. In the course of the trial the government admitted that $4274.48 more in expenses overseas were properly deductible by Hazel Scott Powell on the 1951 return, but that no claim for this extra amount was made by Hazel Scott Powell.

At page 2057 of the trial record, Attorney Williams handed Mr. Emanuel, then on the witness stand, an exhibit marked as Defendant's Exhibit H and asked him to direct his attention to a figure to see whether it refreshed his recollection that the exact computation of the expenses incurred but not deducted which were properly deductible was $4274.48 and his answer was, "Certainly it would."

20. Over and against the charge that Adam Clayton Powell aided and abetted in preparing a false return, is the uncontrovertible fact of law that where a taxpayer acts in good faith on the advice of his attorney, even if such advice is incorrect, as a matter of law, the taxpayer is entitled to act upon it if he has given all the facts to his attorney in good faith.

Adam C. Powell hired Attorney James Johnson, a tax counsel and former Collector of Internal Revenue for Manhattan for eight years. Mr. Johnson was paid $500 to prepare the 1951 Hazel Scott Powell return. Adam C. Powell never saw Johnson in person, but sent along with Mrs. Hattie Dodson, his secretary, a spread sheet upon which were indicated several matters in doubt which Mr. Johnson was to clear up from a legal standpoint. Expert that he was, even Mr. Johnson, it was brought out in the trial, made a $3200 error against Hazel Scott Powell on the complicated return.

21. The 1951 return was a most complex one. It involved income and deductions of two persons. It involved a fifty-one-day professional tour of the United States made by Hazel Scott Powell and a maid,

and a tour of Europe made by Adam C. Powell, Hazel Scott Powell, son Skipper, and a maid, where foreign rates of exchange, foreign taxes, and blocked currency had to be computed. It involved deductions for travel, publicity, and other items usual in the case of a professional entertainer, whose expenses are always extremely high.

22. In addition to these complexities, the 1951 return was prepared in a matter of a few days in order to meet the filing deadline. (Mrs. Powell was out of the city on tour.)

23. In answer to any willfulness which must be present in fraud, in addition to the foregoing facts, the following is relevant:

    (1) The income was overstated on the 1951 return.

    (2) No money in tax was owed on the return.

    (3) $1000 in tax credit, paid in taxes overseas, was not claimed.

    (4) $317 in tax credit, due to an overpayment on the 1950 return, was not claimed in 1951, despite a letter from Internal Revenue on August 1, 1951, advising of same.

24. In the middle of 1956, before the government began subpoena of records and hearing evidence, Adam C. Powell asked Internal Revenue if he could discuss the tax situation with an agent.

    While the interview never occurred, shortly after the Adam C. Powell request, the United States Department of Justice, on official stationery, sent out a letter to every Negro college and every Negro newspaper, stating that a Grand Jury investigation of Adam C. Powell was under way and asking information concerning his speeches for pay.

25. In answer to the above letter written by the United States Department of Justice, Attorney Williams told the Court and jury the following:

"I ask you if they were conducting an investigation into his taxes or if they were waging a political vendetta designed to destroy him?

"I ask you if he was receiving from an agency of his government equal justice under law, or if he was not being the victim of the worst political vendetta engineered by an agency of the government in modern history?"

Whereupon, the following colloquy took place, following an objection by the prosecuting attorney:

MR. ROBSON: If Your Honor please, I object to this. There is not the slightest bit of evidence to warrant Mr. Williams' accusations before this jury and I object to them vigorously. They reflect on me and every member of my staff. I may say that they are lies.

MR. WILLIAMS: I stand on the record. I say, if the Court please, ladies and
gentlemen of the jury, that if these letters were designed
to elicit information helpful to the tax investigation, they
could have been sent to other than Negro papers and
other than Negro schools.

And I say that it was wrong. I repeat, it was wrong. I
believe it was indecent. . . . I say it was wrong because
he had offered to come in and give such information to
the Service, and they didn't want his answers. Rather,
they wanted to tell the papers and the schools that a
Grand Jury was sitting on it.

26. Mr. Williams' closing remarks in his summation were as follows:
"Five years from now this case will have faded into the dimmest
recesses of your minds. It will be a blurred memory. It will be just
a paragraph in one chapter of your lives. His Honor will have gone
on and tried scores of other cases, and so, too, will the prosecutor.
But for this defendant what you do—and this is true of any defendant
—what you do is the most important thing in his life, and it has been
a full life.

"I say to you that all of the dreams and the hopes and the aspira-
tions of over a half century hang on your verdict. I say that. I know
it is true.

"I know that this defendant has been a loud and forceful voice for
his people on a great domestic moral issue in our country. I know that
he has spoken in anger, perhaps in the anger of a soul that feels the
frustrations of being morally and mentally qualified for the ministry
and for the well of Congress, but not to buy meals and lodgings, as
the evidence showed here one day, in some parts of the country.

"And I suppose he has made enemies. I suppose they are many,
and they may be strong and powerful. But I ask of you one thing.
I ask you to consider whether you believe really and truly that there
is behind his trial the charge, recklessly and carelessly put together
in this indictment, or whether he is on trial for political liquidation.

"I say if you believe the latter, then by your verdict you should give
thundering notice, a thundering notice that will reverberate through
the corridors of this courthouse that there is no room for political
trials in this land, and that the indictment is no substitute for the
ballot, and that every man, whoever he may be, whatever his cause,
whatever his beliefs, whatever his heritage, whatever his color, is
entitled under our system to equal justice under law.

"I ask no more for this man."

The case went on for several weeks, longer than it should have, because eight of the jurors were Jewish and wanted to be home for Passover, and those of us who were Christians wanted to be home for Good Friday. But finally, Ed brought our part to a close with his plea: ". . . by your verdict you should give thundering notice that there is no room for political trials in this land, and that the indictment is no substitute for the ballot. . . ."

Now came Judge Bryan's charge. On April 7 two of the three counts had been dismissed by the Court—the personal one involving my own income tax and the one involving my wife's tax. These were dismissed by the Judge on the grounds that there was no evidence. The only count that remained was whether there was any intent to defraud. The charge was made. The jury went out.

After they had stayed out a couple of hours the press came to me with questions: "What's happening? We've been covering this every day and they should have come right back in with a verdict."

I told them I knew nothing. Then the rumors began to fly as the suspense increased and the hours stretched into days. Finally, the jury had to be discharged after they told Judge Bryan twice that they could not reach a verdict. The foreman of the jury told the press that the jury was equally divided, six to six. One of the jurors leaving the courthouse was asked by Norma Abrams of the *Daily News* whether this was true. She said it was not and that the vote was ten to two to acquit me.

One night in the rain on Seventh Avenue, weeks later, I bumped into another juror. I introduced myself and she told me the whole story that night. She said that at one point the vote was eleven to one, but there was one person who held out against me, who had indicated from the very beginning of the trial before any evidence had been introduced that he thought I was guilty.

That last night as we rolled away from Foley Square for the final time, with the two counts having been dismissed by Judge Bryan on the motion of Ed Williams and with the knowledge that the jury had voted ten to two for acquittal on the third, Ed was a little crestfallen. He knew we should have won. As for me, I had more faith in my fellow man than ever before. I realized that if at least ten of the twelve people were able to maintain their objectivity in a climate of prejudice, hatred, and vilification, lies and abuse, with the hundreds of thousands of dollars which had been spent to conduct the case against me, it meant that there was justice in the United States

as long as you could get men and women possessing objectivity. Warren
Olney III, former chief of the Criminal Division of the Department of
Justice, once said in *Life* magazine that justice in the United States depends upon where you are tried, whom you know, and who you are. He was
probably right, but it works both ways.

On April 13, 1961, the wheels of justice turned full circle and my case
was dismissed in Federal Court on a motion by the government, made by
the very same United States Attorney, Morton S. Robson, who had headed
the prosecution. And, to quote *The New York Times* of April 14: "Officials
in the United States Attorney's office had always maintained that the case
against Mr. Powell was 'weak.' " I will add little—for the act of the dis-
missal speaks for itself—except to repeat and underline: ". . . *had always
maintained* . . ."! This was the first time—three years later—that either the
American public or my lawyers or myself were made aware of this admission.

It is impossible to estimate precisely how much the government spent
on this case. Figures given to me by various members of the press varied
from $200,000 to $400,000. Edwin Murray, writing in the *Daily News* on
March 16, said, "It is outrageous to think that our government would spend
$100,000 to prosecute a man like Powell for $3000. There must be something more than that behind this unwarranted scheme." Mr. Murray may
have been right concerning his letter but as for the amount, he was way
off. First, there were seven government lawyers connected with the case:
Paul Williams, Christy, Miller, Boland, Gilchrist, Robson, and Gordon.
Then there were seven Internal Revenue agents working full time: Morris
Emanuel, the chief, Frischman, Kararagheusian, Ellison, Walker, and two
others whose names I never could find out. I also saw many people in the
courtroom who I then learned were on the government payroll. They were
familiar faces—I had seen them in Europe, the West Indies, and many
cities in the United States—and now I knew they were agents who had
been trailing me for years. Beyond all these, there were the various se-
cretarial staffs.

In addition, witnesses were brought in from every country in Europe,
including Israel, where my wife had toured. Each witness averaged over
$1000 in expenses to the United States government. When some of them
refused to come, like Harry Foster of England, or Felix Marouani of
France, our government was able to get the internal revenue department
of their governments to go with our representative to their offices and
demand that they come to New York and testify or they would be in trouble

in their own country. Only one government refused to cooperate, and that was Denmark. The concert impresario of Denmark refused to come, the Danish government refused to force him, and the Danish press approved of his decision with big headlines that were sent to me by the editors of the Copenhagen newspapers.

Witnesses from Europe testified how much the U.S. government was paying them per day to appear in New York City. The amount of money the government was paying them per day in New York was more than the Department of Justice was willing to allow my wife and myself per day while we were traveling on business in Europe during those years in question. The woman who covered for the press of India showed me her first cable: "The United States government could have taken the money it is spending on the Powell case and used it to set up scholarships for Indians that would have done some permanent good."

I learned from that case that unless certain radical changes are made by Congress and all those agencies of the government that are directly involved in Federal cases, there is not much chance for the average American citizen to receive justice in the Federal courthouses of America.

In the first place, the minutes of my trial alone cost over $4000. The average person does not have the money to pay for these vitally necessary minutes. Without them, my lawyers would not have been able to construct, day by day, the kind of case they did. The court stenographers are paid handsome salaries by our government for their services, yet you can obtain the minutes only by paying these government employees eighty-six cents a page. This money goes right into their own pockets. And each page contains not more than a hundred to a hundred and fifty words. I believe it should be mandatory that the minutes of all trials be given free to all defendants. Otherwise, a poor man will never have anything more than a poor case for his lawyers to present.

Second, I believe it should be mandatory that there be no Grand Jury investigations of any taxpayer before the proper government official sits down with the taxpayer and his representative to go over the income-tax returns in question. While my case was exceptional, nevertheless it did happen. And if the government of the United States could do this to me, a clergyman and a Congressman, what chance would John Doe have? It should be mandatory that all American citizens be given the same treatment by the Internal Revenue Service in the discussion of their tax returns.

Third, the average American citizen is not financially able to hire a lawyer of the caliber of Edward Bennett Williams. In fact, not many lawyers are available for acting in criminal cases. I believe that the necessary legislation should be enacted whereby $10,000 is appropriated by Congress for every criminal case that comes before the Department of Justice in which the person charged with the crime can prove that he is not financially able to hire a lawyer. While $10,000 will not hire an Edward Bennett Williams, it most assuredly will give some poor person a better lawyer than he could retain without it. Not a single person of wealth has been executed under capital punishment in many years and, as Edward Bennett Williams asked in one of his articles recently, "When are we going to make available the justice to the indigent that the wealthy are now able to receive?"

Fourth, I believe it is imperative that a law be passed whereby all present tax mills are abolished. No one who is not Federally licensed should be allowed to set up a business to provide help in the preparation of income-tax returns. Furthermore, I believe that all those who fill out such reports should be equally liable in the advent that there is an indictment. My income-tax report involved foreign currency, blocked currency, rise and fall of value, black market, official market, free market—all highly technical questions I know nothing about and concerning which even the instructions of the Internal Revenue Service are vague or at variance. I procured the best services possible to help on these cases. The person who prepared the return testified on the stand to the amazing mistakes that had been made, and yet because of these mistakes, I was the one who went to trial. This system is not just. It must be changed.

Fifth, the system of selecting jurors, in New York City particularly, where there is obvious discrimination, should be vigorously explored by an official committee from Congress. Several outstanding lawyers came to me during the trial and said they would give their services free of charge to break up the rotten system that now exists in the Federal Court in the Southern District of New York. There are more Negroes on jury panels in Southern cities, including Washington, D.C., than in the Federal Court in Foley Square.

Finally, and no legislation can do anything about this, the great, free, and responsible press should seriously examine its own conscience. I would fight to the end against any legislation to stifle the expression of opinion, but I do believe that the press holds a responsibility to the American people to recapture the sense of justice and fair play, and to write from the view that every man is innocent until proven guilty.

14

Castro
and Cuba

"The President pro tem of Cuba would like to see you." This was a phone message I received in February, 1958. The next day I had the first of a series of meetings with Dr. Manuel Urrutia, provisional President of Cuba; Raoúl Chibas, the provisional Treasurer of Cuba; and Dr. Mario Llerena, a Protestant clergyman from Havana who was director of the entire Fidel Castro movement in the Western Hemisphere. At the first conference, held in my New York City office, I found Dr. Urrutia to be a quiet, middle-aged, heavy-set individual, who looked like what he was— a country judge. Chibas was keen, alert, always ablaze with the abundant energy of a revolutionary. Dr. Llerena was the brains—a former professor at Duke University and a graduate of Princeton, he knew his way around. He was dedicated to the cause and brought to it the touch it needed.

Dr. Llerena said to me, "If you will help us, anything you want in Cuba will be yours. Dr. Castro personally talked to me about you when I was in the Sierra Maestra Mountains last month, and he said, 'That's the man to get on our side.' You are in the presence now of the men who will be the President and Treasurer of Cuba. I, myself, have been promised an ambassadorship either to the United States or to the United Nations."

I said, "I don't want anything from you, but what can I do to help the people of Cuba?"

Chibas replied, "Stop the killing of Cubans with American guns."

"But where can I get the facts?" I asked.

Urrutia and Llerena answered together, "We'll get them for you."

On March 20, 1958, I took the Floor of Congress to talk about what the United States was doing in Cuba: "The United States is a partner with the dictator of Cuba, Fulgencio Batista, in the killing of close to four thousand Cubans so far, and it is time we should get out, and get out at once. We not only have been and are supplying arms to Batista, but we have a military mission established with Cuba, actively assisting the Cuban Army. There should be immediate stoppage of the flow of arms and ammunition from this country, and there should be immediate withdrawal of the mission."

I listed in exact detail the contracts between our government and Cuba, contracts 551 through 592, all specifying the exact number of rifles, millimeter grenades, millimeter rockets, mortars, howitzer artillery, machine guns, cartridges, hand grenades, armored cars, and tanks that we had sent Cuba in 1957 and 1958. I also revealed the existence of the United States Air Force contract with the Cuban Air Force, contract number 64, under which we shipped approximately $350,000 worth of bombs in October of 1957, as well as contracts 65 and 66 under which the United States Navy was giving Cuba three hundred 5-inch rockets and twenty-five thousand 20-millimeter caps. The rockets had already been delivered and the twenty-five thousand caps were in the process of shipment. And, finally, I listed contract 6400, under which the United States Navy was then shipping to Cuba fifty magazines for 20-millimeter guns.

I also enumerated the requests of the Batista government for more equipment, automatics, 75-millimeter guns, 60-millimeter mortars, .50-caliber machine guns, six thousand United States caliber-.30 M-1 rifles, and one million .30-caliber caps for rocket launchers.

Where did I get these statistics? From Fidel Castro himself. His undercover agents "borrowed" the documents from the files of Batista's government, photographed them, and sent them to Castro, who forwarded them to me in Washington. Officials of our government pleaded with me not to put this confidential information into the *Congressional Record*. "I will refrain from doing so," I said, "if you will stop the flow of all other arms to Batista." This they would not do, but *within forty-eight hours* after I revealed these facts, it was announced that the flow of arms from the United States to Batista had been stopped.

Batista's record is well known. He came to power in 1933 as a sergeant, staging his first military coup d'état on September 4 during the revolution that overthrew the dictator Machado. After four months of civilian provisional government, he overthrew the elected President, Grau San Martín, and became Cuba's strong man. Batista ruled the country for eleven years, relinquishing power in 1944 after a constitutional election, but in 1952 he went back to Cuba to run for the Presidency. The election was to be held on June 3, and when it became obvious that he did not have the slightest chance of winning, his old military buddies joined with him and on March 10, 1952, eighty days before the scheduled election, he was swept into power. From that day on he reigned supreme as one of the bloodiest and most corrupt tyrants in all Latin American history. He abolished all civil liberties and individual rights. His secret police and armed forces assassinated more than four thousand Cubans.

Our government went right along with Batista up to the end. With the arms that we sold to the Batista regime under the Rio Treaty, we contributed to the slaughter of native Cubans.

What is the Rio Treaty? The Rio Treaty is a treaty we signed with our Latin American neighbors whereby we sell them military equipment for "hemispheric defense." This treaty has been used for no purpose whatsoever except to enable dictators to obtain enough arms to subjugate their own people.

We sent these dictators American military missions under the terms of the military defense treaty. Congress stated that such a mission is supposed to instruct armed forces in the event of "continental aggression." As Dr. Llerena wrote to me, "If Batista's armed forces under the American military mission have been unable to wipe out Castro's guerrillas in a little province in Cuba, Oriente, what could they do in the presence of a mighty invader?"

Our foreign policy in this hemisphere was a joke. Our relationships with our back-door neighbors in Latin America was one of continual tragedy. During all the time that Batista was in power, we not only sold him all the arms he needed but we supported him diplomatically and even increased his sugar quota.

After my speech on the Floor of Congress on March 29 and after the flow of arms to Cuba had supposedly been stopped on March 22, Batista planned to send two gunmen, Miguel Sotolongo and Juan de Dios Soloiziano, to the United States to assassinate Dr. Llerena. When I learned that these two men were applying for visas to the United States at the American Embassy in Havana, I addressed Congress on April 1, had their names put in the *Congressional Record,* and demanded that the Department of State refuse to allow them entry.

On March 27 I received a letter from thirty members of the Congress of Cuba in exile in Miami, led by the former president of their House of Representatives, Dr. Lincoln Rodon. In their letter they pointed out that the entire Roman Catholic hierarchy of Cuba had asked Batista to step aside; that the national associations of professional men, the Federation of Youth, the council of churches, the Masons, the women's club, Lions Club, and eighteen other national organizations had signed a petition asking Batista to resign.

But our policy of cooperation continued. The flow of all arms was to have ceased on March 22. On May 5 Dr. Llerena wired me from Caracas saying that the United States government had violated its open statement and had just gratuitously furnished Batista's Air Force with three hundred rockets from our own United States naval base at Guantanamo. Immediately, I wrote to Mr. William McComber, the Assistant Secretary of State for Congressional Relations, protesting this. It took Mr. McComber three weeks to reply to my letter, three weeks to work out another excuse for helping another dictator, even after the American people had been informed that they would no longer do this. On May 28 I received an official letter from the Department of State: "I can assure you that this Government has not made a grant to Cuba of any rockets—the United States Navy recently effected an exchange of 300 rocket heads which had previously been purchased by the Cuban Government." In other words, we were still doing business with Batista, still lying to the American public, and still undermining all the United States prestige in Latin America.

Here let me recall some further duplicity of our State Department. On March 12 Assistant Secretary of State McComber wrote to Congressmen Charles O. Porter of Oregon that he could not comply with his request for the list of arms the United States had given and was giving to Batista because the list was "classified." Yet I had that list in my hands at that very time. The reason he could not give Porter the list was that he knew the State Department had violated the law of Congress. In Section 105, Subsection B, Part IV of the Mutual Security Act and the Mutual Assistance

Agreement with Cuba, we, the members of Congress, had clearly specified that arms "may be used only in implementation of defense plans agreed upon by the United States and Cuba, under which Cuba participates in missions important to the defense of the Western Hemisphere." Growing out of that same law, the Army Missions Agreement of August 28, 1951, clearly stipulated that the agreement would be subject to cancellation at the initiative of the government of the United States at any time when the United States found that the government of Cuba was involved in *internal* hostilities. No wonder the Executive branch of our government did everything it could to stop me from proclaiming the truth in 1958.

But I would not be silenced. I took the Floor again to point out to Congress that as late as November, 1957, the United States government bestowed one of its highest military decorations on the chief of the Cuban Air Force, directly after he personally had led the bombardment of an open city, Cienfuegos, with American planes and ammunition. I asked why, but never received a reply.

Upon direct instructions from the Department of State, our last Ambassador to Batista, Earl Smith, openly sided with Batista. On March 5, 1958, the Assistant Secretary of State in charge of Latin American Affairs, R. R. Rubottom, testified before the Senate Foreign Relations Committee: "The Cuban government is simply using the military equipment at its disposal to beat back mobs and insurrection." Since the Assistant Secretary of State had so testified, why, then, did our government continue in open defiance of Congressional law and American moral opinion? It did so because the men running our State Department thought they could get away with it. It did so because those men did not think anyone would be able to obtain the secret list that would prove that our government was officially in the business of merchandising death.

Finally, on January 1, 1959, the 26th of July Movement led by Fidel Castro triumphed. Dr. Urrutia was installed as the President of Cuba, and Raoúl Chibas as the Treasurer. I was shocked, however, to learn that Dr. Llerena had been completely ignored. This was the man who had served, by the personal appointment of Fidel Castro, as the head of the forces for the 26th of July Movement in all parts of the world outside of Cuba, who had raised millions of dollars for the revolutionary cause, and who had kept the underground together.

I was immediately asked to see what I could do to get United States recognition of Cuba. On January 4 I cabled Castro that I was demanding immediate recognition and aid for his government.

On January 5 I requested that our government recognize the Castro government; second, that it offer financial assistance; third, that it refuse Batista asylum in the United States; and fourth, that Ambassador Earl Smith be recalled. By January 10 the State Department had acceded to all four of my requests.

I decided to go to Havana and announced my intention on the Floor of Congress during an open discussion on January 15, 1959. I pointed out to Congressman Gordon H. Scherer of Ohio, who led the discussion, the difference between the 20,000 killings that took place under Batista—without trials and under strict censorship—and the executions that had taken place only after trial in the presence of the free press. Congressman Springer of Illinois recommended that the trial of people who were arrested be delayed for thirty days and that they should be tried in a civilian court, and I agreed with him.

What was Havana like in January of 1959? It was a place of chaos, a continuing fiesta. Every day was a Mardi Gras and people were dancing in the streets. I was met by a detail of *Barbudos*—"the unshaven"—carrying machine guns of all types. Most of them were country boys who had fought their way down from Oriente Province, the womb of all revolutions of Cuba. One gun-carrying *Barbudo* was only thirteen years old.

I had gone to Cuba at my own expense, but as soon as I arrived an official of the government told me that I was to be their guest and he escorted me to the Havana Riviera Hotel, where I was ensconced in a beautiful suite looking out over the Caribbean waters and a public park that Batista, in one of his last acts, had sold to a private investor.

The next morning I saw Fidel. He is tall, well built, with the eyes of a dreamer and the fire of fanaticism. Instinctively I knew that this fanaticism could make him a messiah or a menace. He was a man of wealth, born of an upper-class family from Spain, well educated, with a doctor's degree in Law. He had no sense of organization. I was also disturbed by the fact that his brother, Raúl, seemed always to be sneaking around. Much smaller than Fidel, his tiny, glittering eyes somehow gave me the impression of a rat.

I conferred with Dr. Castro at the Hilton Hotel for more than two hours, saw him several times in the midst of that tremendously busy period, stood beside him as he addressed a million people, and sat next to him at his international press conference. When I complained to him about the executions that were troubling the American public, his answer was: "One single execution of an innocent man would destroy the entire 26th of July Movement."

I told him, "Well, I will not attend any of the public trials, although you've invited me, because I do not believe my presence would be of any value to the government of Cuba or to myself. I am against the spectacle of the trials and I will not go."

Fidel looked at me and said, "I am not going either." Apparently by that time he had come to realize the mistake of holding the trials in a public arena and before television cameras. "At first I wanted to do it this way," he explained, "because I wanted the world and my countrymen to see that these trials were conducted fairly, but now I know you are right." On the very next day Fidel canceled the trials in the arena and stopped all executions.

In order to understand those trials and his defense of them, one must understand the Latin mentality. The trials were publicly backed by the Roman Catholic bishops of Cuba, by leaders of the Protestant churches, and even, according to *Time* magazine, which was against the Fidel movement, "by overwhelming public opinion." The principle of justice in Cuba and in most Latin American countries is *"Dos males hacen un bién,"* or, "Two wrongs make a right."

While in Cuba I learned that former Ambassador Earl Smith had been openly anti-Batista until a deal was made with the Freeport Sulphur company concerning the Moa Bay Nickel Mine. This was entirely a venture of United States capitalists. The sums of money involved in the corporations represented tremendous investments of big men in the Republican Party. When this deal was made with Batista, Earl Smith became anti-Castro overnight.

I asked Castro, "What about the contracts and agreements which Batista made with American businessmen, American companies, and our government?" He said, "We will renegotiate all contracts and concessions with the United States and other foreign governments. We will void those which are onerous to our government."

But in time the victorious Castro became increasingly embittered and disillusioned by the attacks being made upon him in the American press. In the beginning he wanted to be friendly with our government. I state here and now, without equivocation, that it was the American press more than any other single group that turned Castro against the United States. Nearly all of our newsmen had been bought and paid for by the Batista forces.

Even after Batista's defeat some of them continued to receive money. As nearly every newspaper in the United States continued to splash stories on page one criticising Castro, the Chicago *Sun-Times'* executive editor, Larry Fanning, spoke up and he spoke up as one who was not a supporter of Castro: "No one is saying that the guys who went down there can be bought, but somehow the context is all wrong for a newspaperman. The implication is that you are being bought, whether or not that is true. We were completely misled before Castro and we're hoping the copy we're getting now is fair." And then he added a revealing detail: "The night before Batista fled and his government collapsed and Castro won, both the United Press International and the Associated Press sent out word on their teletype machines that the Castro forces had been crushed."

I saw the Foreign Editor of *Look* magazine, Bill Attwood, at the Havana Riviera Hotel swimming pool. He said, "When the Hungarian Freedom Fighters were killing in 1956, they were praised by everybody. But Castro does the same thing and he's cursed. Nothing could have prevented riots against the Batista people except the executions."

Herbert L. Matthews of *The New York Times*, one of the world's outstanding newsmen, stated, "In all my thirty-six years of newspaper work I have never seen a worse job of journalism than the coverage of the Cuban revolution during the last three weeks. All you saw in most papers was how many people Castro shot. The real picture of a country under Batista's brutal dictatorship was not made clear."

Castro told me many times that he just could not understand the American press. He said, "I thought your American land was a land of fairness and justice. I thought you would be interested in getting rid of a dictator. People who attack me now never attacked Batista, and are not even now attacking Trujillo. Havana is filled with American newspapermen here at the invitation of my government, all their expenses paid, no censorship. This could have never happened under Batista. Yet, despite this, they are sending out the worst kind of reports and not a word concerning the record of the twenty thousand that Batista killed and maimed. I don't care what they write—my political philosophy is full democratic rights for Cuba and I am going to have the same things for the Cuban people that the people of the United States have, and I am going to demand complete equality of my country with the United States." Then he volunteered this astounding statement: "We will never follow any Communist force and if any attack is made against us, we believe that the United States will help us because we are not Communists, but I still can't understand the American press." And as the press continued to play up the trials held under the Castro regime and to ignore the assassinations under Batista, Fidel became increasingly bitter, and the leaders of Cuba with him.

Early in my visit to Cuba I spoke at the University Methodist Church, as a guest of the Council of Churches in Havana, to about thirty-five leading Protestant clergymen. Nearly all of them had been educated in the United States and, with only one or two exceptions, were members of the underground 26th of July Movement. They were so aroused over the attitude of the American press that spontaneously, without any word from me and even before I spoke, they voted to send preaching missions to the United States to tell the truth. The President of that conference told me, "During the eighteen years of the dictator Batista, he never had in his armed forces a single Catholic or Protestant chaplain. Dr. Castro has had chaplains with him from the very beginning and here are some clergymen who actually participated side by side with the men of the 26th of July Movement. There is complete loyalty and dedication of the people to the regime. Look at the streets of Havana. There rides Dr. Castro without any protection in an open car, and the people have imposed upon themselves a tremendous self-discipline. Why can't the American press state the truth?"

The following week I stood side by side with Fidel as a million people packed one of the plazas all the way down to the waterfront and overflowed into every side street. As I left I walked through the crowd. There was not a single incident; not a single person was drunk. I cannot picture a crowd of a million people in the United States, but if there ever were to be one, there would be some kind of an incident. The Cuban people were so proud of what was happening that even the criminals had given up their pursuits. At the end of the first month of the Castro regime, in a city of a million and a half people, there had been only one case of thievery.

Castro met the press for the first time at his conference in the supper club of the Havana Riviera Hotel. Members of the press from all over the world were there at his expense. They asked as many questions as they wanted. For four hours he stood there, answering everyone openly, indicating his initial honesty. After the conference was over I took him up to the penthouse of the hotel with just a few of his close people and my friends; there were about twenty of us altogether. He threw his arm around me and said, "You're the kind of man who should be the President of the United

States. Why don't you go out and get the nomination? If you do, I'll come to America and campaign for you. If we had a man like you as President, then our country would be treated fairly."

We talked for a while longer, then, pensively, he looked out the window of the penthouse. Not really addressing me, though I was the only one nearby, he said, "I am not the master of my destiny. I renounce any interest of power or money. I need neither, but I am not the master of my destiny."

"But, Dr. Castro," I asked, "why don't you take over a position in the government? It would strengthen the Movement."

He looked at me and placed his hand almost gently on my shoulder and said, "I am so tired. I haven't been able to read in two years. I would like to just rest and read and write poetry now." Then he looked out the window again and repeated once again, "I am not the master of my destiny."

During my stay in Havana I met nearly every member of the Cuban Cabinet. I could sense the increasing bitterness toward America owing to the bad press Cuba was receiving. The Prime Minister, J. Miro Cardona, wrote me after my first visit: "My closing remarks must necessarily be in appreciation for your effective efforts on behalf of Cuban-American relations. You have done a great deal for Cuba and I know of no better way to thank you than by telling you that you are one of the best friends Cuba has in the United States of America. For your benefit and ours I urge you to keep on working for closer ties between our two nations. For our part, we will certainly do."

I came back to the United States to get to work. I did what I could to help the Castro regime. At a meeting soon after my return with a group of men in New York City, I was authorized to present to Dr. Castro, completely free of charge, an entire merchant marine. This fantastic deal was unbelievable. Israel had received from Western Germany, as reparations payments, more ships than she could use or sell, and I had been authorized by a representative of the government, the commercial attaché of the Israeli Embassy in Washington, to give Dr. Castro, practically free, the following: four new ships already built; two tankers and two cargo and passenger ships; four ships in the process of being built in Germany, but whose designs could be altered; and four ships just in the planning stage. As part of the arrangement, Israel would retain a 50-percent interest in the Cuban Merchant Marine, with the proviso that the Cuban government could at any time purchase that 50 percent at a prearranged price representing one half the value of the ships. The ships would be staffed by experienced Israeli crewmen, but serving with them would be Cubans who would take over as they proved capable of performing the necessary duties.

I called Dr. Castro immediately and told him I was coming to Cuba the next day. On February 4 I presented the Israeli ship deal to Castro and his Secretary of the Treasury. By this time the Communists had already moved into Fidel Castro's innermost offices. His number-one personal secretary was a petite blonde, Teresa Cassuso, who had been with the Cuban Embassy in Mexico. She was deliberately placed in Castro's office by the anti-American group within his organization. Her function was eventually to quarantine and isolate Fidel from anyone not serving the purpose of the anti-American forces, though I did not learn this until much later.

The dream of a merchant marine for Cuba had warmed the heart of every one of her leaders through the years. Here was an opportunity to have one worth tens of millions of dollars without a single penny of expense, but the deal was turned down because, in the amazing words of Castro himself, he didn't believe it was possible. I tried to get Dr. Castro to call the private number of the Israeli commercial attaché, who was standing by to take the next plane to Cuba to formalize the contract. This he refused to do.

At the same time I presented a plan on behalf of one of the largest groups of truck-owners in the United States. If the Cuban government would allow them to carry Cuban vegetables and fruits in refrigerated trucks piggy-back across from Key West, they would, without cost, furnish all the equipment and ships necessary. This would have opened up a brand-new market for Cuban produce in the Midwest; forty-eight hours after the trucks were loaded these fruits and vegetables could have been on sale in the streets of Chicago. This offer was also ignored.

Cuba is the site of the world's largest manganese mine—the Charco Redondo. This mine has been such a lucrative producer of manganese that Batista used to give it for a month at a time to various of his followers. In that one month it was possible to clear $1 million from it. I was approached by a group of American mining engineers who felt they could be of valuable assistance to the Castro government and wanted me to intercede for them. They told me that the Charco Redondo was in danger of collapsing because the Administrator of Stolen Property had placed it in the hands of a *Barbudo* who knew absolutely nothing about mining. As a result the mine was beginning to flood, the pumps were not working, and if something wasn't done immediately, the mine would be lost, possibly forever. They offered to move in immediately, get the pumps going, shore up the walls

the mine was collapsing, bring in a new mill from West Germany,
.... tart the mining operations in what had become a ghost town—all
without any cost to the Cuban government. All they wanted as their fee
was 10 percent of the profits; the remaining 90 percent would go to the
government of Fidel Castro. Their offer was refused.

It was at about this time that Prime Minister Miro Cardona left the
government to return to his private law practice, and Castro took over. One
reason for Cardona's resignation was that he loved Cuba more than he
loved Castro. He said to me once, "People should stop saying, 'Give Castro
a chance,' and say, 'Give Cuba a chance!'" He was right.

Members of Castro's Cabinet told me that he had recently changed
almost overnight; he had restored the public spectacle of the trials, and he
was beginning in his public speeches to denounce the United States for its
increasing attacks upon him through the press.

I tried to save the situation by getting Dr. Castro to agree to accept an
invitation if President Eisenhower invited him to come to Washington. On
February 17, 1959, I contacted the White House, indicating the importance of the reestablishment of good relations with Cuba. I received a letter
from President Eisenhower, signed by Jack Anderson, Administrative Assistant to the President, refusing to take the action I had suggested, stating
that, "The President's official commitments would preclude an invitation
at this time"; and "We understand that Mr. Castro has indicated his
intentions to devote his current energies to Cuba's urgent problems."

Not only Anderson but Jim Hagerty, too, ignored what I was trying to
do to help our country's relationship with Cuba. I told them in advance
that Castro was going to accept an invitation to come to the United States
on April 14 as a guest of the American Society of Newspaper Editors. Since
his acceptance was still confidential information, I suggested they move
rapidly so that the President could issue his invitation before the news of
the April 14 visit broke. They still refused to give him an invitation to meet
with the President.

The State Department, which has done more to hurt the United States
than any other agency of our government, went so far as to say, "As a
distinguished leader of the Cuban nation, Prime Minister Castro will
assuredly be welcome, *if he comes.*"

The bitterness in Havana increased. The people began to reflect it on
the streets. My old friends in the Movement began to talk to me confiden-
tially about the rise of anti-Americanism.

At about this time Teresa Cassuso, Castro's secretary, began cutting me off from him. From that point on phone calls, wires, letters, everything that went from me to him or from him to me was deliberately destroyed by her. But I was still unaware of her role.

Information came to me that a relative of hers, serving in the government as a tax collector at one of the ports, had collected money on shipments of manganese ore to Baltimore which he had kept for himself. He was a former Batista man, but through the influence of his niece had been retained in the government and was still stealing from Castro. I sent this information through to Fidel but, of course, it never reached him because Teresa Cassuso destroyed it.

Early in March, I received confidential information that Charco Redondo, the manganese mine, had finally collapsed and that there were casualties. Not a word of this appeared in the press and the incident is still not publicly known. I wired Prime Minister Castro at El Prado: "I understand that Charco Redondo collapsed with casualties. Have warned you and Faustino Perez [the Administrator of Stolen Property]. Will you please take the suggestion I gave you and Faustino? It should be acted on at once or it will be too late. Will telephone you this evening." Of course, he never received the wire and my subsequent telephone call was not put through to him.

One of the senior statesmen of Cuba, Dr. Oscar Gans, called me in Washington, stating it was desperately important that I see Dr. Castro again, that the situation was getting critical, that Dr. Castro himself was worried and requested I come down. He concluded. "Please do this for Cuba . . . for Fidel! He needs you." I promised to call him as soon as I'd made a decision. I decided to go down and called Dr. Gans at his private number in Havana, to tell him that I would let him know as soon as I could get away. I followed this with a cable, notifying him that I could arrive on Tuesday, March 10. He phoned me: "Castro will see us at his hideaway in the country. If you are pressed for time, you can arrange to arrive early in the morning and leave that same night." This I did.

Dr. Gans, who had served as Prime Minister of Cuba and Ambassador to the United States many times, met me at the airport. We drove out to the suburbs and after passing through many armed guards, arrived at the house in which Castro was living, a simple place, beautifully situated on a hill near the sea. It had been selected because it could be easily defended. More than fifty *Barbudos* were living there as guards, and many of the rooms were filled with cots.

After waiting there for two hours with Dr. Gans and his secretary, who was frantically telephoning all over Havana trying to locate Castro, we left the house to have lunch. After lunch the telephoning started again. Fidel Castro could not be found anywhere. I was there, after a week of preparation, at his personal invitation and at the expense of his government. Yet he couldn't be found. I later learned that Teresa Cassuso had deliberately told him that morning that I had not arrived.

We went back to the Havana Riviera. Dr. Gans was so embarrassed that he didn't know what to say. Then and there I washed my hands of Castro and of Cuba. When Castro came to the United States on April 14, I was rigidly excluded from every single affair given by him and the Cuban government. All the old officials of his early regime had gone and he was now a prisoner of the Communist Party.

Ernesto "Che" Guevara had become the boss. He was definitely a Communist and told me so in front of Fidel in February, 1959, at the Hilton.

It did not take long before every man who helped Castro to power was gone from his government. Even the head of the armed forces, General Cienfuegos, was assassinated to allow Castro's brother Raúl to take over.

Gone too was the dream, the hope of the people. Gone too the greatness that could have been Fidel's. Nothing now is left but another dictator, and he has become only a puppet and a pawn.

Later that same year, on August 20, I was invited to a very small luncheon in the Veto Room of the Congressional Hotel in honor of the Perle Mesta of Texas—Mrs. Ada Wilson of Corpus Christi. Just before the luncheon began a gentleman came up to me and said, "I am Señor Balárt, President of the White Rose Society—anti-Bastista, anti-Castro."

My good friend Congressman Victor N. Anfuso, standing nearby, said, "Adam, he wants you to support him. He is the next President of Cuba."

My answer was quick and unhesitating: "No thanks! I've had enough of Cuba and Castro, both going and coming!"

15

The Committee on Education and Labor

As the 86th Congress met in its first session in January, 1959, I was starting my fifteenth year in the House of Representatives. I had been a member of the House Committee on Education and Labor for all fifteen years, and I was now the ranking Majority member. The Honorable Graham Barden of North Carolina served as the chairman for over ten of those years. During the two years 1953–1954, when Republican Samuel McConnell headed the committee, Barden was the ranking Minority member.

The last few years, particularly, had not been easy. Barden ruled the committee like an old-time plantation-owner—controlling the committee members by refusing to call meetings or scheduling them when he knew that most of the members would be unable to attend because of business in the House. He would then adjourn the meeting for lack of a committee quorum and wait until the members absolutely forced him to schedule another meeting.

One year Barden called us for the first committee meeting early in January, naming subcommittees and appointing the members. The next meeting was not called until April and it proved to be brief and unproductive. We met again in July and found that the only item on the agenda was formal adjournment of the committee until the start of the next session in January.

The reasons for Barden's high-handed treatment of the committee were not difficult for me to determine. Barden himself was quoted in 1958, by *The New York Times*, as saying, "Anything that does not concern the Third District of North Carolina cannot be too important."

By 1958, however, things had started to change somewhat. Education and Labor legislation had become a vital public issue and the record of the committee was so barren (during Barden's 10 years, of 2045 bills introduced to the committee only 50 passed, few of them major bills) that the rest of the Democratic Congress helped fill the committee vacancies with more liberal, Northern freshmen.

This additional help, combined with the pressure that some of my fellow committee members and I had been exerting for years, made Barden realize that he must reform or face a total revolt that might be sanctioned by the other Democratic members of Congress. As the 86th Congress began, Barden was promising to hold regular committee meetings twice a month.

Moreover, he had also agreed to appoint subcommittees with specific jurisdictions so that bills could go to hearing without the chairman's consent, a policy that he had totally refused to follow in the past. (In fact, we had tried such a tactic in the past, but when our liberal majority had met and passed bills without Barden's knowledge, the House preserved its unwritten law of not passing any legislation without the approval of the chairman of the appropriate committee, and killed the bills with technicalities.)

But this long battle was not without casualties. When it became time to name the various subcommittee chairmen, Barden announced that he was going to deny me a chairmanship. Positions like the subcommittee chairmanships, and the committee chairmanships themselves, have always been determined on the basis of seniority. Seniority is the very backbone of the Congressional system, but Barden had now decided to punish me for my audacity in questioning his leadership. Actually, it was not his leadership I was fighting, but rather the total lack of progress so far in critical areas of education and employment.

The committee voted on appointing a member of lesser seniority to the subcommittee chairmanship. With Barden's hold over the members, the vote went against me and another member was so appointed, thus effectively stripping me of my seniority on the committee. I was the ranking member of the House Committee on Education and Labor but had practically nothing to do.

The next months were hard, frustrating, and almost totally unproductive for the committee. We had several pieces of important legislation in committee (among them the minimum-wage bill) and Barden clearly intended that they stay in committee. The great promises he had made at the beginning of the session had been all but ignored, and the committee's morale was just about back to where it had been years before. An incident from the old days illustrates the way we felt: a pro-labor committeeman, so frustrated by Barden's obvious stalling and manuevering, ran out of the meeting waving a white handkerchief and crying, "I surrender!"

And then the bombshell hit. Barden announced that he was retiring at the end of the session. With Barden gone, I would, as the ranking Majority member, become the committee chairman.

"The racist attitudes of Adam Clayton Powell, his miserable record as a legislator, and his extreme absenteeism all tend to disqualify him as a responsible and effective Chairman." *The New York Times* (January, 1960), with its usual impartial attitude, had decided I was a racist. (If, instead of fighting for the rights of blacks I had been fighting for white constituents, I imagine they would have called me a true, noble democrat.)

Following the *Times*'s lead, almost every major paper in the country joined in. They had "grave doubts," they had "misgivings," I was "simply not the type." Even some labor leaders (and labor and I had worked closely together since 1930) expressed concern. And as usual, there were motions to strip me of my seniority or to split the committee into separate education and labor groups—anything that would curb the power they were so afraid to let me have.

By now the "get Powell" pattern was very familiar, and after several attempted purges I almost knew my opponents' lines by heart. In the early years they were upset because I ate in their private dining room. Now they were upset because I was poaching on what they thought was their own private power structure. The seniority tradition, however, finally triumphed over the other arguments and the fight degenerated into cloakroom muttering.

I think that when I was sworn in and finally took my place as chairman of the committee in 1961, other than my voters in Harlem there was not more than a handful of people who thought I could do the job. (And even fewer who wanted me to succeed.) But John F. Kennedy had wished me success and I knew that I had whatever support he could give to new social legislation. And there still were a few friends in Congress I knew I could count on.

The first thing I did was to hire a large professional staff for the Committee. We went from twenty-one people to fifty-one, getting the highest-caliber men and women available. (So much research and detail work must be done by the committee that without a large, capable staff, the members themselves would be buried in paperwork.)

I started conducting Committee meetings twice a week, with extra sessions whenever they were needed. I set up subcommittees with the authority to handle a given area, and several special study groups were established to investigate such areas as equal job and educational opportunities.

Almost immediately I started getting results. Within five months of my assuming the chairmanship, the minimum-wage bill had passed the House. This was one of the bills that Barden had stifled so long. In just the first session of the 87th Congress twelve education and labor bills became public law, three of them among the eight most important measures passed by the 87th Congress. My committee held twice as many hearings during the 87th Congress as Barden had held in his busiest years, and mine were almost invariably productive, working sessions, whereas Barden had used the hearings to stifle and delay legislation.

At the end of 1962 the record showed that my House committee had been more active than any other in the 87th Congress. Speaker of the House John McCormack said, "The minimum-wage bill would not have been passed last year if it had not been for Chairman Powell."

At the same time President Kennedy told the press that I had helped, as committee chairman, to lay the foundation of "the Great Society."

In the following sessions of Congress I kept up the pressure, and the results, as measured by enacted legislation, continued to be very good. In one fourteen-month period alone I was responsible for the passage of fourteen bills, a record that no chairman in the history of the United States Congress had ever before (or has since) achieved. In fact, in the six years I was committee chairman, I never lost a bill once it got to the House Floor.

The success of my chairmanship surprised many of my more ardent opponents. They had predicted that I would plunge the entire Congress into a battle over civil rights through controversial bills and amendments. My battle plan was just the reverse.

Instead of fighting to attach the "Powell Amendment" to legislation to bring about equality, I evolved the tactic of getting a *written* promise from the Cabinet Secretary concerned that fair employment practices and standards would be maintained in the implementation of each program. This guaranteed that minority groups would have their civil rights protected, while avoiding the long battles that sometimes were occasioned by my not so popular amendment. In fact, in many cases in which the "Powell Amendment" was no longer necessary we removed it from the legislation as an outmoded tool. One example of this was the School Lunch Act to which, years before, I had fought so hard, and successfully, to get the amendment added. Then, in mid-1962, I had it removed since the Supreme Court had ruled to void the "separate but equal" clause.

By 1964 I had helped with the passage of several major pieces of legislation. In a personal letter to me on January 30 Speaker McCormack again thanked me for my work. He said:

> The 88th Congress is already a historical one because it has passed, in the field of education, (1) the Higher Education Bill and (2) the Vocational Education Act of 1963. These two measures came out of your Committee and passed through Congress under your brilliant and courageous leadership.
>
> I am always happy when there is a Bill on the Floor of the House that has come out of your Committee because I know that, under your leadership, its chances of passage are excellent, even when it receives the "blind opposition" of the opposite Party.

The committee work was demanding. It took thousands of committee man-hours to investigate and prepare the material properly. I worked the committee, the staff, and myself around the clock on more occasions than I can remember. But we were making progress. After so many years of a do-nothing Education and Labor Committee, I was now seeing many of my dreams and goals made into law.

On my fifth anniversary as chairman, the record showed that I had guided to passage from my committee sixty major laws. By then I was receiving active support from a great many people in the Congress—some of it unwilling, but support nonetheless. At that time I received a letter of appreciation from President Johnson:

THE WHITE HOUSE   March 18, 1966.

Dear Adam:

The fifth anniversary of your Chairmanship of the House Education and Labor Committee reflects a brilliant record of accomplishment.

It represents the successful reporting to the Congress of 49 pieces of bedrock legislation. And the passage of every one of these bills attests to your ability to get things done.

Even now, these laws which you so effectively guided through the House are finding abundant reward in the lives of our people.

The poverty program is rapidly paving new pathways to progress for those whom the economic vitality of this land had previously bypassed.

The education measures are being translated into fuller opportunities for all our citizens to develop their God-given talents to their fullest potential.

Minimum wage, long a guarantee of a fair return for an honest day's work, has been increased and greatly extended.

And the problems of juvenile delinquency are being met and curtailed by positive and determined action.

Only with progressive leadership could so much have been accomplished by one Committee in so short a time. I speak for the millions of Americans who benefit from these laws when I say that I am truly grateful.

Sincerely yours,
LYNDON B. JOHNSON

The laws passed covered the spectrum of human rights, wages, education, youth, and old age. The following is just a partial list of the many laws that resulted from my chairmanship:

Public Law   *Title*

87–22 Amending vocational education laws to include and help practical-nurse-training programs

87–30 Increasing the coverage of minimun-wage legislation to include retail clerks; also increasing the minimum wage to $1.25

87–87 Increased benefits for longshoremen and harbor workers

87–262 Establishes a teaching hospital for Howard University; transfers Freedmen's Hospital to Howard University

87–274 The Juvenile Delinquency and Youth Offenses Control Act

87–344 Extension of the laws providing funds for school construction and maintenance in Federally impacted areas

87–339 Amending the Federal Employee's Compensation Act

87–400 Amending the National Defense Education Act regarding student loans
87–415 The Manpower Development and Training Act, making more jobs available
87–581 The Work Hours Act of 1962, establishing standards for pay and work of laborers and mechanics
87–715 Educational and training films for the deaf
87–729 Amending the Manpower Development and Training Act regarding railroad unemployment insurance
88–38 Equal pay for equal work
88–204 Higher Education Academic Facilities Act
88–269 Increasing Federal assistance for public libraries
88–452 The War on Poverty
88–582 Registration of contractors of migrant workers
89–36 National Technical Institute for the Deaf
89–73 The Older Americans Act of 1965
89–77 Amending Public Law 815, providing for school construction in Puerto Rico, Wake Island, Guam, and the Virgin Islands
89–287 Financial assistance for students attending trade, technical, business, and other vocational schools, after secondary education
89–313 Providing for assistance in construction and operation of public elementary and secondary schools in areas affected by major disaster
89–329 Strengthening the educational resources of our colleges and universities; and financial assistance to the students
89–752 Higher Education Act of 1966

16

The Plot
of 1966

As 1966 and the 89th Congress drew to a close, I was starting to think that perhaps my life was stabilizing. Through the years my public life (as well as my personal life) seemed to run in patterns of glorious peaks of accomplishment followed by valleys of dissension, bitter fighting, and ill health. But now this seemed to be a thing of the past. We were finally starting to make some progress in the fight against discrimination (even though the 89th Congress had only six black Congressmen), my committee's work was producing results, and it looked as if the longtime anti-black elements in Washington had finally adjusted to my presence and my long, and very vocal, fight for equality—both for myself and for my race. I even thought that the old "get Adam" conspiracies had gone out of style.

The only real dissent I knew of at that time came from one of my committee members, Sam Gibbons of Florida. Gibbons had told me one day that my support of "Black Power" was going to get me into trouble. Considering that I had heard the same thing from that day in 1930 when I helped desegregate the Harlem Hospital, I didn't take his threat seriously. As events developed his threat proved to be accurate, and I ended up fighting the most bitter battle of my career. A battle that I finally won, but only after going to the United States Supreme Court.

I've always respected a white Southerner more than a white Northerner. A white Northerner is one who says openly that he has no prejudice and yet who practices it every day of his life. The white Southerner is the one who says, "I am prejudiced, but I have certain friends [not always just Uncle Tom friends] I would do anything in the world for." In other words one is a hypocrite and the other is bluntly honest.

This was never brought home to me more incisively than when Representatives Frank Thompson of New Jersey, John Brademas of Indiana, and Jim O'Hara of Michigan came into my office one day and said they had a complete typed-up copy of what they were going to do to the House committee structure—they were going to strip me of all of my power.

This, despite the fact that I had treated every subcommittee better than subcommittees had ever been treated. Each member could travel wherever he wanted. There was a letter from me allowing them to use what we call counterpart funds. These are United States funds held in various nations throughout the world which cannot be used in the United States but can be used by our government in those nations. And I treated all the members of my committee with more fairness and justice than any other chairman in the House or Senate.

It was a producing committee and a committee that produced more laws without a single defeat than any other committee has ever produced in the history of the Republic.

And when Patsy Mink came from Hawaii in her first term, I did the unprecedented: I gave her the authorship of two laws.

But these three men, who posed as white Northern liberals, knew that I had too much power because I controlled most of the domestic legislation of the United States of America. But I controlled it with fairness. I controlled it not only with fairness to my colleagues but with justice for all people. It was a deliberate plot by these men, with the help of two white Southerners, Sam Gibbons of Florida and Bill Dickinson of Alabama.

In mid-September of 1966 the fight started within the committee. Led by Gibbons (and triggered by the power of the Democratic Study Group), a group of the younger "liberal" Democrats demanded that the organization of the committee be drastically revised. The net effect of the reorganization would be an enormous reduction of the powers of the committee chairman and a vast increase in the authority of the subcommittee chairman. It also began to look like an outright battle against the overall seniority system that governs all House conduct.

On one side was the powerful Democratic Study Group and its chairman, Frank Thompson; allied with them were the various enemies that I had made throughout twenty-four years of battling in Congress. I had recently lost a potential White House ally when Jack Valenti, a fair liberal and a personal friend, was replaced by a bitterly anti-Negro Texan, Marvin Watson. At the same time Speaker McCormack was politically weak and decided on a course of neutralism, while another powerful friend, Majority Leader Carl Albert, was suffering the aftereffects of a serious heart attack and was unable to bring his considerable influence to my aid.

Contributing to the emotional pressure at that period was my proposal for "Black Power" and my alignment with Stokely Carmichael—not to mention my announced intention of holding the first National Black Power Conference. The conference, and the new dimension it signified in black-white relations, was a source of irritation and worry to a great many Congressmen who rightfully recognized the threat it could be to their political power.

This was the atmosphere surrounding the seemingly minor revolt that caused the complete revamping of the committee structure.

Gibbons had drafted, and was demanding adoption of, a proposal that would place *all* administrative and procedural powers in the hands of six subcommittee chairmen. In my committee—or any House committee—such a move would leave the chairman with, as one reporter put it, "nothing but the gavel."

After several skirmishes we finally fought it out. Gibbons' original proposal was discarded and in its place the committee adopted (by a twenty-seven-to-one vote) new rules that made all important decisions regarding legislation and staff hiring subject to concurrence of the committee majority. Even in the watered-down version it was obvious that I had lost. And it was becoming even more obvious to me that this was merely the first round in what must certainly be a new "get Adam" vendetta.

The next move occurred while I was out of Washington preparing for the new session. I received an urgent telephone call from one of my staff; he told me that Lionel Van Deerlin, the Republican Congressman from California, had announced in Washington that he planned a House motion refusing to seat me until I had purged myself of the contempt-of-court citations and judgments resulting from the Esther James case. My lawyers were at that time still fighting the case through various appeals (which, ultimately, vindicated me) and certainly the only way to purge myself was to continue those appeals. This fact was certainly known to Van Deerlin, so his announcement of his intention to prevent my seating was a thinly disguised declaration of war.

A week later it was announced that the House had set up a special subcommittee to investigate the records of the Education and Labor Committee. The subcommittee, headed by Wayne Hays of Ohio, had already announced that it expected to prove that I had misused committee funds —particularly for travel. (The rather bitter irony of Hays's heading the subcommittee must have given many Congressmen a laugh—Hays was once the center of Washington gossip because he took a House dining-room headwaiter on a junket to Paris.)

Within days Hays told the press that more than half of the hundred and fifty committee trips made during the 89th Congress were made by persons other than those in whose names the tickets were purchased. Without refighting the entire Hays Committee case, there are a few points worth considering in relation to his well-publicized charges.

First, Hays himself set the number of individual trips at a hundred and fifty—for a two-year period. At that time we had a committee staff of almost a hundred and fifty, and the committee itself numbered thirty. That meant that a group numbering almost a hundred and eighty used only a hundred and fifty tickets in a two-year period—an average of slightly over six tickets per month divided among a hundred and eighty people.

Hays also tried to make a major point of the fact that many times committee members, staff, or I had used tickets made out to another member. I would like to ask any traveling businessman to count the number of times he has traveled on a co-worker's ticket because of a last-minute change in plans. It takes three minutes to switch a ticket made out to an associate; it takes much longer to have that ticket canceled for eventual credit and a completely new ticket issued—if space is still available.

Even Hays privately admitted that if I had taken all the trips myself, and had every ticket made out in my name, they would still be considered as valid committee business—it was simply the switching of tickets that he was questioning.

But more important than all this was the fact that I did not sign the vouchers used to get the tickets. All the vouchers with my name on them had actually been signed by Maxine Dargans, one of my senior staff members. And yet she was not asked why she signed my name to the vouchers or if I had known that she was signing them. The other major point in the Hays findings was that I had supposedly endorsed paychecks made out to my estranged wife Yvette, and misused the money. Again it was Maxine who had endorsed the checks. In fact one day, in Maxine's absence, I tried to sign my name to the check and the Sergeant at Arms (who runs a private bank for the House) would not accept my endorsement. I had to wait until Maxine returned and have her take care of the check for Yvette. Yvette and I had only one checking account in the world. From this I paid all her expenses. She handled all my Latin American cases. I paid income tax on both of our incomes.

In spite of Maxine's close knowledge of so much of the finances of the committee, she was not questioned by Hays. In fact Maxine was the only black member of the committee staff who was retained by the new chairman after my exclusion. Not only was she retained, she was given a much better job with the committee and a large raise in pay!

Another oddity, and a point that could indicate some slanting of Yvette's testimony, is the fact that the committee paid her expenses from Puerto Rico to Washington, gave her a fee for testifying, and paid for a top Washington attorney, Joseph Rauh, to represent her at the hearing. But since we were still married, Yvette was under no legal compulsion to testify. A wife does not have to testify against her husband, yet Yvette came all the way to Washington to talk to the committee.

By this time I should have become accustomed to the continual sniping from my fellow Congressmen. I remember the criticism of a trip I made to Europe in 1962. My expenses (as shown in public records) totaled $1544. That covered three people traveling in every country from England to Greece for almost eight weeks. The same year one of the severest critics of my trip, Otto Passman of Louisiana, spent $4588 for a trip to Europe and another around the world. And yet Passman and his colleagues were disturbed by my spending. I told *Newsweek* that December, "I do not do any more than any other member of Congress, and by the grace of God I will not do less."

The hypocrisy of the entire Hays Committee action passed almost unnoticed by the world at large, but within Congress the members were aware of it. I refused to be meek and let them off the hook easily. If I had to go down, I was going down swinging. When I was asked to appear before the Hays Committee, I stipulated that I would do so only if I were allowed the right to cross-examine witnesses, including Congressmen. This sounds like a basic right, inherent in the American judicial system. But my fellow lawmakers knew very well that if I started to ask them questions, we could easily end up drawing lots to see who was the guilty Congressman who should be punished. I could have asked Hays himself who paid for the almost fifty flights between Washington and his home in Ohio.

Needless to say, my request was denied.

Sam Gibbons brought the fight out into the open in September. By mid-January, when the 89th Congress opened, my enemies were ready and the first step was to castrate me politically in the Education and Labor Committee; which I had led so successfully for six years. A closed Democratic caucus met and voted 140 to 70 to remove me as chairman and name the ranking member, Carl Perkins, as the new chairman.

The next day the House voted 364 to 64 to exclude me from my rightful seat until a new committee investigated my fitness to serve in the Congress. The committee was to be made up of five Democratic members and four Republicans, and was supposed to report within five weeks. Promptly the next day, the committee members were named: Democrats Emanuel Celler, James Corman, Claude Pepper, John Conyers, Jr., and Andrew Jacobs, Jr.; Republicans Arch Moore, Charles Teague, Clark MacGregor, and Vernon Thompson.

All five Democratic members had fought, unsuccessfully, against my exclusion. Emanuel Celler, chairman of the new committee, had described the action as "a kangaroo court" and John Conyers had voted against any form of investigation. The four Republican members, not surprisingly, had supported my exclusion.

At this point I formed my own committee, the best civil rights lawyers I could find. There was former Judge Hubert Delaney, Arthur Kinoy from Rutgers University, Herbert Reid from Howard University, the NAACP's Robert Carter, William Kunstler, William Chance, Edward Bennett Williams, Henry Williams, and George Donald Covington. This group represented the finest collection of legal minds that could be assembled. And they worked without a fee, simply for justice. While the members of the Congressional committee were deciding if, in their opinion, I was "fit to serve," I was determined to prove that the Constitution of the United States sets only three qualifications for House service—age, citizenship, and residence. According to the Constitution a man (or woman) is fit to serve in Congress as long as he is twenty-five years of age, a citizen of the United

States, and a resident of the state in question. That was the legal issue. Equally important was the moral issue: I had been elected by an over-whelming majority of the people in my district—at the very height of the virulent anti-Powell campaign that was carried on in every newspaper and magazine in the country.

Nine Congressmen were sitting in judgment on my fitness when more than four hundred thousand citizens of my District had already passed judgment and given me a mandate to represent them in the House.

In the aftermath of the committee's appointment the black community of America rallied around me. Black leaders like Stokely Carmichael and Julian Bond denounced the House's action. Even Martin Luther King, Jr., a longtime black moderate, denounced the move, stating that an investiga-tion of my conduct should not be held without a comparable investigation of other Congressmen. In Washington a hundred black clergymen pro-tested; one of them, the Reverend Jefferson P. Rogers, was quoted by *Time*: "The only reason Adam Clayton Powell draws this kind of attention is that he is a Negro and wields power like a white man wields power."

The "Hands Off Powell" movement produced more solidarity among blacks than any event in recent years. But to no avail; Congress had started something that it would not stop. What had begun as an involved political move against the system had turned into a runaway purge. My committee had been the arena, so I became the sacrificial lamb.

The leaders of the House had completely lost control of their members. Speaker McCormack was being so heavily criticized by his own Democratic colleagues that the *Washington Post* urged in an editorial that he "step down gracefully" because he no longer brought to the Speakership the "energy, shrewdness and fighting capacity it deserves." Ever since my support of Eisenhower ten years earlier, many members of the Democratic Party had been waiting for the opportunity to get me. They could never understand that, in 1956, I had had to support the man who was going to do the most for my people. Any other act would have been a complete betrayal. In addition my stand on Black Power and my years of dedicated fighting for the black people had made enough enemies so that I became a common target.

I had realized that there had been some realignment of power when, in September of 1966, I had attended the signing of the War on Poverty Bill in President Johnson's office. The President refused to shake my hand when I arrived, and his entire attitude toward me was one of complete detachment—as if I were already a dead man and he would have preferred not to have a corpse in his office. At the same time he warmly embraced Gibbons, so I knew that whatever Gibbons was planning, he obviously had strong Democratic backing—all the way to the White House, in fact.

In a sense the Democratic Study Group ran out of control. The press immediately jumped on the bandwagon and every politician who wanted to impress his voters started making speeches about what should be done with Adam. I knew that the affair was becoming a personal grudge fight for many Congressmen, and a tip from Jack Anderson (then Drew Pearson's assistant) confirmed it. Anderson called Chuck Stone, my special assistant, at home late one night and told him that the House leadership had told him that they now knew that they did not have enough support in Congress to control the upcoming vote on my exclusion. But even though they could not prevent it, they were going to put up a phony fight for me, just to protect the Democratic Party's reputation!

Shortly after the Anderson tip, Emanuel Celler, chairman of the special House committee, presented its recommendations: I should be publicly condemned, stripped of my twenty-two years of seniority, and assessed $40,000. They also asked the Justice Department to take any appropriate action on the evidence the committee had gathered. (The Justice Department did set up a grand jury to consider the material. After sitting for several weeks, they decided that there was not evidence to justify an indictment and the jury was dismissed. Then the Justice Department took the unusual step of putting the material before a second grand jury. This jury also recommended against any prosecution and finally the matter was dropped.) Publicly the leading House members were assuring the press that the special committee's findings would be the end of the case. Privately they knew, as I did, that Congress was in revolt and would not stop until I was out.

The next day the House met to consider the committee's findings. There were three rapid votes. First there was a motion to preclude amendments to the resolution containing the committee's $40,000 assessment and loss of seniority formula; that was defeated 222 to 202. Next came a motion to substitute complete exclusion in place of the Celler proposal; that passed 248 to 176. Last came the actual vote to bar me from my seat; 307 to 116 was the final tally—I was not going to be allowed to serve.

Again the black world rose in protest, not because I was a man named Adam Powell but because I was a symbol for blacks everywhere. Stokely

Carmichael said, "The issue isn't Adam Clayton Powell, it's his power." If a black Congressman with years of accomplishments could be arbitrarily dismissed from the House, what protection—what rights—did that leave the black man in the street or ghetto? I knew my exclusion was unconstitutional; my lawyers were already preparing the briefs for the United States Supreme Court. I felt that only the Supreme Court could be far enough removed from the House pressures and prejudices to make a fair decision. The Supreme Court takes time, however, and in the interim all I could do was wait.

There are over 400,000 people in the 18th District, from which I was elected—the great majority of them black and Puerto Rican—and some years more than 100,000 of the 126,000 registered voters cast their ballots. My exclusion automatically created a vacancy; a special election had to be scheduled to elect a Representative to fill it.

When the results of the voting were announced that April, I felt as humble as any man under God could feel. I was a Congressman who had been excluded from the 90th Congress; there was no possible way I could serve, and yet the people of Harlem had elected me again—by a margin of seven to one.

As a public protest, to put forever on record their feelings regarding the exclusion, an entire Congressional District had decided to go without representation in Washington for two years.

I have several walls covered with various decorations and awards that I have been fortunate enough to receive throughout the years. Haile Selassie named me a Knight of the Golden Cross, churches have honored me, business and fraternal groups have given me tokens of appreciation; but the honor that the people of Harlem gave me that day in April must certainly be the highest award that I could ever receive in this life.

17

Jack Kennedy and LBJ

T he New Frontier. The Great Society. These were the dreams of the two greatest Presidents this Republic has ever had and both of them were killed, one physically, the other politically.

The Warren Commission never revealed the true facts of the physical assassination of Jack Kennedy. The average library has two volumes of the Warren Commission Report. I have in my possession twenty-six volumes. Even in those twenty-six volumes many portions of testimony were not printed, including testimony by Kennedy's widow and the Deputy Sheriff of Dallas County.

LBJ was assassinated politically by the albatross he inherited from the Kennedy days. Let us not forget that it was Jack Kennedy who sent the first American troops to South Vietnam—seventeen thousand Marines. LBJ inherited the same men who advised Jack Kennedy to send those troops in. And they were the ones who mired him deep in the quicksand of blood and death.

When Harry Truman succeeded Franklin Roosevelt, he had his own Cabinet and his own heads of the important bureaus in the Executive branch of the government within thirty days. LBJ was astute in the Senate, especially as long as Mr. Sam was the Speaker of the House. But he was foolish not to put his own men in key White House positions when he became President. It's hard for a poor Southern boy, even if he's white, to stand up against the kind of polished, sophisticated Irish Mafia with whom Jack Kennedy had surrounded himself. They were the ones who killed him.

Jack Kennedy and I were always friends. In fact it's very interesting that, out of the committee of which I was chairman, came Senators Griffin of Michigan and Goodell of New York; a Vice President, Richard Nixon; and two Presidents, Jack Kennedy and Richard Nixon. All of them served on the Education and Labor Committee.

Jack and I were very close. He never had his secretary call me, but would always telephone directly. One day he called and one of my clerks answered the phone—Kennedy was President at that time—and he said, "This is Jack Kennedy calling." She said, "Yes, and I'm Liz Taylor," and hung up.

There was not a single social occasion at the White House, whether it was for Pablo Casals, André Malraux, or a host of others, to which I was not invited. I remember sitting in back of Mrs. Kennedy at one affair when Casals played the cello after dinner. When he finished, I touched her shoulder and said. "Are we going to go upstairs now and do the twist?" She said, "Adam you're a naughty boy, I'm going to send you home."

It took me almost one entire year to realize that Jack was dead. I hadn't shed a tear. The night it finally struck me I was almost hysterical for the entire night. It took a night for me to get rid of a year of pent-up tears.

I do not think conditions would have been radically different had Jack Kennedy lived. All the ideas of the New Frontier were pursued by Johnson under the name of the Great Society.

In my opinion Kennedy's assassination was the result of a conspiracy on the part of Texas billionaires. Oswald was merely a patsy. His wife, who was Russian, could not speak English at that time; when she did finally appear before the court, she had been coached by government officials in English so that she could answer certain questions; any other questions she could not answer, since she had not been coached in them. It is significant that seventeen people who knew some of the important facts surrounding the assassination have died natural deaths or been killed since it occurred.

Jack Kennedy had the milk of human kindness in his veins, but his brother Bobby had ice water in his. Bobby had a bitter hatred of Lyndon Johnson, and not without reason. I remember dropping in to see him in

June, 1967, just as I was about to leave for Geneva as United States
Congressional observer at the International Labor Organization. He told
me he had just had a wonderful conference with the President. "Look,"
I told him, "I know your office is tapped; it always has been. LBJ will chew
you to ribbons the first time he gets a chance—when you're not looking."

Johnson was certainly not involved with Robert Kennedy's death,
however. Bobby's death was engineered by the same group that had Jack
killed.

The so-called credibility gap of which LBJ was accused was the result of
many things. He had lost interest in being President of the United States.
Lady Bird was insisting that he resign, or at least not run again. His press
corps was, to say the least, not the best. Finally, he felt he was going to
be a loser and didn't want to lose. With all these conditions operating, he
just didn't give a damn any more. It wasn't a credibility gap that caused
him to get out—it was just the case of a man who was tired of his work
and wanted out.

He knew the Vietnam war was hopeless. He knew that the American
economy was about to collapse, that we would have not only a rising cost
of living but rising unemployment as well. He thought he could pass the
mantle on to Hubert Humphrey, but Hubert Humphrey couldn't have
won, a point that is well made in a story told by Hale Boggs of Louisiana,
the House wit, in which I also figure.

Boggs was more or less presiding informally over a get-together of Southern Democratic Congressmen prior to the 1960 Democratic Convention.
Various names were mentioned as Presidential candidates. Someone mentioned Jack Kennedy. Boggs said, "No. He's a Catholic." Someone else
mentioned Stuart Symington. "No," Boggs said. "He's too stiff. Can't
project himself." Another brought up Hubert Humphrey. "No. Talks too
much." Then Boggs, just for fun, said, "Well, now, what about Adam
Clayton Powell?"

The group of Southern Democrats was speechless, and before anyone
could answer, Boggs said, "You're right. The country's not ready for a
Baptist preacher to be President."

That is the story of Hubert Humphrey, however. He talked too much
and said too little. He did not campaign the way a pro should. My advice
on the campaign was sought twice but was not heeded by the crowd around
Humphrey—not that I was Zeus thundering from Mount Olympus, but
I had been a political pro for forty years.

After Jack Kennedy's death LBJ tried to carry the torch, but he had that inheritance, the Irish Mafia, around him. They were out to get LBJ. They wanted Bobby Kennedy to be the man who was running the game, not him, and they halfway succeeded in their job.

On the day after the election LBJ called me from the ranch in Texas and said, "Adam you're the second man I'm calling. I just called Speaker McCormack, and I'm calling you because you were the first person, black or white, North or South, to say that I should be President of the United States." Editorials in Northern papers, especially the black ones, condemned me when I made that statement, but I knew that if the breach of regionalism and racism in this nation was ever going to be healed, it would have to be healed by someone who came from the South.

LBJ still maintained, however, the taint of Southern prejudices.

All during the years that he was in the White House he never invited me to a single social affair. We used to sit together in the President's upstairs private quarters to talk over matters concerning the Committee of Education and Labor. During those times he always asked his servant for a glass of Dr. Pepper. Of course I knew that the Dr. Pepper was well laced because LBJ loved his Dr. Pepper with good old Southern Bourbon.

LBJ is really a Southern country boy who was skilled in the Senate but not in the White House. His rhetoric could not be compared to Jack Kennedy's, even in private. One was to the manner born and the other was to the Lord born. The two, of course, do not have to make a difference, but it did make a difference. One will go down as a prophet, the other will go down as a hard-working man who somehow or another was able to get to the finish mark on time or ahead of others. It was with deep regret that I marked the passing of those two great men of the New Frontier and the Great Society.

18

"The Cat's Only Living"

During the days following my exclusion from Congress, I had taken refuge in my favorite "home away from home," Bimini. I was obviously not welcome in Washington, and the contempt charges were still being battled in the New York courts, so Bimini was the only place where I could let down and be comfortable. I had been visiting the island regularly since 1963, when a friend first told me that if I wanted the greatest fishing in the world, I had to go to Bimini. He was so right. Fishing has been a lifelong passion of mine and in Bimini you can catch almost anything, from monster-sized blue marlin to frying-pan-sized grunts and snapper.

Bimini also gave me a place where I could relax—a place where I was Adam baby, or sometimes Mr. Jesus, to the people. In Bimini they cared less about my being a Congressman, or an ousted Congressman, than they did about my ability as an angler, a preacher, or a dominoes player. Dominoes, as we play it, incidentally, is not the childhood game you may remember. It is played with four people, and the action is faster than any board or card game. I had first started playing in Puerto Rico and I introduced the game to Bimini. Within a few years there were players there who could hold their own anywhere.

Another aspect of Bimini that I liked was the people. They reminded me of my church congregation in that everybody knew at least part of everyone else's family. By now I know most of the people on the island and it is still the place to which I go when I want to escape from the world. Escape can be very difficult and very precious for the person in public life. As a Congressman I did not really have a private life—or if I did, it was buried so deeply inside me that only I could see it. What to most people would be a private life was my public life. I belonged to the people and my life belonged to them as well. But I was still determined to live that life to the full and enjoy every minute of it.

I can remember when, many years ago, Elmer Carter, chairman of the New York State Commission Against Discrimination, and my lifelong friend, was chosen by the Republicans to run against me for Congress. With his sonorous Harvard accent, Elmer went out into the streets to campaign and in a speech from a sound truck at the corner of 125th Street and Seventh Avenue, he made the mistake of starting to list all the material things he thought I possessed. He pointed out that while I claimed to be a man of the masses, I had a "big house in Fleetwood, where Negroes can't live; owned an apartment house on Riverside Drive, a beach house at Westhampton"; and that Hazel Scott had "scores of thousands of dollars' worth of diamonds, twelve fur coats, an English maid, and a Cadillac limousine with a French chauffeur." A wino who had been standing at the curb, rocking back and forth, listening to Elmer Carter, finally couldn't stand it any longer and screamed out, "Quit your wailing, Jack. The cat's only living!"

Writing from Walden Pond in 1854, Thoreau said, "I wanted to bite deep and suck out all of the marrow of life." This is the way I have tried to live all my life, and in my thrust for the marrow there always was a tremendous sex drive. Perhaps I married because I wanted to legalize the act. For when I had just reached the age of puberty, I was introduced to sex.

It was in the summer of 1920—or was it 1921?—when my family went to Atlantic City and stayed with friends there. There were three boys in the family, all older than I, and when I arrived I found that they had just settled down to a nicely scheduled summer of sexual activity. The daughter of the family cook, who was about fifteen, had a body mature beyond her years and a capacity for sex that only someone who was mentally ill could have. Every morning and afternoon, and sometimes in the evening after she finished doing the dishes for her mother, we would repair to the tent far at the back of the Davenports' huge yard, where she promptly took on all of the boys, including any friends or visitors who might be around. I hadn't the slightest desire or knowledge. The girl was totally unattractive to me. But that was the beginning.

What is beauty to me? People have asked, "What kind of woman do you like—redhead, blonde, or brunette; tall or short; petite or large; blue-eyed? Just what is your type?" I like all women who are beautiful. It matters not whether they are black or white, tall or short: color or eyes or hair mean nothing. If they are beautiful, I like them. Beauty to me is the sum total of a woman. There's a something I can't describe. It is the total impact of a woman that registers upon me. For me she can be as exquisite as the late Dorothy Dandridge or as Elizabeth Taylor, but if there isn't something there that moves the something in me that has to be moved, then that woman is not beautiful to me.

I remember liking one girl because she had a way of smiling out of the corner of her mouth, showing just a little bit of the whiteness of her teeth. It was only after a while that I actually began to look at her. There was another who, when she walked, threw each foot as if she were about to turn a corner. I went to a party one day and heard a woman laugh across the room, and before I turned around I knew I would like her, because that laughter could have come only from the totalness I looked for.

My first real love was Lil Handy, slim, talented, beautiful daughter of W.C. Handy. At all the high-school parties I attended she was my only girl; whenever our basketball team played, she was there—lovely, gay, and warm. Then I went away to college. She got married. I never saw much of her later in life, until one day years later there came word that Lil was fatally ill. And so I stood in the white marble pulpit of the Abyssinian Baptist Church and said, "Ashes to ashes, dust to dust" over this piece of skin that now could not even know the comfort of prayer. I was glad we had never married, for by then I was beginning to feel the total impossibility of my having a successful married life.

During my junior year at Colgate, I met an exciting creature, Isabel Washington. She and her sister, Fredi, were without doubt two of the most talented sisters in the entertainment world. Fredi had just finished starring in the successful motion picture of Fannie Hurst's *Imitation of Life*. Isabel was the star of *Harlem*, one of the most successful dramas then on Broadway.

A whole new exciting world had opened up for me by that time. While going with Lil Handy, I had met some of the greats in the music world, but now there was a wide-open highway with the most exciting personalities of that day, and others who, though still unknown, were soon to become stars. I remember sitting in the Cotton Club when it was uptown and owned by the mob. A keen-looking, handsome fellow was hanging around in those days. He was a friend of but not part of the mob that controlled the underworld of New York. He was interested in show business, but couldn't seem to get anywhere at that time, and in order to pick up a quarter here and there, and to bask in the hot lights of glamour, he hung around the Cotton Club. One night backstage I asked him to go out and get something for one of the girls, and when he came back, I gave him a half dollar. His name was George Raft.

I used to sit in Duke Ellington's apartment and listen to the greatest of the great. The Duke not only plays a beautiful piano, but uses the most interesting language in the English-speaking world. I've always marveled at the vastness of his wardrobe and the tremendous bags under his eyes.

Probably the most interesting man I have met in my entire life at that time was Sascha Iskander Hourwich, who was deeply in love with Fredi. It was in his Greenwich Village apartment that the Coordinating Committee for Employment later held its meetings. Hourwich was an anarchist and a Wall Street broker. He believed in his political ideal as the purest form of government. He maintained that if there were no laws at all of any kind whatsoever, men would be able to live together in greater peace. He held the theory that laws caused crime and war; that without any law, we would have a society that would be raceless, classless, creedless; that nationalism would therefore have to disappear because nationalism becomes an entity only through the legalization of laws. His hearthside was filled with books —books that both stimulated and angered me.

He laid for me the basis of my knowledge of wines, changing me from the rotgut of the Prohibition Era to a taste for that which was good. Sascha was a gourmet. He not only introduced me to the best wines, but also made me welcome at wonderful meals in his own home.

All this was a new way of living for me. My tastes became refined. The favorite restaurants we went to were the Lafayette and the Brevoort, both now gone. And just the other side of town on Avenue B was a fabulous eating place, the Café Royale, directly across from the Yiddish Art Theatre. There, Luther and Stella Adler's mother, the dowager queen of the café, would always be seated at the first table by the door. To the degree that she greeted you or failed to greet you, to that degree the captain would decide whether your table would be at a good location or under the stairs. She had no financial interest in the café but accepted the divine right of being the mother of the outstanding stars of that day.

The busboy at the Café Royale carried no dishes but always had between $10,000 and $15,000 on him, lending money to people he knew at exorbitant rates of interest. He made more money than the owners of the restaurant and kept his position as busboy in order to maintain an office for usury without paying rent.

I had no intention of marrying Isabel. She had no intention, I think, of marrying me. She was older than I, at the peak of her career—and her career then was much more important than mine, for I had no career. I was going to college. Possibly I married Isabel because my father and mother opposed it. They did everything they could to break us up, and they were probably right. She was married, she had a child, she was older than I, and she had her career. But I'm the kind of person who, when opposed by anyone, even though I know he is right, usually fights to prove that I am right. This is especially true when people base their arguments on some ancient creed or ancient, false morality. Isabel was married, but separated and getting a divorce. I had come to like her little boy. And why should the pulpit look down upon the world of the theater? I found more practicing Christianity in terms of brotherhood there than I found within the church. There are sinners in both, but in the theater, it seemed to me, there is less hypocrisy.

Isabel was excitingly beautiful. She had dark red curls piled all over her head, a beautiful mouth, lovely light-brown eyes, and an exquisite figure. As long as we weren't married we had wonderful times together, but our marriage was a great injustice to her. She determined that when we married she would give up the stage. But as I now know, this was a mistake. Why should any human being have to give up a career because of another's way of life? When one is married to a career, there should be no marriage to another human being. Just before we were married in 1933, Isabel was offered the leading role in *Showboat*, which had just been made famous by Helen Morgan. There would have been a transcontinental tour, a revival on Broadway, and then the lead in the motion picture—and she gave up all of this.

At our wedding thousands were turned away into the streets, mounted police were there to keep the crowd from being hurt, automobiles could not get through, the auditorium of the Abyssinian Baptist Church was packed with the greatest names in show business and the church. I remember coming down from the community center, just prior to the ceremony, and looking out the door into the face of the staid Father Bishop, priest of the largest Episcopal church in the United States, St. Phillip's, ruthlessly pushing through the mob, trying to get in the door.

But my father and mother were right. I should never have married Isabel. It was a grave injustice to her, not because she was divorced, not because she had a child by her former husband, not because she was on the stage, not because she was older than I—but because one day I caught up with her and then passed her.

She loved me completely and utterly, yet I grew and she stood still. And as I grew there was absolutely no understanding between us. When I was elected to the City Council, she said, "Darling, I know I am going to lose you." And when I told her I was going to run for Congress, she did everything to dissuade me, until one day I finally said, "This is the end," and walked out. I gave her every single thing I had accumulated—money, property, and, for me in terms of my income at that time, a very handsome sum per month for the rest of her life.

I've seen her only once since. It was at the funeral of the great prize-fighter and star of *Native Son*, Canada Lee. Time had taken its toll on both of us. I did not speak. One day, when I was about to undergo the massive surgery for a possible malignancy, I received a lovely note of cheer from her.

I married Hazel Scott on August 1, 1945. A West Indian, born in Trinidad, Hazel is, without a doubt, one of the most intriguing women living. Her mind is brilliant and I shudder to think of how it might have been blunted had she ever gone to a college or university. She is remarkably gifted and speaks several languages fluently. In fact, she is the only person I know who can speak Yiddish with both Galician and Litvak accents. She is never anywhere without a book by her side, usually the heavy, challenging, demanding type. And as she reads she grasps that one phrase or sentence that is the thesis of the whole book. She has the worst temper of anyone I know, except myself. Someday she will write the story of her life and it will be one of the most exciting books ever written.

I met Hazel during the World War Two years. She had just made her seventh motion picture. She was the darling of Café Society, a wonderful night spot run by Barney Josephson, and had already broken every show-business record for a one-star show at a supper club. Café Society was then *the* supper club of New York, and Hazel Scott was its *grande vedette.* No one came to challenge her domain on East 58th Street just off Park Avenue.

There was nothing like Café Society and there has been nothing like it since. Way at the end of the long room was the black concert grand piano sticking its nose up out of the audience. All the lights would go out, Hazel would make her way to the piano, and then suddenly a spotlight would catch her. For a moment the audience would gasp, because it looked as if she were seated there nude—the height of the piano, the bare-shouldered dress, nothing but the golden-brown shoulders and arms, the super-talented fingers.

She had a lovely home high on a hill in North White Plains, a car and a chauffeur. Her home in the country was just what I like, with a lake nearby where I put a rowboat for fresh-water fishing; and her mother cooked tingling, peppery West Indian dishes. I practically moved in. Again, there was no thought of marriage.

Wonder of all wonders, Hazel and my father got along beautifully. The first time they met we went to Reuben's for dinner. I wasn't worried about Hazel. I knew she would make an impression on Dad, because this girl could sell herself to anyone. But I was worried about my father, who was such an old curmudgeon. They hit it off. As the crowds came by with their adoration and adulation asking for Hazel's autograph, Dad suddenly reached across the table with his fork poised and asked, "Are you going to eat that fat on your steak?" She looked at him and laughed, "Of course not." "May I have it?" he asked. There was nothing my father liked better than steak fat.

Sometimes we would take Hazel and her mother fishing. Since Dad and I preferred salt-water fishing, we often drove out to the seashore and chartered a boat. One night, though there had been no previous discussion of plans of marriage, on the drive back from a wonderful day of fishing at the sea something "clicked," and the wedding date was set. Meanwhile, I had just been elected to Congress.

I did not want to go through the same kind of wedding for the curious that I had been through with Isabel, so Hazel and I were married in a church in Connecticut with only three people other than the minister present. Then we went down to Café Society where Barney Josephson gave the most fabulous wedding reception possible. Five thousand people—from cafés and society, from my Congressional District, mayors, governors, Congressmen, Senators, stood in line all the way up to Park Avenue and then up Park Avenue to 59th Street. Champagne flowed all day.

But there was no place to go for a honeymoon. I had leased a lakeside chalet in Vermont for the summer from the former Chief Justice of the Supreme Court of Vermont. The night before the wedding I received a call from him: "My neighbors have had a meeting and have voted they will not allow a single Negro to live in any of these houses. Come ahead and I will support you, but they have the power to turn off the water, although you can have it from the lake, and to cut off other services of the community. I don't think you would like to have this kind of a honeymoon." The best we could do was to take a suite at the Waldorf-Astoria until we could find somewhere else to go.

Hazel was due to start her first transcontinental concert tour the very next month. She met with tremendous success everywhere. It marked the first time anyone had played classics and jazz on the same program.

With this brilliant girl, moving ahead in her career, I felt that I had a marriage that would last. And when in October we learned that she was pregnant, then I knew this would be the kind of family in which, while each of us made a separate contribution, we could at the same time live together as a unit. I was totally wrong.

This child was meant to be something more than a child for me; I think his birth had tremendous meaning for my father, although he and I never never discussed the matter; for with Dad's passing I would be left alone in the world without any flesh and blood. He wanted to see the Powell name continued, and that's why he wanted a boy. All I wanted was a child, so that somewhere in the world there would be a someone who had some of my blood in him. And Adam III was born on June 17, 1946. He had Hazel's looks, my early curly blond hair, and bones that said he would one day be bigger than his father. He also had inherited the knack of ending all breakfast meals with turning the bowl of cereal upside down on his head . . . or is that common to all children?

As soon as he was old enough Skipper traveled with me wherever I went. This sometimes made for complications, as on the occasion when I was in Panama investigating the wage differential between the black workers and the white workers in the Canal Zone, where blacks were being paid about one-fourth as much as whites for the same jobs. Skipper was with me and we were hurrying to board a private train that would take us from the Pacific coast to the Atlantic coast, where we were to board a Panama Line ship for New York. Skipper was immaculate, dressed in white from head to foot. He was sitting in his high chair eating oatmeal just before we were due to board our train. Just as I turned my back for a minute he took the bowl of cereal and turned it upside down on his head. He had to be completely changed, bathed, and shampooed before we could start our trip.

At the age of five he was being interviewed on the Junior Celebrity Hour of the Mutual Radio Network. The interview took place in the back room of Billy Reed's Little Club. The interviewer said to Skipper, "Now, your mother is a famous concert pianist and movie star, and your father is a member of Congress and a preacher. What will you be when you are older?"

"Six," he replied.

A number of years later I took him on another trip involving use of the Panama Line, which was owned by the United States government and on which all members of Congress traveled free. I was questioned by the press as to how I could take a nine-year-old boy on the line, free, at government expense. "He's my secretary," I told them—and that was the truth. He had a Hermes portable, was by this time an excellent typist, and did a lot of work for me on the boat, both going down and coming back.

The little house in North White Plains eventually became too small, and we bought a house in Fleetwood, Mount Vernon, and a beach shack on Dune Road next to the Swordfish Club in Westhampton Beach. I invested our money very carefully. We reduced the mortgage of the $50,000 Fleetwood house to just over $6,000, sold the beach house at a large profit, and bought two apartment houses on 111th Street and one on Riverside Drive which were later sold, again with considerable profit.

But Hazel and I began to drift apart after eight years of marriage. It was not her fault, but mine. We had gone on long trips to Europe in 1950 and 1951—I on appointed business for the United States Congress and she for the furtherance of her career. It was then that she fell in love with her first real home—Paris. Years later, when a newspaper reporter asked her when she was going to return home, she replied, "Home? This is my home— Paris."

Hazel tried her best to help me in the church. But I think she resented the people, because subconsciously she realized that they were the ones standing between us. I tried my best to help her in her career, but here again I probably subconsciously was jealous of her work and the affection she gave it. After six months of drifting apart, it was suggested that we both seek professional assistance. I was advised to take a Rorschach Test.

When I had completed the test and had received the report on it, for the first time in my life I knew definitely and objectively what I had thought all along but wasn't sure of: the specialist who administered and interpreted the Rorschach said I had a great love for people and an incapacity to love individuals as long as I served people en masse. I knew this was the end and Hazel did, too.

For a while she drank rather heavily, and then there took place in her life one of the greatest acts of faith I have ever seen. She was living on the Left Bank in Paris, with Skipper's godmother and our lifelong friend Mabel Howard. They lived just across the Seine from Notre Dame, whose spires they could see shimmering in the dawn. One morning, accompanied by Mabel, Hazel went to Notre Dame, got down on her knees in front of the altar, and vowed she would not move until God gave her strength. She stayed there until her knees actually became bloody. When she finally did rise to her feet, she had the power and strength and the faith never again to touch or desire a drop of alcohol. She became an exceptionally religious person. When I say religious, I use the word in the broadest sense—she became not a Christian, but a religious person. She looked for something of value in every religion of the world. She carried a rosary, which she used, yet she loved the Baptist Church, too. She studied very carefully the best elements of Judaism and Christianity, and incorporated them into her philosophy of life.

And in October 1956, despite the fact that we were both deeply attached to Skipper, the one last link of the chain that held us together, we agreed that our futures would be best separate. In the presence of her lawyers, my lawyer, and our accountant, I gave her my share of every single thing we had held together—house, mortgage, the furniture, all.

When I walked out of her lawyer's office that cold October night, with everything gone for the second time in my life, it was with a sense of knowing that at last the obvious truth had been driven home to me—that under no circumstances should I ever marry again until my wife knew and understood that my first love was the masses of people everywhere.

And so I began to live the life of a bachelor. I had many personal habits that were not conducive to good homemaking. I was meticulous, exacting, impatient, and I possessed a tremendous temper. Whenever I went to bed, everyone had to go; when I got up, that was the beginning of the day for everyone also; I could not stand any disorder, whether with my possessions or others'; I wanted everything always in its place.

I moved to a room in the heart of Harlem and a room in Washington, and began to allow my abrasive way of life to have full sway in my solitude. I do not mind being alone. Emerson once said, "The test of a man's character is what he does with his solitude." I like being alone. It's not that I am antisocial, but when one is forced to be exposed to thousands of people, day in and day out, it is a luxury to be able to close the door and shut off the phone and the world. In fact, one of the first things I did was to get rid of my personal telephones.

My sleeping habits are very irregular. If I feel like going to bed at eight, I do. I rarely sleep more than five hours in a stretch, but I sleep that five hours without the slightest bit of help, and then I am wide awake. Alongside my bed, wherever I am, I keep a scratch pad, pencils, and a dictating machine with a disc on it, ready to work at a twist of the knob. After my first five hours of sleep I do my best thinking, reading, and dictating. Frequently, I take a sleeping pill, just enough to give me about five additional hours, because I love ten hours of sleep. I sleep late in the mornings because nearly every night I work until eleven or twelve o'clock.

I am not as miserly as my mother was, but I surely am frugal. I smoke eight-cent cigars from Manati, Puerto Rico, which I keep in the refrigerator, taking out a few each morning for the day. I smoke cigaritos, too, but do not like cigarettes; I have a feeling they are only for women, which is, of course, absolutely wrong. I use leather-covered pipes from France, Longchamps, which I buy for a little over $2 apiece at the American Embassy in Paris. My favorite pipe tobacco is Balkan Sobranie.

I read probably more than most of the members of Congress, and my reading habits have changed a great deal in recent years. My personal library consists of a hundred and sixty-five feet of shelving, packed with about two thousand volumes, with scarcely any fiction among them. I never bought fiction, or any book I felt could be read only once, but when I had the Library of Congress at my disposal, most of my reading was fiction because I did not have to purchase it. Is this frugality? It surely is not intellectuality.

I love cheap wines. I drink a very light Scotch, preferably on the rocks with a twist of lemon peel. My favorite martini is made by filling a cocktail glass to the brim with gin and pouring it over ice in a mixer; then I fill the same glass with vermouth, stir the gin in the mixer until it is very cold, throw out the vermouth and pour the gin into the glass—that's what I call a dry martini!

One thing on which I will not limit myself is food. I love the very best, but I do not eat starches, desserts, fried foods, or any food with a thick sauce. I am a real weight-watcher, despite the fact that in recent years I have been inching up about a pound a year. I pride myself on being an excellent cook, but hate to entertain.

I used to drink a quart or two of milk every day until I read that some scientific authorities said milk is not necessary for the human body. They even went so far as to state that it isn't necessary for children. So I cut it out overnight. I drink coffee black—no sugar, no cream. I like it best *"tinta"* —the Latin-American dark-espresso way of brewing it.

When I travel by plane, I travel coach. I never buy anything unless it is at a sale, and that goes for food as well as for clothing. In fact, I haven't bought much clothing in many years. When the double-breasted styles changed to single-breasted, I shipped fourteen suits to an Austrian tailor about forty miles from Salzburg, at lovely Bad Ischl. There the *Schneidermeister*, Herr Thalhammer, is located. I was told about him by Ambassador Llewellyn Thompson's wife. He makes the most wonderful clothes of the finest fabrics for from $60 to $70, and that includes three fittings. He took all my double-breasted suits and made them over completely, at a cost of $12 per suit.

Some of my shoes are ten and fifteen years old. I still have beautiful custom-made shirts purchased from Austin Reed of London in 1950, which cost me just £3 each, or about $8.40. While I have scores of ties, most of them gifts, the tie I usually wear is a black knit. In fact, I love everything in black—wallet, cigar case, card case, tobacco pouch. I have a beautiful black lacquer case, given to me by Olga Baclanova, in which I carry my cigaritos.

I wear no undershirt, winter or summer. I never wear rubbers, and rarely wear a hat, but now and then will carry a homburg in my hand when the occasion demands it.

I do not like to write. In fact, I never write letters to anyone except the very closest of friends, and these I dictate. I read all my mail but rarely dictate a full reply; instead, I merely mark in the corner "Regrets," "Accept," "Refer to—," "Agree," "O.K.," or "No." My secretary, who has been with me for many years, carries on from there.

I do not go to the movies often, but I rarely miss a Broadway opening, and when I do, I see to it that I drop in as soon after the opening as possible.

In 1950 I bought a Jaguar Mark V drophead for $3800—it is still running and is a collector's item. If I had bought an American car, I would have had to purchase at least three or four since then, in order to keep up with the styles. In 1952 I bought a car that the Nash Company put together— the body made by Pininfarina of Torino, Italy, and the engine by Healey of England—which still looks like the car of tomorrow. These are the only cars I have had in ten years.

During my terms as a Congressman, once a month I was in New York for a Friday night board meeting at the church. Saturdays I generally reserved for Skipper, although there was usually business of some sort as well. I tried to be in bed with the lights out by nine o'clock because Sunday was a big day. I never had visiting preachers at the Abyssinian Baptist Church except during the summer when I was away. I preached every Sunday, giving the sermon twice, each time to a packed auditorium, one right after the other. On Sunday afternoons there were always speaking engagements, so that by the time Sunday evening came I was ready to relax and have a good dinner. On Mondays of this once-a-month long weekend I slept late; in the evening after a meeting with the deacons of the church I saw constituents at the local Democratic club from nine P.M. on. Invariably other meetings were also larded into this weekend—the United Democratic Leadership Team, the executive committee of the Alfred Isaacs Democratic Club, meetings of Baptists and of the interdenominational ministers' group, Tammany Hall organizations, and so on.

In Washington, I rarely went out except on the various embassy parties, which were innumerable.

How could a human being of my exacting personality, the minister of one of the largest churches in the nation, a senior member of Congress, possessed of my peculiar living habits, be married to anyone and get along? When I met Yvette, I thought it was possible.

Yvette came to Washington to work on my staff at the lowest point in my life—when friends had turned their backs on me, when politicians were out to purge me, when enemies in high places were out to get me. She stood by me when every relative except my lovely stepmother, Inez, left me. She nursed me through my trying illnesses and introduced me to the relaxing, wonderful Latin-American climate of Puerto Rico and a new way of life in the States. We lived in an alley house in Washington, a beachcomber's driftwood shack in Puerto Rico, and rented a room in New York.

As I look back through the years now and think of the many women in my life, I realize that I loved all women as long as they didn't interfere with my work. There has never been a woman in my life who didn't remain my friend after we broke up. Sometimes we loved each other and sometimes we were just two human beings—friends.

Therefore I never thought that the day would come when Yvette would turn on me. But it did happen. She came to Washington (with all expenses paid by the United States Congress) to testify against me. She did not have to testify against her husband—the law is perfectly clear on that—but testify she *did*. She also sold an article to the *Ladies' Home Journal* for what I heard was a very considerable sum.

In the days gone by I would rather have sat and talked with Eartha Kitt or Faye Emerson than date any other woman. Kitt had a great brain. When she returned from a trip to India, the first thing she wanted to know was, "What is your opinion of Nehru?" I told her that I thought Nehru had turned his back on Gandhi and had thrown away the concept of nonviolence, and that as a result one of the greatest fratricidal wars in history—the war between the Hindus and the Moslems—had broken out. She said, "Exactly. No one else in the world had agreed with me except you, but I know I'm right and will not change my mind."

Faye Emerson is undoubtedly one of the finest human beings God ever created; a "real good Joe" in every sense of the word. She packs a wallop in her fists in the best Texas tradition, but few people know this until it's too late. When she blows her top, even if you're twice as big, she lets you have that right wallop.

Then there was the girl who was Miss Puerto Rico in the Miss Universe contest (which year? I won't tell you), a wonderful, shy person; Dorothy Dandridge and Abbey Lincoln—two exquisitely chiseled women; and Jean Pochna, who always blew in like a gale from some strange place—her skiing chalet in Switzerland, her town house in Paris, or a lovely villa on the Riviera; and Sally Blair, whom I saw for the first time when she was sixteen. They, and many more, were all friends.

I remember the night at Montego Bay, dining at the lovely Bay Roc Hotel with my good friend Dick DeLisser, when a tall flaxen-haired Texas girl came over and said, "I don't know who you are, but whoever you are, take me out tonight." And I did. I later learned that her doctor had purposely been giving her morphine and that he was doing this in order to hold her. Fortunately, she had not become an addict. I got her out of there and back to the States, and she has always been my buddy. Some time later we had arranged to meet at Penn Station one night as she was passing through New York; I was unexpectedly detained in Washington and couldn't meet her, so I telephoned one of my secretaries in New York and asked him to meet her at Penn Station and explain that I couldn't get there. He asked, "How can I find her?" And I replied, "Just look around the concourse for the most beautiful girl." He told me later that as he walked down the steps from the street, he caught one glimpse of that girl . . . said to himself, "There she is". . . and went right to her.

One seemingly uneventful day, during one of my later trips to Europe, as I was seated on the terrace of the Excelsior Hotel, the wonderful playground for the "in" people on the Lido just across from the Grand Canal of Venice, I looked up and there was the cutest green-eyed redhead staring at me. I spoke no Italian, and she spoke no English, but for two months we had a most wonderful friendship . . . Princess Maria Louisa Branciforte of Rome, fabulous swimmer, crack skier, who never missed a night at the Casino, playing the grand table. That summer I saw her toss away over $25,000. When we went back to Rome in September, I met her husband, a wonderful man, at the opening of a new musical comedy. He spoke perfect English and the Prince and I had delightful conversation. They, of course, were separated.

I will never forget the night the President of Italy gave a white-tie reception. When I arrived with the Princess, Mrs. Clare Boothe Luce, our then Ambassador to Italy, who had previously served with me in Congress, came over to her and said, "Don't you know that's the worst man in the United States Congress?"

Maria Louisa, by that time, had learned a little English: "For you, yes; you do not know him. But for me, the best!"

And of all the friends I had through the years, there was not one closer to me than Sally Backer, daughter of George Backer and his former wife, Dorothy Schiff, who owns the *New York Post*. All sorts of stories were told about us. All I can say is that our relationship was one of confidence and the genuine love of two different beings for each other, and not man for woman or woman for man. I met Sally at the Anta Theatre when she was seventeen years old. We became friends and that friendship deepened through the years; a love of tenderness, a love in which there was not a thought regarding man or woman. She is one of the most poised, lovely little persons I have ever met. I recall the evening I went to her mother's home and there, sitting in the living room in front of one of her paintings by Grandma Moses, I assured her that she need not worry about Sally, that Sally was getting understanding from me that she never got at home; and that she, being so busy running the affairs of the *New York Post*, could not give Sally what I could. Sally worked hard on political campaigns, came to church regularly. She is happily married now and writes me frequently.

And there was the tall Welsh girl, with cornflower eyes, whom I met in the drizzle at Hyde Park in London, just across from the Marble Arch, where we sang Welsh hymns on Sunday evenings. Her name was Powell and she came from Cardiff. I saw her for a few summers and then she got married. I can still remember her as she walked away for the last time, swinging along, her trench coat bunched up around her neck, walking with that stride that is indigenous only to an Englishwoman.

And there was Cyn, a wonderful little rabbit, who had a smile and a laugh any hour of the day or night.

And Sue, with the soft eyes that always looked like they were about to break into tears. She, too, is married now and lives in Miami.

During the period when Yvette refused to come to the United States, I had to go to Puerto Rico at least once a month, sometimes twice, to see her and my new son. Then a very lovely, charming girl was introduced to me by Herb Wright, one of the executives of Philip Morris. She was the first soul sister to be in the Miss Universe contest. She was Miss Ohio; her name was Corinne Huff—Huffi is what I called her. She stood by me for many years and carried her burden in the heat of the day. And I will never forget what she did to help me when everyone had turned their backs upon me. She is now married and lives in Bimini, and I will always wish her the very best the rest of her life.

After I started to fight my battle against the cancer that was proliferating in my lymph glands, there were Mrs. Dorothy Johnson and Tee Dantzler who stood by me and nursed me through those awful months of cobalt and betatron and intense radiation. I beat cancer of the lymph glands and then the most gorgeous woman—inside and out—ever to enter my life walked into my office one day. She had been working on the hill for four years for Congressmen Samuel Friedel and Frank Thompson. I took one look at her and said, "You are the most beautiful woman I've ever seen." She's jet black with skin like satin, and she came up the hard way from Hattiesburg, Mississippi. When she was a youngster she even picked cotton. Now she is brains, perception, and above all, love. She told me one day, "All that I want to do the rest of my life is take care of you." And all I want to do the rest of my life is to take care of her—Darlene Exposé.

I have been criticized during my life for admitting that I enjoy the company of women. And there have been times when I have been told that it would be better not to let photographers shoot me with a glass in my hand. I have also been accused of almost everything—of being a black racist, an Uncle Tom, a rabble-rouser, a pleasure-seeker, a slanderer, and much more. But I have never been accused of being a hypocrite, of saying anything I did not believe in, or doing anything I did not enjoy.

19

The Exile's Return

In spite of its being the twelfth time, it was still a thrill as I walked to the well of the House and raised my hand to be sworn in as the 91st Congress met. I was the last member to be seated; there had been a long debate (almost a reprise of the one two years earlier) on the conditions the House would impose before seating me.

Although my exclusion had died with the 90th Congress, the members were still determined to remind me to keep my place. They intended to let me back in but there had to be one last punishment to show the world they were vigilant. The final agreement was to permit me to be admitted if I would accept a $25,000 fine and the loss of my 22 years of seniority. I could not refuse the terms. If I had been the only one involved, I would have fought forever. But the people of Harlem had been without representation in Congress for two years and I could not allow them to be forced into suffering another two without a voice.

My actual return to Congress was almost anticlimactic. I had been back in the country from Bimini a year and I had spent the first two months on the lecture circuit. But instead of talking at ladies' teas or political gatherings, I had been making a sweep of all the major colleges in the country. I went out there to teach the students what I knew and I stayed to learn from them what they thought of our world.

I could not help but contrast my youth and college days with what I was seeing day after day on the tour. When I was at Colgate (which was, and still is, a solid, conventional school), one of our biggest worries was where we were going to get the bootleg liquor to bring back and sell on campus. Had anyone asked us to join a demonstration, we would have considered him some variety of practical joker. In those days a student's knowledge (even a college student's) of the actual world, and what his country was doing in relation to it, was incredibly limited. Student participation in politics was not discouraged—simply because almost none of the students of that day had ever thought of participating.

And here, day after day, I was talking with thousands of young people who were vitally concerned and involved with every aspect of the country, from our foreign policy to our treatment of emerging nations. They had facts, they had knowledge—many of them had traveled on their own money to areas of the world where America is involved just to see what was really happening—they had commitment, and they had the burning desire to better the world they are about to inherit.

I talked at Berkeley, at UCLA, Stanford, San Diego State, Duke, Smith, Amherst, and dozens more. In every case they wanted to know why and what: Why is the country doing many things that seem to be nothing short of suicidal, and What can they do to stop it? I could not give them any golden answers. I could, and did, encourage them and at least prove to them that they were not totally alone. And I could talk with them. My speeches were only half-speeches; the other halves were the question-and-answer sessions that I always incorporate. I have had tougher debates in many field halls and gymnasiums than I ever had in the House of Representatives.

And I hold one record not many speakers can match: I have never been shouted down or had a session of mine disrupted on any campus. I know of several governors who would like to be able to say the same thing.

Those months of speaking to the youth made a distinct impression on me, and since then I have made it a standing policy to speak (and be spoken to) at as many colleges and universities as possible. I may be forty years older than most of the audience, but I am still in step with their thinking.

After the lecture tour I went home. To my real home, Harlem. I landed at Kennedy Airport very late on a Friday night, with only my staff aware of my arrival. The next morning was as cold as only late March can be in New York, and it was raining as if the second flood were on its way. We drove to 125th Street and Seventh Avenue and I got out of the car and started walking toward 135th. I never made it down the first block. There are close to half a million people in my Congressional District of Harlem and that Saturday morning, I think, they all were packed into that one block. People were jammed so closely together that I doubt if anyone even got wet. With the crowd chanting "We kept the faith," I finally led them up the street to my church. After so many months it was good to be home.

The first order of business after getting back was to start campaigning for the upcoming election. My campaigning always took an entirely different form from that of the usual office-seeker, however. Rather than run around and tell the people what I wanted to do, I always conducted countless private and public sessions and gatherings to give the people a chance to tell me what they wanted and what needed to be done in the district. My staff and usually I ended up with pages of grievances, from broken street lights and crooked landlords to missing welfare payments and irregularities at a local draft board. From lists like those I could draw up priorities and often detect and cure problems before they became major trouble. Once again that fall the people voted me back to Washington— the vote was 86 percent in my favor—to claim the seat I had been excluded from two years before.

Once the session began, things were uneventful and again I thought that my life might be leveling off. But again I had several surprises. First was a dramatic announcement from the Supreme Court. My lawyers had fought my exclusion case through all the various appeal courts, and a few months earlier the Supreme Court had ruled that it was a proper matter for consideration by that tribunal—the highest court in the nation. There was speculation at that time that the Court, although admitting that the case did fall within its jurisdiction, might still refuse to consider it in order to avoid a direct confrontation between the Court and the Congress. This speculation proved to be unfounded, however, and the Court had taken the case. Now the Supreme Court of the United States ruled that Congress had acted unconstitutionally in denying me my seat. Although it was a dead issue in that I was seated in the current Congress, the decision still raised a hail of protest. The Congress never likes to be told that it is wrong, particularly by another branch of government.

I rejoiced in the news, first because it forever vindicated me and, more important, because it dramatically proved to the world that there was still justice left in the United States. The decision also raised some other questions that have not yet been (and may never be) decided. If the seat I had been denied was rightfully mine, was the salary that goes with the seat also due me? (I had lost $55,000 in that period.) And if the House did not have the right to exclude me from the 90th Congress, did it, in fact, have the right to strip me of my twenty-two years of seniority and fine me $25,000 in the 91st Congress? Considering that the difference to me is twenty-two years of service and $80,000, these are questions that my lawyers are making every effort to resolve.

The next major event in my life was a delightful surprise to me but—judging by the mail I received—a shock to the entire country. My son, Skipper, Adam Clayton Powell III, had announced his wedding plans. Skipper was going to be married in May, 1969, to Beryl Slocum, a beautiful girl who traces her family back to the *Mayflower*. Needless to say, Beryl is white. Her ancestors had been among the founders of Rhode Island long, long before my father had been born. Of course our family's antecedents had also come to America by ship—but they had traveled in chains in the stifling hold of an African slave ship.

The mail that came in after the announcement was, in part, sickening. I collected baskets of the worst threats and turned them over to the FBI. But there were also kind, warm letters. As Drew Pearson said in his column that day, "There will be many wishing happiness to this young couple, whose diverse ancestors made America."

Just recently Skipper and Beryl made me a grandfather; there is now another male Powell loosed on the world. At this rate, we may still end up with a Powell as President.

Not long after Skipper's marriage came an occurrence that was more stunning to me personally. In the late summer of 1969 my doctors told me I had a malignant growth—a cancer—centered in my lymph glands. After a series of tests, examinations, and consultations, they decided that an operation was not advisable, that radiation treatments would offer the greatest chance of stopping the growth. I went to the Cornell University Hospital and was started on a series of radioactive cobalt treatments that, before we were through, stretched over almost five months. The almost daily doses of radiation gave me a barren area on the back of my head and softened the structure of my teeth (which had always been almost indestructible), but it was a very small price to pay when the doctors finally announced that the growth was stabilized and that I could return to a normal life.

I have never been able to determine, however, just what a normal life would be for me. Congress certainly could not be considered a normal environment. What sort of normality is there when that body, spurning the Justice Department's offer to take over the legal work necessary during my exclusion, hires a New York law firm for over $200,000 to carry the case, and only through the appeal court stage at that? The estimates on what it cost Congress to exclude me—just in outside legal fees—is close to $500,000. My lawyers fought the case for me out of a sense of justice; I never paid them one cent.

Or what sort of normality have we finally arrived at when in 1969 I was made an honorary deputy sheriff, in Alabama! I was sworn in by Lucius Amerson, the first—and only—black sheriff in Alabama. They never believed that when I got back to Harlem.

Then there were the honorable gentlemen who started the drive to oust me from Congress. One of my most severe critics was big Bill Dickinson, the Alabama Republican. To hear Bill tell it in those days, I had taken just about everything but the dome on the Capitol. And then Jack Anderson reported that Dickinson might have something to hide. In the *Washington Post* (September 30, 1970) Anderson reported: "We have compiled evidence that Dickinson, who served on the committee that investigated Powell, may have violated the bribery and kickback laws himself."

This may be normal, but only in Washington.

And then there was the primary election in New York in the late summer of 1970. My people in Harlem asked me to run again and I agreed. This time I was being challenged for the Democratic candidacy by State Assemblyman Charles Rangel. In New York, as in many states, a voter can cast his ballot in the primary only for a candidate representing the voter's party. In other words, a registered Republican can legally vote only in the Republican primaries and a Democrat only in the Democratic primaries. In the actual Congressional election, of course, the voter may select any of the candidates on the ballot—candidates whose names have been placed there by the results of the party primaries.

As the results came in from the primary election in June my staff and I began to realize that something was wrong. Although the primary vote is generally much lighter than the November balloting, we had made an advance estimate of what percentage of the vote I should receive—and after more than thirty years of running for public office, I can usually come very close in that estimate. But now the results didn't fit. I was receiving just about the number of votes I had expected, but my opponent was getting more. The final results gave Rangel the election—by a hundred and fifty votes.

My election workers immediately went into action, getting ballots re-counted and examined. As they began to report in, we could see where some of those votes might have come from. My workers found machines with more votes recorded than the total of voters who had signed in to vote. They found voting machines that had not been guarded by police before and/or after the polling (to prevent additional, illegal votes from being registered on the machine).

Just a rough count showed that my opponent had received over 12 hundred ineligible votes—Republican, Liberal, Conservative; even twenty-seven dead men had faithfully cast their vote for Rangel! We uncovered over twelve hundred votes that should not have been counted. And I had lost by only a hundred and fifty votes.

I immediately filed suit in the New York State Supreme Court. The material supporting my claim to the election victory filled twenty pages when, for the benefit of history, I read the material on the floor of the House and it was printed in the *Congressional Record.*

I have great faith in the courts, and the eventual justice of their findings, but by the time they decide that I was the actual winner of the 1970 primary, it will be much too late for me to be seated in the House and serve the people of my district who had elected me.

Perhaps, looking back over the period since my cancer was arrested, this is my normal life. Fighting somewhere—in a courtroom, a picket line, in the Congress; fighting to prove what will end only as a principle, since the wrong it was meant to correct is long forgotten by the time the battle is ended; fighting to squeeze a little more justice from the system, not for myself but for those downtrodden or discriminated against for skin color or other irrelevant causes.

20

___

Black Power and the Future of Black America

Every single black leader in America with a strong national following has been bought off, assassinated, imprisoned, or exiled. While I know I was not directly responsible, in a way I have a deep sense of guilt concerning the assassinations of Martin Luther King, Jr., and Malcolm X.

Martin Luther King came to see me once in Washington, bringing with him Ralph Abernathy. Chuck Stone, my administrative assistant, and the chief investigator of the Education and Labor Committee, were also present.

King and I talked for about three hours. I told him that the concept of total nonviolence had become outmoded. I reminded him that when Gandhi died, even Nehru, his closest follower, gave up the concept in the course of the fratricidal war between the Hindus and Moslems that resulted in the creation of Pakistan. King then told me that he was giving up the concept of total nonviolence.

Following our talk I went on to California to speak on campuses there, and in the course of a press conference during my trip reported that Martin Luther King was giving up total nonviolence—as he had said in front of witnesses during our talk in Washington. King immediately called his own press conference and denied that he had made such a statement. My puzzlement over this action was dispelled several days later when he received a foundation grant for several hundred thousand dollars.

Subsequently, however, King preached a sermon at the Riverside Baptist Church in New York City, in which he did state as a matter of record that he could not continue his concept of total nonviolence as long—and I quote him—"as my nation is the greatest purveyor of violence in the world."

During our Washington talk King also did not tell me the truth regarding his financing, and Ralph Abernathy corrected him on that score. I had asked King, "Martin, how much money are you getting from white people?"

"None," he said, "except what comes in through the mails when we send out our form letters for appeals through the Southern Christian Leadership Conference."

"Martin, you forgot that just last week we got over a hundred thousand dollars from a foundation," Abernathy said.

No comment from Martin.

King later visited me several times at Bimini. One night we were with a crowd of Biminians and went into a restaurant for something to eat. After we were settled—all of us black—one of the younger fellows with us said, "Do you think Dr. King would preach us a little sermon? We've never heard him."

I said, "How about it, Martin? These young people have never heard you preach." So he leaned back and preached an old-fashioned Baptist sermon. While he was preaching, a stranger, whose identity we were never able to discover, came up to one of the men in our group and said to him, "Please tell Dr. King not to go to Memphis because if he does, he will be killed."

I passed this along to Dr. King, who apparently thought little of it. Two weeks later he was dead.

Malcolm X, one of the great minds we black people lost, was a dear friend of mine. As time went on we became extremely close because I was able to give him a better understanding of his religion. At the time we became acquainted he thought that Christianity was the white man's religion and that Islamism, or Muslimism, was the black man's religion. I pointed to the Coptic cross in the Abyssinian Baptist Church and said to him. "This is where Christianity began—in Ethiopia. It wasn't until A.D. 329 that Constantine recognized Christianity, but long before that there was the Coptic Church."

I also taught Malcolm that his concepts of Muslimism were incorrect, and I urged him to go to the Arab countries and if possible to Mecca to find out what Islam really was. This he did. After his return from Mecca he held a press conference at which he stated that he had found outstanding leaders of the Muslim religion who were white, with blue eyes and blond hair, and that he knew he had been wrong in his previous thinking on that point. Evidently his changed attitude did not find favor with all his followers because two months after this Malcolm X was assassinated.

Stokely Carmichael had great charisma and showed great promise for the future of black people. An activist, he traveled to Communist countries where I, a United States Congressman, couldn't go. Eventually he became involved with my old friend Kwame Nkrumah, the deposed redeemer of Ghana. He lived with Nkrumah for some time and then returned to America, preaching Pan-Africanism, which is the gospel of Nkrumah. But his speeches did not go over too well; in fact, some audiences in the States and the Caribbean booed him when he spoke.

What we blacks are suffering from—and white America is suffering from also—is a fragmentation of leadership. There is no leader among blacks and there is no leader among whites.

Even the Black Panthers have no leadership left. Whether one agrees with them or not, one must give them due respect as being the first organization of black people since Nat Turner's to commit themselves to a willingness to die for the cause. And any time a man like J. Edgar Hoover can call the Panthers' 100,200 members a threat to the security of this vast nation of 200 millions plus, then you know they are a power.

Jesse Jackson is one of the brightest hopes for the future. Jackson, who worked for Dr. King in Chicago, setting up the successful Operation Breadbasket there, has brains, looks, charisma, and is a gifted orator besides. I see him as the only man on the horizon who can come forward and provide leadership, not only for black America but for blacks and whites together.

What, then, for the future? I believe—no, I know—that we are passing through a revolution. And I believe that we are also on the edge of a civil war. That war will be a war not of racism or regionalism but of young people, black and white, campus people, poor whites, Chicanos, and blacks —in all a group that will number 100 million by 1972.

Black people need to make a decision, however, before they achieve this unity of the majority—they need to decide what they are going to believe about integration and separatism. My own opinion is that we cannot afford the luxury of differences among ourselves now. But the one point on which we can all definitely afford to agree is unity on the basis of desegregation, regardless of whether we are joining with Black Muslims, Black Panthers, or the Negro bourgeoisie. After desegregation is accomplished, then we can afford the luxury of differences among ourselves.

BLACK POWER!
BLACK POWER!

During 1968, 1969, and 1970 I made more than one hundred speeches all over the United States. I spoke to entirely white audiences in the South and to entirely black audiences in the North. And I found that no phrase strikes more terror to the hearts of white Americans than Black Power.

Black Power was founded half a century ago by Marcus Garvey, the semiliterate immigrant from Jamaica, at whose feet I sat as a youngster and listened while he talked. I held the first National Black Power Conference in this Republic. Therefore I write with authority.

Black Power does not mean antiwhite unless whites make blacks antiwhite.

Black power does not mean violence, but it does not mean total nonviolence. It does not mean that you walk with a chip on your shoulder, but you walk letting the chips fly where they may.

Black Power means black dignity. Pride in being black. Pride that black is beautiful. Pride that blacks are not second-class citizens as our forefathers were.

Black Power means a complete separation from Negroes. Especially the Negro bourgeoisie or, as I call them, Negro bushies.

Black Power means pride in heritage. Pride in knowing that before the first white man, a savage in what is now England, could ever comb his matted locks, black men were carving statues, painting, creating astronomy, mathematics, and the alphabet.

Black Power means pride that the first man who died on Boston Common that America might be free was a black man, Crispus Attucks. Pride that a black man, Benjamin Banneker, planned the city of Washington, the capital of the Republic—and before him another black man from France, Pierre L'Enfant.

Black Power means that blacks have a willingness to die for their cause —no cause has ever been successful without the willingness of the people who believe in it to die for it, whether they died or not.

Black Power means we are no better—and above all no less—in terms of equality with any other ethnic group in the United States.

Black Power means we are going to lead our own black group and do not want any white leadership. Whites can help us with troops, maybe a corporal or sergeant, but above all no white generals. We will command our destiny. We ask those who want to help us to help us. With or without you, we're going to win.

Black Power means that we have paid the price in Watts, in Newark, in Detroit, in Harlem, in a hundred and three cities after Martin Luther King, Jr., was assassinated.

Black Power means we're not afraid of anyone even though others may have the weapons that we do not have—although some of the Black Power groups do have weapons.

Black Power means we are proud of our Black Panthers. We may not agree with them, because few people really understand them. But we are proud of any group that's willing to die for its cause.

Black Power means we are searching for truth always. Not the truth of J. Edgar Hoover's wiretapping of Black Panther Headquarters and infiltrating of Black Power movements. It means the kind of truth that we discovered on the scene in Chicago when we went to the Black Panther Headquarters. The truth that the Attorney General of Illinois had publicly denied—but that later made him dismiss the charges against the Black Panthers he had arrested.

The truth about Fred Hampton's assassination by the police of the city of Chicago. We saw the truth—the door with every bullet hole made from the outside in. Not one shot fired from the inside out. We saw the truth —that Fred Hampton was killed while he was sleeping; they came through an outside door on the back porch and shot him in the top of his head.

Black Power calls on all Americans to stop the genocide against the Black Panthers and black people everywhere.

Black Power says don't forget the executive secretary of the NAACP who was murdered in Mississippi. Don't forget the two white boys from Manhattan and a black soul brother who were bulldozed into the earth in Mississippi. Don't forget the assassination of Jack Kennedy. Don't forget the assassination of Bobby Kennedy.

Black Power says power to the people. The gaunt man who walked at midnight on Pennsylvania Avenue said it once—power to the people. He said the only government that would not perish from the earth would be a government of the people (power to the people), by the people (power to the people), and for the people (power to the people). But what does this power, this Black Power, come from? Let me tell you what I have been telling my brothers, what I call a Black Position Paper.

1. Black organizations must be black-led. To the extent to which black organizations are led by whites, to that precise extent is their black potential for ultimate control and direction diluted.

2. The black masses must finance their own organizations; at least such organizations must derive the main source of their funds from black people. No other ethnic or religious group in America permits others to control their organizations. This fact of organizational life is the crucible for black progress. Jews control Jewish organizations; there are no Italians or Irish on the board of directors of B'nai B'rith. Poles control Polish-American organizations. But the moment a black man seeks to dominate his own organization, he's labeled a "racist." And frightened black Uncle Toms quickly shun him to cuddle up to Mr. Charlie to prove their sniveling loyalty to the doctrine that "white must be right."

3. The black masses must demand and refuse to accept nothing less than that proportionate percentage of the political spoils, such as jobs, elective offices, and appointments, that are equal to their proportion of the population and their voting strength. They must reject the shameful racial tokenism that characterizes the political life of America today. Where blacks provide 20 percent of the vote, they should have 20 percent of the jobs.

This is not true of other ethnic groups, who usually obtain political favors far in excess of their proportion. A good example for comparison are Chicago's Negroes and Polish-Americans. According to the 1960 census, there were 223,255 Polish-Americans and 812,637 Negroes in Chicago. As late as 1970 there were three Polish-American Congressmen from Chicago and only one Negro Congressman. Thus, with approximately one-fourth as many persons as Negroes, Polish-Americans nonetheless had three times as many Congressmen. That kind of inequity is not due to racial discrimination. It is due to racial apathy, stupidity, lethargy, indifference, ignorance, and lack of courage.

4. Black people must support and push black candidates for political office first, operating on the principle of "all other things being equal." This

is a lesson Chicago Negroes might well learn. In a primary in the heavily black Sixth Congressional District, Chicago black people actually elected a dead white man over a live black woman. A young white candidate, who had going for him only the fact that he was young and white, defeated an intelligent, dedicated black woman who was backed by all major civil rights groups for alderman in a predominately black ward.

5. Black leadership in the North and the South must differentiate between and work within the two-pronged thrust of the black revolution: economic self-sufficiency and political power. The Civil Rights Act of 1964 had absolutely no meaning for black people in New York, Chicago, or any of the Northern Cities. De jure school segregation, denial of the right to vote, or barriers to public accommodations are no longer sources of concern to Northern blacks. Civil rights in the North means more jobs, better education, manpower retraining, and development of new skills. As chairman of the House Committee on Education and Labor, I controlled all labor legislation, such as the minimum wage, all education legislation, including aid to elementary schools and higher education, the manpower training and redevelopment program, vocational rehabilitation, and, of greater importance today, the "War on Poverty." This is legislative power. This is political power. I use myself as an example because this is the audacious power I urge every black woman and man to seek—the kind of political clout needed to achieve greater economic power and bring the black revolution into fruition.

6. Black masses must produce and contribute to the economy of the country in strength proportionate to their population. We must become a race of producers, not consumers. We must rid ourselves of the welfare paralysis that humiliates our human spirit.

7. Black communities of this country—whether New York's Harlem, Chicago's South and West Sides, or Philadelphia's North Side—must neither tolerate nor accept outside leadership, black or white. Each community must provide its own local leadership, strengthening the resources within its own local community.

8. The black masses should follow only those leaders who can sit at the bargaining table with the white power structure as equals and negotiate for a share of the loaf of bread, not beg for some of its crumbs. We must stop sending little boys whose organizations are controlled and financed by white businessmen to do a man's job. Because only those who are financially independent can be men. This is why earlier I called for black people

to finance their own organizations and institutions. In so doing, the black masses guarantee the independence of their leadership.

9. This black leadership—the ministers, politicians, businessmen, doctors, and lawyers—must come back to the blacks who made them in the first place or be purged by the black masses. Black communities all over America today suffer from "absentee black leadership." The leaders have fled to the suburbs and, not unlike their white counterparts in black communities, use these communities to make their two dollars, then reject those who have made them in the first place as neighbors and social equals. This kind of double-dealing must stop.

10. Blacks must reject the white community's carefully selected "ceremonial Negro leaders" and insist that the white community deal instead with the black leadership chosen by black communities. For every "ceremonial Negro leader" we permit to lead us, we are weakened and derogated just that much.

11. Blacks must distinguish between desegregation and integration. Desegregation removes all barriers and facilitates access to an open society. Integration accomplishes the same thing but has a tendency to denude the Negro of pride in himself. Blacks must seek desegregation, thereby retaining pride amd participation in their own institutions, just as other groups, the Jews, Irish, Italians, and Poles have done. Negroes are the only group in America that has utilized the world "integration" in pursuing equality.

12. Demonstration and all continuing protest activity must always be nonviolent. Violence, even when it erupts recklessly in anger among our teen-agers, must be curbed and discouraged.

13. No black person over twenty-one must be permitted to participate in a demonstration, walk a picket line, or be part of any civil rights or community acvitity unless he or she is a registered voter.

14. Black people must continue to defy the laws of man when such laws conflict with the law of God. The law of God ordains that "there is neither Jew nor Greek, there is neither bond nor freedom, there is neither male nor female: for ye are all one." Equal in the eyes of God, but unequal in the eyes of man, black people must press forward at all times, climbing toward that higher ground of the harmonious society that shapes the laws of man to the laws of God.

15. Black people must discover a new and creative total involvement with ourselves. We must turn our energies inwardly toward our homes, our churches, our families, our children, our colleges, our neighborhoods, our

businesses, and our communities. Our fraternal and social groups must become an integral part of this creative involvement by using their resources and energy toward constructive fund-raising and community activities. This is no time for cotillions and teas. These are the steps I urge all of America's 25 million black people to take as we begin the dawn of a new day by walking together. And as we walk together hand in hand, firmly keeping the faith of our black forebears, we glory in what we have become and are today.

Index